STUDIES ON HOSPITAL MANAGEMENT TRANSFORMATION

STUDIES ON HOSPITAL MANAGEMENT TRANSFORMATION

Jian Di

Beijing Jingyi Wanjia Technology Co., Ltd, China

World Scientific

NEW JERSEY • LONDON • SINGAPORE • BEIJING • SHANGHAI • HONG KONG • TAIPEI • CHENNAI • TOKYO

Published by

World Scientific Publishing Co. Pte. Ltd.

5 Toh Tuck Link, Singapore 596224

USA office: 27 Warren Street, Suite 401-402, Hackensack, NJ 07601

UK office: 57 Shelton Street, Covent Garden, London WC2H 9HE

Library of Congress Cataloging-in-Publication Data
Names: Jian, Di, 1950– author.
Title: Studies on hospital management transformation / Jian Di.
Description: New Jersey : World Scientific, [2020] | Includes index.
Identifiers: LCCN 2019042854 | ISBN 9789811211638 (hardcover) |
ISBN 9789811211645 (ebook)
Subjects: LCSH: Hospitals--China--Administration. | Organizational change--China.
Classification: LCC RA971 .J475 2020 | DDC 362.110951--dc23
LC record available at https://lccn.loc.gov/2019042854

British Library Cataloguing-in-Publication Data
A catalogue record for this book is available from the British Library.

For any available supplementary material, please visit
https://www.worldscientific.com/worldscibooks/10.1142/11589#t=suppl

Desk Editor: Ong Shi Min Nicole

Typeset by Stallion Press
Email: enquiries@stallionpress.com

About the Author

Jian Di is a management consulting specialist in China, an internationally Certified Management Consultant (CMC) and one of the 2018's Influential Men in Management Consulting and Training in China. He is an employee of Beijing Jingyi Wanjia Technology Co Ltd. (JYWJ), which was awarded the "CMC-Firm" upon review by the International Council of Management Consulting Institutes (ICMCI) in 2018. In addition, JYWJ was ranked 4th among the top 50 domestic consulting firms in 2018 and rated as one of the most trustworthy management consulting firms in China for the year 2018. It has served more than 600 hospitals in China. Jian started providing management consulting services for hospitals back in 2001, and he has carried out a lot of research on the development strategy of hospitals over the years, including some typical theoretical research topics such as "Destruction and Reconstruction of Hospital Culture", "Evaluation Model for Hospital Department", "Building of a Medical Service Community", "Execution Capability", "Proposal and Implementation of Hospital Disciplinary Focuses and Key Discipline Construction", "Sudoku Theory of Development Strategy of Hospitals", "Proposal and Implementation of the Theory of Rapid Chinese Medicine Specialization", "Initiation and Implementation of the Theory of Medical Risk Control and Prevention" and "Social Value Model of Hospitals". His research has been delivered in international forums several times. Jian's main published works include *Discussion on New Medical Reform & Expanding of Domestic Demand* and *Destruction & Reconstruction of Hospital Culture*.

Foreword

The "patient-oriented" hospital culture needs to go beyond China and be shared with the world. How to build a hospital culture, and how to build it soundly and effectively are exactly what drove Mr. Jian to complete the manuscript *Evaluation & Construction of Hospital Culture* against all odds. This also inspired my feelings and made me reflect on my own career.

As is known, attitude determines one's vision while direction decides what one will see. As I often emphasize at conferences, "Culture is the core competitiveness of hospitals, the true reflection of hospital service quality, the manifestation of employees' cohesiveness, and the engine driving hospital development." However, if the original intention — being patient-oriented — is cast aside, the cultural development would just be a slogan. Furthermore, external factors always play their roles based on internal factors. Development depends more on internal factors. Therefore, the hospital's identification towards culture will determine the quality of hospital culture development. This perfectly echoes with Mr. Jian's ideas.

The word "culture" was first seen in the *Commentaries on Yi* at the end of the Warring States Period: "Observe the natural laws to know the changes of the season; focus on human ethics and morals to enlighten the whole world". "Human ethics and morals" are closely related to "enlightening the whole world" here. The philosophy highlighting culture and education was quite clear. Of course, there may be different cultures in different hospitals or in different stages of one hospital. For instance, our hospital is an old one in Guizhou with a long history and profound cultural deposits. We have grown into the first county-level Grade 3B general hospital in Guizhou from the former Dejiang County Health Clinic established in 1939 (the 28th year of the Republic of China). Over nearly 80 years, the hospital culture may fade or be diluted by the various ups and downs. Then, how should we explore and inherit the previous cultures? How do we establish the hospital culture for the new era based on previous ones? How do we preserve the excellent cultures while introducing new elements? We've been aimless and confused, too. I am very lucky to know Mr. Jian. Whether in the county's traditional Chinese medicine hospital or people's hospital, Mr. Jian and his team have helped a lot, and the hospital culture development has become clearer in my mind. In recent years, our hospital's overall service quality has been improving, patient satisfaction is increasingly higher and the brand effect is getting more prominent. Last year was celebrated as our hospital culture development year. We promoted the building of the "patient-oriented" hospital culture and achieved remarkable results. I hereby express my sincere gratitude to Mr. Jian and his team.

Hospital culture is not constructed to follow some trends or to show off. In this era, with rapid medical development, the medical-seeking pattern has changed fundamentally. A hospital's prosperity depends on its transformation results. Some hospitals neglected the strategic position of hospital culture development while planning performance incentives for their employees. However, it is culture, not incentives, that will work in the long term. Culture development is done to promote self-consciousness in management, services, learning and actions. There are always people hoping to make changes but feeling powerless.

This refreshing book is the fruit of Mr. Jian's labor. The connotations of hospital philosophy and culture are presented here in detail. I wish all readers can explore this masterpiece with the mind that "good books deserve reading". You will feel the noble professional sentiment of JYWJ and its dedication to the hospital culture development. The book will certainly bring you new inspiration and greater benefits.

Zhang Yonghong
People's Hospital of Dejiang, Guizhou
June 3, 2018

Preface

Hospital culture is a type of enterprise culture. As a typical representative of the service industry, hospitals are researched by many management masters all over the world. Philip Kotler, an American, quoted hospital stories in his famous book *Marketing Management* repeatedly. In addition, Leonard L. Berry, former President of the American Marketing Association, brought the "patient-oriented" service principle and philosophy of Mayo Clinic to the world through his book, *Management Lessons from Mayo Clinic.* Many peers in the Chinese medical circle, including our consulting firm, learned about Mayo Clinic from this book.

At the end of April 2015, I visited Mayo Clinic in Manchester, Minnesota, USA, under the organization of the Management Consulting Committee of China Enterprise Confederation. We were welcomed by Sun Xiaofeng, a Chinese American who has been working for Mayo Clinic for more than 20 years. We had a fruitful experience in Mayo Clinic, and I am still grateful to him for answering almost all the questions that we raised. After returning to China, I made many special speeches throughout China, to share the inspirations gained from the visit to Mayo Clinic.

Specializing in management consulting, we want to get an intuitive judgment on a certain matter or concept as well as clear criteria and evaluation systems, which is the only way to describe matters clearly and realize the fact-based and proper management consulting process. The points of correct methods, clear measures and strong performance form the basis of customer acceptance, of consulting services, and principles in conducting theoretical research and management consulting over the years.

A company concerned with hospital strategic management consulting will inevitably engage in the study of hospital culture even though there exist problems such as how to describe and evaluate the characteristics of hospital culture and how to improve the situation on the basis of evaluation, problems that have plagued us for many years. As we all know, this is difficult to solve because hospitals are different from other companies and organizations in the service industry. Fortunately, this condition was changed during a consulting project for a hospital in Beijing in 2013. During the course of this project, I was inspired to establish a "patient-oriented" evaluation model for hospital culture and develop a methodology for improvement of the hospital service system based on the evaluation results. In 2014, we published a book entitled *Destruction and Reconstruction of Hospital Culture* in China. On May 5, 2017, we presented the research results at the Asia Pacific Regional Hub of the International Council of Management Consulting Institutes (ICMCI) in Singapore.

In the nearly five years since, we have provided special consultations for more than 100 hospitals in China based on this theory and have achieved good operation results. Seeing doctors and nurses respond with more frequent and heartfelt smiles and provide better services, as well as seeing more patients and residents feeling the changes in the frequented hospitals, my colleagues and I were very happy. I believe that this research result not only belongs to China but also to the world, and so we now want to publish this book for the world.

Over the past five years, we have supplemented and improved the evaluation system of the "patient-oriented" hospital culture greatly. In particular, we put ourselves in the shoes of patients and their families to view and modify the original indicator system while formulating the evaluation indicators. This change is significant since we all know that the feeling that the patients and their families get from hospital services mainly comes from what they see, hear, smell, taste, touch and sense. The research on the improvement of service in hospitals and the building of the "patient-oriented" hospital culture based on these feelings represent a breakthrough in researching ways to improve services. Overall, we have updated the original evaluation indicator system significantly, and the number of indicators has increased from 410 to 501.

Over the past five years, we have been paying more attention to the improvement of the service process via special consultation projects to establish the "patient-oriented" hospital culture. We have carried out much innovation and implemented many practices in providing organizational forms of quality services, staged improvement plans, created flexible improvement methods, etc., which were some of the hurdles faced in the preliminary exploration five years ago. These valuable experiences and methods will be introduced in this book.

We believe that the "patient-oriented" hospital culture is not self-promoted, but comes from the comprehensive comments made by patients and their families. All doctors, nurses, and administrators in a hospital are exposed to masses of people who need medical services on a daily basis. Their emotions, words, deeds and the service culture are presented to patients. Just as no evaluation system in the world can reflect all aspects of its target, one should not expect a single evaluation system to cover all aspects of the hospital's service personnel. However, there is still a need for the establishment of an evaluation system. It couldn't be better if a set of methods were established through assessing the fulfilment of the "patient-oriented" culture in hospitals in order to practice the "patient-oriented" hospital culture and to make such value a voluntary obligation of all employees.

Only when all service staff members in the hospital acknowledge that they should adhere to the values they promised can they provide better services. The story below shows the importance of adhering to the "patient-oriented" hospital culture in the absence of systems.

During summer a few years ago, I visited a hospital in Southern China. The pungent smell of paint rushed into my nose when I walked through the Outpatient Department. At this moment, I subconsciously recalled the harmful effects of xylene on people. In 2017, WHO's International Agency for Research on Cancer listed this type of substance, often used as a solvent in coatings, resins, dyes and inks, as a Type 3 carcinogen. I asked the person in charge of the hospital accompanying me where the smell came from; he replied that several outpatient clinics were under renovation. I pondered over this for a while before continuing with my visit.

I mentioned the above episode in my lecture that night. As hospital operators, we should have realized the harmful effects of xylene in the paint and its effects on the respiratory tract before commencing the renovation. We should have known that such a risk should not be allowed in the hospital and that we should have taken preventive measures before the renovation to avoid the harmful vapor from dispersing in the Outpatient Hall. This reflects the values the hospital as well as all its employees hold towards their patients. Employees are indifferent to the feelings of patients and their families. For a hospital highlighting a "patient-oriented" culture, measures should have been taken to relocate the patients who were in the Outpatient Hall during the painting; if not, there should have been a way to remove the the smell of paint entirely from the Outpatient Hall.

Jian Di
April 15, 2018 in Brunei

Introduction

An Indissoluble Bond with Hospital Culture Construction

It has been over 5 years since I embarked on hospital culture construction in 2013. During these years, hospital culture developed as I grew. From engaging in indicator compilation in the very beginning to implementing the hospital culture system in over 100 hospitals, every step was inseparable from the devotion and effort of many management consultants, hospital leaders and Cultural Management Department leaders, as well as the commitments of medical staff from all hospitals. Hospital culture is like our child. We witnessed its early formation and birth, and now its growth. Now it has been brought onto the international stage with the support of all these medical institutions and consultants, particularly Mr. Jian. I love it so much, and I am proud that it is recognized throughout the world.

I. *Love at first sight*

Many people have no idea about how to construct hospital culture or how to evaluate the results. This was until 2013 when Mr. Jian proposed an innovative hospital culture knowledge system — patient-oriented hospital culture. I was still a consultant in August when we brainstormed about the indicators. I had given several dozens of smile trainings earlier, so I was more concerned about the services. I also tried to think about how to make our etiquette training more effective in the long run. I was thrilled at the new interpretation Mr. Jian had about the patient-oriented hospital culture. This is the entry point for service improvement and the true hospital culture we need. I fell in love with this philosophy at first sight.

II. *In-depth contact*

In 2014, I was lucky to join the project team of Liuyang Maternal and Child Health Care Hospital and, more fortunately, I was in charge of the hospital culture construction under the supervision of Mr. Lan Xiaofeng, which represents me having in-depth contact. From the investigation method, time, location and type for each indicator to the final improvement measure, responsible department, responsible person, acceptance department and acceptance time, I was able to carry out a profound and deep analysis of the 410 indicators for hospital culture version one. Then, I considered the improvement measures of each indicator.

During this process, I appreciated the profound connotations of "patient-oriented" culture. The 410 entry points cover the whole hospital process, from the person falling sick and arriving at the hospital to waiting at the outpatient clinic, followed by examination, hospitalization, publicity, hospital guide and finally discharge and return visit. These results could help to improve patients' sense of gain and make them feel at home. This makes me realize the charms of hospital culture from various aspects. I once felt aimless and frustrated about how to implement these indicators, and I was confused about how to allocate duties. Looking back, I found everything worthy. Everyone grew during the implementation of hospital culture, and the hospital also evolved with fast development.

III. *Interpretation communication*

I began to direct and supervise many projects since 2015, two of which were regarding hospital culture. The cultural projects were growing in number and popularity at that time, and cooperating hospitals began to embrace the patient-oriented idea. I created the JYWJ hospital culture WeChat group to bring together the leaders of Cultural Management Department who are familiar to me. I hoped that we could discuss about how to implement the patient-oriented hospital culture through the group. But the group turned out to be inactive for some time. Then, I wondered if we could gather together around some main theme. It would be the hospital cultural theory system, no doubt. On December 25, 2015, we began to interpret the 410 indicators of hospital culture. A lecture was given on one of these indicators each day so that the connotation of patient-oriented hospital culture would be understood by people and the philosophy would take root in more places.

I embarked on this journey with the permission of Mr. Jian. I would discuss about the interpretation of "patient-oriented" cultural indicators in the chat group with Mr. Gu every day at 10 p.m. "Patient-oriented" became a slogan since then, and it marked the beginning of a practicing journey. Over the course of around 400 days, we detailed the patient-oriented hospital culture to the hospital workers using nearly 1 Gigabyte (GB) of data in the form of texts, images and voice recordings. I met more and more friends at these lectures, thus leading to a constant increase of hospital culture "fans". The practice of patient-oriented hospital culture was getting more attention in hospitals.

As for implementation, Mr. Jian proposed to make hospital culture construction something pleasant. He even proposed a guideline: "full participation, indicator decomposition, module guidance, key assessment and system support". This guideline was strategic for the implementation of hospital culture in 2016 and later. Thanks to the guidance of Mr. Jian and the concern of Jian Bingbing, Lan Xiaofeng and Zhang Shujun, and under the joint effort umbrella of hospitals, the cultural practice cases of Liuyang Maternal and Child Health Care Hospital and People's Hospital of Dejiang were selected as excellent management consulting cases in China. The theoretical system proposed by Mr. Jian was nominated for the Constantine Award[1] as it

---

[1] The international "Constantine Award" is the first international evaluation award for management consulting achievements among all countries. It serves as the stage for countries to showcase their national management consulting capabilities. Through recommendations of member associations of various countries and review by the International Review Committee, the ICMCI selected the acclaimed outstanding management consulting cases.

was an outstanding management consulting case. It was highly acclaimed by management consulting experts all over the world. I am sure this will make all hospitals and friends who know the hospital culture proud.

IV. *Culture Business Department*

With the development of the company, the implementation of the cultural project is making more achievements thanks to the guidance of Mr. Jian and his constant efforts as well as support from hospitals. In August 2017, Mr. Jian released the second version of the "patient-oriented" hospital culture based on the implementation of the first version and the latest social trend. He proposed to establish a Cultural Business Department and make the cultural project a special project. This marked the beginning of another upgrade in the journey.

The "patient-oriented" hospital culture was carried out as an independent project, lasting for 3 months. Personnel in the project team elaborated 501 experience points of 32 procedures, starting from persons falling sick to discharge, from five aspects — environment, service, etiquette, convenience and management — and in six dimensions — vision, hearing, smell, taste, touch and perception. The second version emphasizes implementation, to realize efficient management organization, wider participation, specific focus of managers and quantified result display.

Through the repeated in-depth practical guidance of Mr. Cheng Songlin, the director of the Cultural Business Department, the forms of implementation become more diverse. The etiquette indicators were not only implemented through hospital-level trainings in batches but also through guidance in the departments. Within 3 months, the etiquette trainings were seen in all departments during morning shifts. The hospital held more than 30 single etiquette trainings, making it clear to everyone how to apply etiquette practices in their work, and make it a habit. For environmental indicators, the most fundamental 5S management was implemented in every aspect of each of the departments, including sorting, rectification, clean-up and quality, to make sure that everything was tidy and neat even after work was completed. This was also applied to management, service and convenience indicators. The hospital strives to offer more advanced medical technologies and warmer services to the residents based on actual situations of the hospital and local consumption standard.

The grateful old mothers make insoles for us, stitching their blessings therein. The hospital guides supported patients when needed, and medical staff came to work with light make-up and greeted patients actively. They also celebrated birthdays for their patients, helped them to wash their hair, trimmed their nails, etc. Warm scenes like this emerged one after the other. The doctor–patient relationship thus returned to what it should always have been through the construction of a "patient-oriented" hospital culture. Patient satisfaction also improved significantly.

Meanwhile, the hospital held a series of activities during the cultural festivals, such as etiquette demonstrations, sending of blessings, hospital cultural knowledge debates, speech competitions and even a baby climbing race. These enriched the employees' work and lives, and brought the patients and medical staff closer together. In addition, the hospital was recognized and approved by residents and governments, elevating its brand influence.

V. *Five-year review*

After five-years of promotion and practice, over 100 lectures on patient-oriented hospital culture and investigation and implementation in multiple hospitals have been given. I have a deeper understanding about the significance of patient-oriented service system to the service improvement of hospitals. I feel that patients need more care from the medical staff, and all hospitals should bear the social responsibility to keep improving patients' medical experience.

The "Spark Plan" training class of JYWJ was officially launched in April 2018, emphasizing the construction of quality service system in hospitals in the first session. Our practices in the past 5 years were summarized, enlightening 67 trainees from over 20 hospitals through 6 modules — awareness improvement, problem diagnosis, improvement method, case sharing, special rectification and brand building. After the training class, the trainees had a clearer understanding about the idea of constructing the patient-oriented service system. I hereby sincerely appreciate everyone's attention and support.

This training class, as I see it, is both a summary and a review of the patient-oriented hospital culture. JYWJ's Cultural Business Department will carry on with unremitting efforts to create a patient-oriented hospital service system together with other hospitals. I believe that the strategic "patient-oriented" hospital culture will boost the hospital's healthy development. I sincerely wish it a promising future!

Gu Lili

Executive Director of Business Department of JYWJ

May 1, 2018 in Anshun, Guizhou

Core Values of Massive Health Service Industry

I. *About massive health*

The concept of massive health was initiated by General Secretary Xi Jinping at the National Sanitation and Health Conference on August 20, 2016.

> "We should advocate a healthy and civilized life style, develop a massive sanitation and health concept, make a shift from the disease-centered idea to the health-centered one, and establish and perfect the health education system to improve the whole nation's health literacy and drive the in-depth integration of nationwide fitness and nationwide health."

Extensiveness of massive health, in addition to the development of health service, lies in its human health-related aspects, such as economy, politics, culture, education, science and technology and environment.

It can be accurately expressed as the "integration of health and all policies" and "the united front of sanitation and health".

It is also reflected in the connotation of "full life cycle" health of "all the people".

The concept of massive health caters to the fundamental demand of the development of human society. Everyone wants to be healthier and live longer. Advancing the construction of a healthy nation has become a major national policy. It will certainly play an immeasurable role in propelling the healthy development of the Chinese nation.

II. *Concept and market segment of massive health*

General concept of massive health: It refers to a green development idea based on the human health.

Narrow concept of massive health: It refers to the management and intervention of the society and social institutions towards the physiology and psychology during people's full life cycle.

Massive health market segment

III. *Core values of massive health industry*

In China, the layout and construction of the massive health industry is not as difficult as the development of the core values of the service industry. Because the former can be supported by the direction and support of policies, true "patient-oriented" value requires hospital operators and service providers to have customers in their hearts and to adhere to the principle of "client-oriented".

What the service industry desperately needs is a loving heart. It should be integrated into the core values of enterprises to form criteria for all employees. By this, the enterprise will grow. If there is no walk after the talk, failure will be inevitable.

The following part will focus on the introduction to the research achievements of the "patient-oriented" hospital culture.

Contents

About the Author v
Foreword vii
Preface ix
Introduction xiii

Part 1 Defining Hospital Culture using Basic Values **1**

Chapter 1 Hospital Culture without Core Values **3**

Empty Definitions and Complicated Practices 4
Typical Characteristics of Traditional Hospital Cultures 5
Inspiration from Mayo Clinic 7
Hospital (Enterprise) Culture — The Carrier of Core Values 7
Hospital (Enterprise) Culture — The Inheritor of Core Values 9
The Protective Effect of Culture on the Health of the Hospital (Enterprise) 10
Discouraging Doctors from Pursuing Self-interested Goals 11

Chapter 2 Defining Hospital Culture **13**

Definition of Hospital Culture 13
Differences between Two Cultures 15

Chapter 3 Basic Ideas for Research and Implementation of Participatory Hospital Culture **21**

Full Participation 21

Starting from Patient Service Details 22
Prioritising the Experience of Patients and Their Family Members 23
Experience Depending on Practicality 25
Always Approaching and Always Lagging Behind 26
Developing Persistent Habits in Standard Practices 27

Chapter 4 Establishing a Hospital Culture Evaluation Model 29

Hospital Culture Evaluation Model 29
Patient Experience Process — The Value Chain Delivering Warmth 30
Enterprise-type Hospital Culture 31
Charitable Hospital Culture 33
Indifferent Hospital Culture 33
Pirate-type Hospital Culture 34
Discrete Hospital Culture 34
Design and Evaluation of the Service Level Indicator System 34
Design and Evaluation of Profit-seeking Degree Indicators 35
Evaluation of the Hospital Culture Type after Investigation 40
Evaluation Results 40
Improvement Direction in Hospital Culture Construction 40

Part 2 The Experience of Patients and Their Family Members 45

Chapter 5 Catering to People's Visual Sense 47

Reducing Visible Inconveniences 47
Where Improvement is Needed According to the Patients 52
Services Needing to Be Improved for Patients 60
Management Issues Noticed by Patients 66
Etiquette — The First Impression of Patients and Their Family Members 76

Chapter 6 Using Warm and Pleasant Words 83

Creating a Quiet Environment for Patients 84
Satisfaction from Clear and Pleasant Words 86

Patients' Auditory Feelings Needing to Be Managed 92
Standards Existing in Hearing Etiquettes 94

Chapter 7 Providing Fresh Air for Patients 101

Chapter 8 Pleasant Smells and Palatable Food 105

Chapter 9 Warmth and Comfort 109

Convenient Facilities Required to Get Satisfactory Temperature 109
Never Ignore Impacts of Environment on Touch 111
Let Patients Feel Warm During Contact 113
Patients' Touch Needing to Be Managed 117

Chapter 10 Leaving a Good Impression on Patients 121

Resident Awareness and Timeliness — Approach to Convenience 123
Impact on Patients' Mood Even from Slight Changes in the Environment 126
The Essence: Willing and Active Service 129
Patient Satisfaction Comes from Efforts in Many Aspects 147

Part 3 Hospital Culture Construction 151

Chapter 11 Diagnosis of Hospital Culture 153

An Objective, Accurate and Quick Investigation Plan 153
Objectivity — The Soul of Hospital Culture Survey 156
Evaluating Hospital Culture Type Objectively 158
Show the Gaps to Prepare for Systematic Improvement Measures 159
Plotting the Radar Map to Show the Current Status of Hospital Culture 169
Plotting the Schematic Diagram of Hospital Culture Type 169

Chapter 12 Formulating Measures of Improvement for Hospital Culture Construction 173

Measures — The Carrier of Responsibilities 173
Improvement Measures for Convenience 174
Improvement Measures for Service 178
Improvement Measures for Management 181
Improvement Measures in Environment Link 182
Improvement Measures for Etiquette 184

Chapter 13 Implementing Hospital Culture Construction 187

Empowering Management Functions to Hospital Culture 187
Organizational Form of Hospital Culture Construction 191
Responsibility List Based on the Implementation of Improvement Measures 193

Chapter 14 Various Hospital Culture Construction Activities 199

Hospital Culture Construction — Implementation Is Better than Mere Paper Talk 199
Conducting Concerts in the Hospital 200
Region/Community-Rooted Public Relations 204

Chapter 15 Executive Force in Hospital Culture Construction 209

Launch of New Hospital Culture Construction Requiring Confidence 209
Emphasis of President and Executive Force of Leaders of the Cultural Management Department 211
Prerequisites for Being a Good Leader — Capabilities to Raise and Solve Problems 212
Resolution — The Start of All Practices 214
Higher Emotional Quotient Required by Leaders at All Levels 216
System Destroyer — Leaders Instead of Employees 217

Chapter 16 Cases of Management and Assessment of Hospital Culture Construction **219**
Organization, Division of Labor and Duties of Hospital Culture Improvement 219
Establishment of "Hospital Culture Construction" Quality Control Circle 221
Workflow of Hospital Culture Construction 221

Annex: Quality Control Circle Management Scheme of Cengong County People's Hospital 229

Index 263

Part 1

Defining Hospital Culture using Basic Values

Chapter 1
Hospital Culture without Core Values

In order to differentiate the "patient-oriented" hospital culture mentioned in this book from the traditional hospital cultures, all other hospital cultures that do not advocate the "patient-oriented" value are collectively referred to as traditional hospital culture.

In the early days of China's reform and opening up initiative, due to long-term planned economic system and typical social characteristics of material shortage at that time, the theory of enterprise management had not been exposed to the market economy or shown any innovation. The upsurge in the introduction of advanced management philosophy and theories from the west began then. Textbooks about management theory in Chinese universities are still based on management theories from developed countries.

China witnessed a wave of research and application of enterprise culture since the mid-1980s. The *Enterprise Culture — The Spiritual Pillar of Modern Enterprise* published by Professor Terrence E. Deal of Harvard University and consultant Allan A. Kennedy from McKinsey & Company, William G. Ouchi's *Theory Z: How American Business Can Meet the Japanese Challenge*, Tom Peters' *In Search of Excellence: Lessons from America's Best-Run Companies* and *The Art of Japanese Management* jointly written by Professors R.J. Pascale and A.G. Athos from Harvard Graduate School of Business Administration and Stanford Graduate School of Business were all influenced by it. All of these books have met with extremely good responses from around the world. Researching enterprise culture became an international trend, even involving China. The trend was called the emergence quartet of enterprise culture research in China. Research and application of this enterprise culture also penetrated into the medical industry.

For hospitals — a special service industry — culture will affect their development imperceptibly. Unfortunately, the enterprise culture was applied mechanically to the hospital culture construction for some time, resulting in a hospital culture that did not take patients into consideration. A hospital culture lacking the core values of "serving patients" surely deviates from the hospitals' tenet. The definition of "hospital culture" in Baidu Baike does not even mention "patient" at all, obviously overlooking the fact that healthcare is a special service industry. The core value of serving patients is clearly overlooked. It is universally true that hospitals are built to provide health services to patients and residents, rather than anything else.

All cultures are governed by some core values. In hospitals, it should be "patient-oriented" service. Many other values such as "employee-focused" or "profit-driven" ones, deviating from the tenet of serving patients in hospitals, are what we don't want to see.

Empty Definitions and Complicated Practices

The typical characteristic of traditional hospital culture is the absence of "patients" in its values. Normally, the traditional hospital culture has generalized and narrowed concepts.

In a broad sense, hospital culture refers to the total sum of certain materials and spiritual wealth created by the hospital's subjects and objects after long-term medical practices. It includes the explicit culture of the hospital (medical equipment, building, environment, medical technology level and benefit) and the implicit culture of the hospital (ideas, consciousness, concepts and behavior patterns with distinct hospital characteristics, as well as the supportive system and organizational structure). The explicit culture of a hospital is tangible and objective and its subject is material, while the implicit culture of a hospital is developed during the long development of the hospital and its subject is people.

In a narrow sense, hospital culture mainly refers to implicit culture, i.e. the value concepts with distinct characteristics that the hospital developed during its long-term medical activities that are recognized and observed by all employees. It is the sum total of the hospital's operating standards, management style, spirit, moral codes and development goals.

Obviously, neither the generalized nor the narrowed definition of hospital culture has anything to do with the "patient". According to Terrence E. Deal and Allan A. Kennedy, enterprise culture consists of five elements, enterprise environment, values, heroes, rituals and cultural network, with values being the core element. Therefore, the "patient-oriented" value is the soul and the spiritual pillar of hospital culture construction.

At Mayo Clinic, the core philosophy of being "patient-centered" runs throughout the entire decision-making process, right from the top level. When the leaders are facing numerous complicated issues, different opinions will be raised, and then the core value may play a decisive role. Any final decisions benefiting the patients must be favourable and embody the leading role of the "patient-oriented" value in hospital culture construction.

Typical Characteristics of Traditional Hospital Cultures

In addition to the absence of a "patient-oriented" core value, traditional hospital culture also has other features, which are as follows.

First, the hospital culture construction is too broad and lacks a boundary concept. Hospital culture construction includes material culture, behavior culture and spiritual culture. Such abundant concepts make the hospital a basket that can be filled with anything, leading to difficulty in practical management. Hospital culture construction early on was set against a unique historical background. The trend of constructing hospital cultures in China originated in the late 1990s and developed in the early 21st century. At that time,

Chinese society was rife with official standards, money worship, formalism and extravagance, and China's hospital culture construction also reflected that. The hospital culture that evolved at that time extended to infinity in terms of both concept and contents. Hospital culture construction was worshiped as the almighty top-level management, and a plethora of studies on hospital culture appeared. Thus, the understanding and description of culture deviated further from the "patient-oriented" value. Ideological confusion, distortion of values and proliferation of formalism became typical features of hospital culture construction in that era. Some scholars even proposed the establishment of an "employee-centered" service philosophy in hospitals, and this was once even recognized by certain people. Numerous academic papers on hospital culture research were produced during that period. Many of the papers did not even mention the idea of "serving patients" at all, indicating the serious formalism of "empty words".

Second, hospital culture construction focuses on management organization and hospital employees, rather than on patients. This runs counter to the main hospital tenet of serving patients. At that time, hospital culture construction mainly focused on internal employees and attached great importance to the improvement of employees' images, teamwork awareness, professional skills and service attitude. All of these aimed to improve the quality of the hospital staff. However, all would be in vain without any "patient-oriented" values. Patients would still face poker-faced medical staff, tedious formalities and poor hospital wards. The service provided by a hospital directly determines the satisfaction of a patient. Good service means that it is a good hospital and vice versa. That's it.

Third, formalism was deeply rooted in hospital culture construction, mostly serving as a political ploy. Therefore, ideological construction rather than behavior changes was the focus. This period was characterized by more slogans with few actual measures of improvement. The fundamental reason for this was that many hospital administrators didn't really realize that the value of hospital culture construction was better patient services and that an operable patient service standard was required for cultural construction. The traditional hospital culture construction was poorly operable. Although hospitals have formulated relevant codes of conduct, spirit, mission and service philosophy; made banners; created slogans; held flag-raising ceremonies; formulated a hospital song and organized various cultural activities, the lack of a "patient-oriented" value was noticeable in all of these. Therefore, patients and their families felt little or no service improvement despite the vigorous hospital culture construction.

Fourth, the achievements of cultural construction were evaluated by the hospitals or their superiors themselves, without an objective standard or without the firm foundation of public opinion. Of course, this was common throughout the world, not just in China. Enterprise culture evaluation will be further discussed in subsequent research.

Inspiration from Mayo Clinic

The book *Management Lessons from Mayo Clinic* brought the American Mayo Clinic style to China and even the world. The Clinic has been praised as a world-level medical palace since its establishment over a century ago, and its core cultural value is "patients' requirements come first". Patients choose Mayo Clinic because of the care, confidence, hope and superior services it provides rather than any other advantages such as magnificent buildings, advanced technology or famous doctors. Mayo Clinic is committed to providing the best care and service for each patient every day. Everyone at Mayo Clinic cares about their patients. This, in simplistic terms, is the core value of Mayo Clinic.

Hospital (Enterprise) Culture — The Carrier of Core Values

Hospital culture is the manifestation of values rather than a single element in the organization's operation. It is not parallel to but dominant over the various other elements in the organization's operation.

Hospital culture is the carrier of core values, and it runs through the hospital operation, serving the transportation function. The hospital needs to construct its core values and practice them in all aspects with culture as the carrier. Such core values will be reflected in human resources, product and service innovation, quality management, cost management, marketing and decision management. It is only after being equipped with core values can the counterintuitive concepts and actions in the daily operation of hospitals be eliminated, which will thus conserve and protect the healthy metabolism of the organization. The highlighting and practicing of the "patient-oriented" core value requires hospital leaders to emphasize the core value and act in strict accordance with it. This is not easy. Once a deviation from the core value occurs at a certain stage, the function of hospital cultures to convey these values will be weakened and the future organization and operation of hospitals will be morbid. It is clear that leaders need to constantly undertake self-reflection and warn all employees on this topic in order to prevent any morbidity.

The external social environment, rapid development of technology, extensive application of the Internet technology and the emergence of WIT120 indicate the high requirements for hospital operation and management. Hospitals must adapt to environmental changes; however, the hospital culture should remain unchanged, let alone the core values that lead the hospital culture. New policies, technologies and medical patterns should be integrated into the "patient-oriented" version of hospital culture. Other values under the guidance of core values will adjust the operation of organizations via cultures.

In fact, a successful organization should develop a unique philosophy or methodology regarding human resources, quality management, marketing, innovation management, teamwork, etc., all of which are governed and led by core values.

The universal model for the core value-governed traditional hospital culture construction is shown in Figure 1.1, in which the shift from the original philosophy of hospital culture construction into the core value-governed hospital culture construction is also depicted.

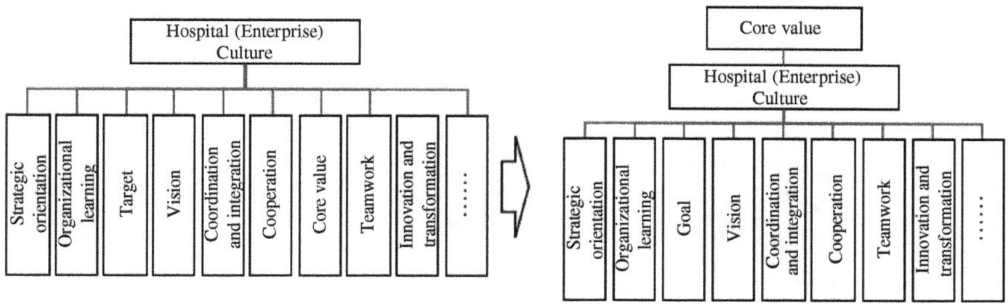

Figure 1.1 Core values leading hospital culture construction

Hospital (Enterprise) Culture — The Inheritor of Core Values

During our visit to Mayo Clinic in 2015, a Chinese American, who had worked at Mayo Clinic for over 20 years, received us and told us many stories about Mayo. The visit turned out to be beneficial. What amazed us most was that there were no advertisement banners about Mayo Clinic on the walls — something quite different from many other hospitals.

A hospital culture must be stable since something that is constantly changing cannot become a culture. Mayo Clinic's inheritance of this over a century old "patient-oriented" hospital culture relies on its consistency with and practice of it over the years.

This culture must be useful and play an important role in the sustainable development of hospitals. It should go beyond the flowery slogans hanging on the wall and the profound comprehension of the hospital leaders about their values, which have nothing to do with the actions taken by management. We must bear in mind that the core values are there for us to implement and carry forward. We noticed a leaflet at Mayo Clinic. It is marked with "Welcome to Mayo Clinic" in the front, and the expression "Patients are our first priority" (Figure 1.2) is included in the introduction.

In fact, many enterprises or hospitals would describe their values at their beginning. But these values are usually meaningless in practice, and are just created for show. Only those organizations that

Figure 1.2 A Mayo Clinic leaflet

have existed for a long time and achieved considerable growth will comprehend their core values and unique cultures. The leaders of these organizations will be able to realize the importance of cultural inheritance to the existence and development of the organization, and pass it on as a treasure.

The Protective Effect of Culture on the Health of the Hospital (Enterprise)

There must be some reason for a hospital's existence and prosperity for over a century, and the very gene is imprinted in the core values of its hospital culture. This core value-governed culture will constantly resist and remove interferences from unfavorable external ideologies and behaviors. At the forefront is the Mayo culture, which all employees must adhere to or leave, without any alternatives. We were shocked by such a strong and unshakable cultural inertia. In fact, only culture can make a hospital or an enterprise healthy and long-lasting since only the introduction of values will maintain the relative stability of the organization, enabling adaptation to any external environmental changes and maintaining its leading position. In particular, the protective culture can lead to the removal (clear-out) of employees who do not approve of, adapt to, or who violate the hospital (enterprise) culture, regardless of their titles or designation. In this way, the healthy operation of the organization is guaranteed. The so-called clear-out includes, first, the actions of the organization to drive out any employees seriously deviating from the organization's culture and discipline; and second, firing employees who fail to fit into the culture and want to seek opportunities that suit their preferred organizational cultures.

Like enterprises, a hospital, especially a society-benefiting and healthy one, would be home to some employees who think highly of themselves, overlook the organization rules and put their individual will, interest and values over those of the organization. What an organization needs are employees who recognize the organization's values, integrate their abilities into the organization and grow together with the organization.

Discouraging Doctors from Pursuing Self-interested Goals

We didn't know that the Mayo Clinic was a non-profit hospital until we walked in. The list of enterprises who gave in donations is put up on the wall in the Outpatient Hall, to be remembered forever. More amazingly, along the corridor leading to the canteen on the first floor, we saw a long wall engraved with the names of individual donors.

As the name suggests, a non-profit hospital is not profit-seeking by nature. Corresponding to its non-profit nature, Mayo Clinic sets a unique salary system — all doctors and nurses will get almost the same salary after working at Mayo Clinic for 5 years. A doctor with 5 years of experience at Mayo Clinic will make about the same amount of money as those with decades of experience, or even more famous doctors. This is different from what we had known about hospitals in many countries, including the US.

In Mayo Clinic, a doctor's salary is not related to his or her medical actions at all. Such a pure salary system nullified the interview outline I had prepared. China's hospitals usually adopt a performance-based salary system, highlighting "more pay for more work, and better pay for better service". How to avoid the "profit-driven" behaviors of hospitals was the question on our mind while visiting Mayo Clinic.

I was enlightened by the idea of distinguishing the profit-pursuing behaviors of hospitals from those of doctors.

In fact, hospitals in all countries must obtain sufficient funds to maintain normal operation, and the funds usually come from the government, insurance agencies, charitable donations from individuals and donations from organizations. Hospitals have to bear the expenses of the medicines as well as auxiliary costs during its operation, and also pay long-term or short-term debts seen in the balance sheet. Of course, there will be human resource expenses as well. Therefore, a hospital must seek profit to avoid the loss of major doctors and nursing staff due to low salary standard.

The success of Mayo Clinic is also attributable to its remarkable practice of preventing doctors from chasing personal gains. The prerequisite for this practice is the ability to implement a corresponding system. If a hospital does not have sufficient funds to support its operation, any system that discourages doctors from pursuing their self-interest will fail. Hence, an institution needs to be profit-driven, regardless of the sources, and this is the top priority of its operators. If a doctor's salary is linked with workload and his or her contributions to the institution, problems will arise. There will inevitably be medical behaviors that damage the interest of the patients and society and run counter to the "patient-oriented" core values. This is why the hospital must be profit-driven while doctors must not. In reality, all around the world, very few hospitals do this. What we often see is that the profit-seeking behaviors of the hospital are copied by doctors. Preventing doctors from pursuing their self-interest needs more social restrictions and changes to the operating capacity and system design of hospitals. There is still a long way to go.

Chapter 2
Defining Hospital Culture

The definition of hospital culture shouldn't be infinite and boundless. Some Chinese scholars understand hospital culture as being both a generalized and a narrowed concept. The generalized hospital culture is "the sum of certain material wealth and spiritual wealth created by the hospital's subjects and objects" during its long medical practice. This is a concept easy to explain but hard to explain clearly. The narrow concept refers to implicit culture, i.e. the values imprinted with the distinct characteristics of a hospital developed during the long-term medical activities and recognized and observed by all employees. It is the sum of the hospital's operating standards, management style, spirit, moral codes and development goals. This concept categorizes the hospital culture in ideology. However, both generalized and narrowed definitions deviate far away from "patient-oriented" nature of hospitals. All hospitals in the world are built to treat patients. A hospital would be useless if it fails to serve patients. Thus, hospital culture construction must highlight the core of serving patients, and all research and practices should be carried out based on the "patient-oriented" value.

Definition of Hospital Culture

It is meaningful to accurately define a culture in such a way as to reflect the core strategic contents to maintain long-term and healthy development of an institution. Conceptually, hospital culture reflects a hospital's attitude towards patients, its employees' attitude towards patients, as well as the direct or indirect satisfaction level of patients and their families.

First of all, we should be clear about the fact that hospitals are places that provide medical services to patients and their family members. The targets of all services offered by hospitals are patients and their family members. The connotations of hospital culture should be based on the core value that it should be a "patient-oriented" one. Therefore, anything that cannot be directly or indirectly felt by patients or their family members does not belong to the concept of hospital culture. This changes the infinite and boundless traditional hospital culture. Thus, the hospital culture construction transforms from an abstract concept to an operable, targeted and effective practice. This is the most fundamental difference between our new understanding and the previous understanding of hospital (enterprise) culture.

Second is the profit-seeking degree of hospitals. The majority of hospitals in the world are profit-seeking. We are not suggesting that profit-seeking behavior is unfavorable. Institutions need to maintain their normal operations, whether they are social capital–funded, non-profit or for-profit. What matters is whether the profit-seeking degree matches your service level. For a hospital with poor service, the residents would hate it regardless of its type, because it is against the basic tenet of hospitals. The profit-making nature of a hospital requires it to make profits, but it must also provide good medical services. A public-benefiting hospital also needs to make profits; however, the profit it makes from providing medical insurance services will not be too high; otherwise, it will step away from its public-benefiting nature. It is a whole other story if it also provides non-medical insurance services.

In Singapore's hospitals, inpatient wards are divided into A, B and C classes. Class A inpatients are not covered by medical insurance, and they receive top-level services and treatments, which is directly related to their paying capacity. While Class B and C inpatients will be covered by medical insurance based on their paying capacity, even Class C inpatients are provided with effective treatments and satisfactory services. Hospitals earn more profits from Class A inpatients, less from Class B inpatients and much less from Class C inpatients. However, the hospital will still have surplus in general; otherwise, it couldn't operate at a normal level. What Singapore hospitals did give was a lesson for all countries in the world — all residents can choose different medical services based on their actual economic capability. The experience of Singapore hospitals can be summarized as "Affordable Excellence".

Below are the in-depth understandings of this concept from six aspects:

1. The "patient-oriented" hospital culture construction will be carried out from the fundamental point of "patient experience".
2. All service-related problems arising in a hospital are the direct reflections of the hospital's attitude towards patients and their family members. A hospital should care about its patients and their feelings.
3. Hospital culture construction is characterized by "full participation", with every employee being a participant and practitioner.
4. Hospital culture construction is not targeted at providing the best environment and services, but with the patient satisfaction as the top priority. It aims to provide the most satisfactory environment and services. The socio-economic development level in different countries and regions varies, and populations with different economic income levels will have different requirements and perceptions about their service experience.
5. Hospital culture construction should be initiated by the leaders of the hospital, with a focus on standardizing the basic environment and behaviors through management and assessment.
6. Profit-seeking behaviors are commonly seen in many hospitals, but such behaviors need to match the service levels of hospitals.

Differences between Two Cultures

The new "patient-oriented" hospital culture is different from the original one owing to its insistence on "patient-oriented" value as the basic tenet of the hospital. This results in multiple differences from the traditional hospital culture. The differences between traditional hospital culture and patient-oriented hospital culture are summarized in Table 2.1 and annotated as follows:

1. The concept of traditional hospital culture is too complicated and abstract, boundless and infinite, and hard to understand and implement. However, the new hospital culture concept of "satisfying the needs of patients and family members" is easy to understand and implement.
2. In terms of management, the traditional hospital culture is subordinate to ideology, and is obviously political, mission-oriented and ideological. The new hospital culture is part of business management.
3. In terms of objectives, the traditional hospital culture construction is endowed with strong administrative and organizational features, and clearly targeted at serving the administrative or organizational operations. On the other hand, the sole objective of the new culture system is to serve patients, and keep improving the service quality.
4. In terms of research objectives, the two cultures show different emphases. The traditional one emphasizes continuous improvement of employees' ideological level, while the new one sets its roots firmly on the feelings of patients and their family members on ideas related to hospital's services.
5. The traditional and new hospital culture constructions have different strongholds. The former adheres to the core value of "enterprise culture" construction, seeks to improve employees' qualities and makes them care about the hospital, while the latter aspires to make employees care more about patients, and improve their patient service level.
6. The traditional and new hospital culture constructions are subordinate to different departments. The former is governed by the political administration department of the hospital (in China). The latter, on the other hand, is divided under the hospital business management umbrella, and the management

functions can be divided into medical matters, nursing and hospital-acquired infection departments. Or it can be an independent business management department dedicated to improving the hospital's service level.

7. The traditional and new hospital culture constructions also differ in their contents. The scope of the former is extremely wide, while the latter focuses on serving patients.
8. The traditional and new hospital culture constructions adopt different approaches to improve the level of serving patients. The former seeks to realize the above objective by changing its ideology, while the latter focuses on standardizing employees' actions in all aspects.
9. The traditional hospital culture construction stresses employees' consciousness during the process. The new construction emphasizes employees' execution of actions based on a specific standard.
10. The traditional and new hospital culture constructions also differ in their manifestations. The former focuses on the external form, showing serious formalism, while the latter pays attention to actions of the hospital leaders and employees, and determines specific directions and requirements for improvement.
11. The targeted participants of the two hospital culture constructions are different. The former highlights the role of leaders, and its participants are mainly administrative leaders at various levels led by the president. The latter, new hospital culture construction, engages all employees of the hospital and makes systems covering the whole hospital process to constantly improve the patient service quality.
12. The investigations undertaken to judge the levels of traditional and new hospital culture constructions are targeted at different objectives. The former mainly surveys employees, and rarely or never takes patients' feelings into consideration as there is no "patient-oriented" idea in this system. The latter mainly surveys patients, or judges the level of hospital culture construction from the standpoint of patient experience.
13. The operability of the traditional and new hospital culture constructions varies greatly. For the former, there are few

measures that can be used directly to improve patient services, leading to an extremely poor operability. It features emptiness, formalism, slogans and low innovation. The new culture construction is more concrete and practical, and it can clearly reflect the specific problems existing in hospital culture construction. With it, the improvements required are clear, the responsibilities are well-allocated and evidences are ready for assessment. Hence, hospital culture construction becomes a practical activity, rather than just theoretical research.

14. The traditional and new hospital culture constructions vary greatly in planning. Without a clear idea, the planning of the traditional construction is usually a copy of already existing ones and can be repeated for years. The latter develops accurate improvement plans on the basis of diagnosis.
15. The traditional and new hospital culture constructions vary widely in continuities. The former suffers from poor continuity as it lacks a system to evaluate its continuity, and the status quo of hospital culture construction is hard to evaluate. This further leads to the fact that no one can draw up continuous improvement measures for culture construction. The new culture construction system, on the other hand, has a specific evaluation system, making it possible to carry out continuous hospital culture construction to solve problems at different stages.
16. The traditional and new hospital culture constructions are evaluated by different groups. The former is evaluated by the hospital itself, which is kind of self-glorifying, as it is evaluated by a known superior. Both evaluation methods lack the participation of patients and the results may not be "patient-oriented". The new system consists of direct or indirect feelings of patients and their family members towards the hospital services, and the evaluation results reflect the satisfaction of patients.
17. The traditional and new hospital culture constructions are obviously different in evaluation. The level of the former is hard to evaluate, and a hospital's culture construction level is often approved or disapproved qualitatively, lacking scientificity. New culture construction can be accurately evaluated, making it more scientific.

18. When considering horizontal comparison of traditional and new hospital culture constructions, the traditional hospital cultural levels cannot be compared horizontally among different hospitals, due to the high consistency of their service procedures. The latter takes the experience and feelings of patients and their family members as the criteria for evaluating the hospital culture. Therefore, it is possible to evaluate hospitals' cultural construction levels. Horizontal comparison of hospital culture construction levels thus becomes practically possible.
19. Traditional and new hospital culture constructions are different in terms of their effect. The former works slowly since it mainly depends on ideological education, instead of codes and systems. In addition, this is also due to complicated and unclear objectives. As regards the latter, problems are easy to diagnose, and can be solved quickly if the hospital decides to do so.

Table 2.1 Differences between the two hospital cultures

S.N.	Comparison item	Original hospital culture	Patient-oriented hospital culture
1	Concept understanding	Abstract and complicated	Simple and easy to understand
2	Subordination	Ideology	Management content
3	Goal	Serve the politics	Serve patients
4	Research object	Internal employees	External patients
5	Foothold	Improve employees' quality	Improve the patient service level
6	Management department	Political and ideological work	Business
7	Content	Extensive	Focus on serving patients
8	Approach	Ideology	Regularize behaviors
9	Emphasis	Consciousness	Executability

Table 2.1 (*Continued*)

S.N.	Comparison item	Original hospital culture	Patient-oriented hospital culture
10	Pattern of manifestation	Focus on the form	Focus on actions
11	Participation	Leaders at all levels	All members
12	Investigation subjects	Mainly survey the employees	Mainly survey patients
13	Operability	Few measures	More measures
14	Planning	Disoriented	Accurate improvement
15	Continuity	Hard to continue	Continuous improvement
16	Evaluator	Itself or the superior	Patients
17	Evaluation capacity	Unable to evaluate	Accurate evaluation is possible
18	Horizontal comparison	Unachievable	Achievable
19	Effect	Slow	Quick

Chapter 3
Basic Ideas for Research and Implementation of Participatory Hospital Culture

The basic ideas for the research and implementation of hospital culture can be analyzed from three aspects. First of all, full participation; second, patient service details should be the priority; and third, there must be an everlasting determination to implement various improvement measures, making patients and their families more satisfied with the hospital's ever-improving service level.

Full Participation

In today's service industry, hospitals, even those with very high levels of intelligence, have the most complicated and tedious service process among all sectors. Therefore, the most important step for hospital culture construction is to engage all employees throughout the entire process. Upon entering a hospital, a patient needs to go through a series of service processes to get medical diagnosis and treatment. The patients or their family members are usually dissatisfied with one certain link in this process, and not all of the processes. Over its long life, the world-renowned Mayo Clinic keeps perfecting all the links of the patient service chain, ensuring patient satisfaction with the hospital's constantly improving services. Meanwhile, the continuous improvement of medical services also makes the Clinic more reliable in the eyes of the patients.

"Patient-oriented" philosophy is the core value of hospital culture construction, which is practiced by each and every medical staff. This value won't be recognized by the residents unless it has been carried out for a long time. None of the employees in the hospital can be excluded from it.

Starting from Patient Service Details

We are all clear about what details refer to. However, it is not so easy to show perfect details in every aspect and to take details as the focus of hospital culture construction all the time.

Can you politely greet all the patients and their family members you receive every day?

Can you keep smiling whenever you are in front of a patient or their family members?

Can you keep your clothing tidy and clean every day?

Can you make sure that the patient doesn't feel a sudden chill when you put the stethoscope on his or her chest in winter?

Can you gently call their name whenever you contact a patient?

Can you remain careful and patient during an inquiry? Can you listen to patients carefully and patiently?

Can you insist on cooperation with different experts to provide services for one patient (consultation)?

Everything, including services, that is involved in hospital culture construction amounts to details. Once a hospital can shine bright in all the details, it will also make great improvements in other significant aspects. The technical advantage that Mayo Clinic possesses wasn't built in one day. Residents choose it because of its constant improvement in these tiny details. After over 100 years of earnest practice of "patient-oriented" values, Mayo Clinic has finally been recognized by people, making the brand a renowned one not only in the US but also worldwide.

Hospital culture can be felt by patients. The objective of hospital culture construction is to make patients feel satisfied with the medical services offered to them. In fact, a patient can feel the influences of hospital culture as early as the time they get sick. The choice of which hospital to visit for treatment is the very result of hospital culture influence. All the different medical services received since arrival at the hospital will impact the patient's feelings about the hospital. From this point of view, "hospital culture" is actually a "detail-oriented culture". We need to study hospital culture and its construction using details appreciable by patients. Only in this way can we ensure that the hospital culture serves the needs of patients and their family members. However, what we commonly see in hospital culture construction are things unrelated to patient experience at all. When a patient comes in, all the doctors care about is whether he or she can be cured, rather than wondering if they feel comfortable with the services. They do not care about other aspects unrelated to treatment. On the contrary, we can see tons of non-medical advertisements in many hospitals. Some management departments require placement of all those banners unrelated to patients' treatment, and this is even taken as a standard for assessment. In fact, for a public benefit hospital, it is fulfilling its social responsibilities in providing good medical services. Without that pre-condition, all banners and slogans, no matter how beautiful they may sound, are useless.

Our hospital culture and its construction do urgently need radical reforms in order to retain the serving of patients as the priority. Hospital culture is meaningless until it is recognized by patients and family members. It is not a tool for self-glorification or an evaluation from the superior that matters. Hospital culture construction is a process which standardizes the behavior of employees using the above-mentioned details and keeps finding ways to improve patient service levels.

Prioritising the Experience of Patients and Their Family Members

Hospital culture is an objective reality. As long as hospitals exist, there will be medical and nursing behaviors and interactions between the medical staff and the patients. This interaction is quite long-lasting, and it is during this time that the hospital would send various signals to patients. All these signals are collectively called hospital culture, and they are in sum the feelings of patients and their family members, and not something that is self-awarded. Hospital culture objectively exists, despite whether it was intended to or not. Hospital culture differs from the cultures of other organizations as the prime goal here is to save people's lives. Hospitals are established for patients, and so hospital culture should be "patient-oriented".

Leonard L. Berry explained the objective existence of the "patient-oriented" hospital culture of Mayo Clinic for over 100 years and expounded on the significance of the inheritance of such a culture in his book entitled *Management Lessons from Mayo Clinic.* Inheriting a "patient-oriented" value (and other related values and philosophies) was, is and will always be the first priority of Mayo Clinic's management, and the "patient-oriented" core value is deeply rooted in the Mayo culture.

The "patient-oriented" hospital culture we highlighted values the direct or indirect feelings that patients and their family members have towards the hospital service. Their satisfaction with the services provided by the hospital is the objective of the existence of the "patient-oriented" hospital culture. We should give a systematic description of patients' feelings at various links of the medical services chain process. Their feelings towards the hospital services mainly come from two aspects. One is their experience with the respective medical services at each link, and the other is the cost. The former kind of feeling refers to the fact that all links of the medical service institution can instil a sense of warmth, convenience and curative instinct. Then, every patient would have such feelings, which have nothing to do with the nature, grade and size of the hospital. Different patient groups would have different feelings towards the charge level, which is directly related to the nature of the hospital and the social medical security level. For instance, if the self-paid aspect of the hospital is too costly, most patients will feel that "getting medical treatment is expensive", resulting in their dissatisfaction. This is something the society, especially the government, needs to handle.

Profit-making hospitals must, however, cater to patient groups with a certain paying capacity, as such groups of patients demand more services.

Experience Depending on Practicality

The "patient-oriented" hospital culture highlights the practicality of hospital culture construction. It studies and standardizes the hospital culture construction from the perspective of patients and makes a quantum leap forward in quantitative research about hospital culture construction. While the traditional hospital culture construction is hard to examine or assess, a complete patient experience model is established based on patients' feelings towards hospital services. Using this model, the experience of patients from all aspects is surveyed, and so standards covering all aspects of medical services and satisfying patients and their family members are developed. Using these standards, we can clearly determine the type of "patient-oriented" culture of the hospital, precisely show the direction of improvement of the "patient-oriented" hospital culture and formulate explicit improvement measures, thus making hospital culture construction a true management tool for the hospital to improve its service quality, instead of an abstract aspect as in traditional hospital culture construction.

The "patient-oriented" hospital culture can easily be felt. It means that patients and their family members can clearly feel the results upon the implementation of a series of continuous cultural improvement measures from all aspects of hospital environment, definite indicating system provided for patients, access to information required by patients, service attitude of doctors and nursing staff and reduction in waiting time. It indicates a transformation from the "patient-oriented" commitment to the real experience of patients and their family members. For the design of a "patient-oriented" hospital culture indicator system, scenes that are intuitively visible to patients and their family members in hospitals should be deemed as the starting point. For instance, an unlit signal lamp in the Emergency Department will surely make it harder for an emergency patient to get to the requisite department. Other examples are gentle reminders around the hospital, such as “Mind Your Step”. This is similar to the physical evidence seen in the seven elements of service marketing (service marketing 7P, i.e. product, price, place, promotion, people, physical evidence and process).

Always Approaching and Always Lagging Behind

The “patient-oriented” hospital culture cannot be constructed in one day. It requires constant improvement along with socio-economic development and keeping up with increasing patient requirements. In the traditional hospital culture construction, it is difficult to show progress due to the absence of a basic evaluation system. We can say the hospital culture construction level is improving, but it is just a generic statement since there’s no quantitative evidence. We are not clear about the current picture of the “patient-oriented” hospital culture, nor can we propose any plans for progressive improvements. This book proposes to construct an evaluation system for the “patient-oriented” hospital culture, providing an intuitive and quantifiable standard for hospital culture and to help make the progressive improvement of “patient-oriented” hospital culture construction a reality. This progressivity also lies in the constant perfection of the evaluation system with the constant increase of patients’ service needs. The evaluation system will gradually expand as the services become diverse, and a progressive increase of the service standards can be observed.

Constant improvement of the level of serving patients is an eternal issue that hospitals have to contend with. It is always lagging behind when assessed with the expected hospital culture construction, suggesting the very hysteresis of hospital culture construction. Yet in many cases, we don’t realize that it is lagging behind, and even if we do we don’t know in what way and how to improve it. The constructed “patient-oriented” hospital culture diagnosis model provides a systematic evaluation indicator system for the hospital’s service level, which can clearly diagnose the hysteresis of hospitals’ services, and thus provide a practical basis for the hospital to construct the "patient-oriented" culture more effectively.

Developing Persistent Habits in Standard Practices

The "patient-oriented" hospital culture weakens the "ideology" of traditional hospital culture construction and strengthens the "normativity". It establishes the basic standard and codes of conduct that must be observed by the leaders, the medical staff and other service personnel in the various links that the patient goes through during a hospital visit. This changes the lack of normativity in traditional hospital culture construction and bridges the long-separated status of hospital culture construction and hospital management.

It is very hard for medical staff and other service personnel to develop a habit of serving the patients actively and without complaints through constant ideological education. In fact, any good habit, especially the habit of actively serving the patients, will not be formed among employees spontaneously, and it can't rest on "self-consciousness". Systematic basic codes and rules concerning patient service and a rigorous assessment system are the basic necessities to ensure that hospital employees fulfill the "patient-oriented" hospital culture.

The "patient-oriented" hospital culture is obviously mandatory for hospital employees to satisfy the patients and their family members. It aims to make sure that employees at all posts can provide satisfactory services for patients under a set of relatively complete standards and restraint mechanism, transforming the hospital culture management (management culture) from emphasizing the "self-consciousness" to highlighting the "mandatory" execution of hospital cultural systems.

Any task, including hospital culture construction, wouldn't last long if it solely depended on mentation. In European and American countries, people would consciously sweep the snow in front of their houses after a snowfall. It is not because of the high awareness of their citizens, but the legislations which require the homeowners to clean the snow in front of their doors as soon as possible. If they fail to do so, they would be fined or would have to bear the medical expenses for anyone who falls in front of their houses. Over time, this quick snow-sweeping became a culture. This is the behavioral habit driven by cultures formed by institutional constraints.

Hospital culture construction needs persistence, while the traditional hospital culture is too complex, lacking institutional constraints and emphasizing ideological education. Hospital culture, as an ideological and political task, inevitably lacks persistence while the "patient-oriented" hospital culture construction puts forward a series of specifications as the standard for hospital culture construction, which greatly enhances the persistence of hospital culture construction.

Chapter 4
Establishing a Hospital Culture Evaluation Model

There is no model that can quantify and evaluate hospital culture types and guide the hospital to constantly improve its level of hospital culture construction in any academic report worldwide.

Hospital Culture Evaluation Model

To come up with a mode, first of all, we selected two decisive indicators to evaluate hospital culture, developing an "S–P" hospital culture evaluation model, where the first indicator "S" is the service level, which is proposed based on the core value of hospital culture, and the second one "P" is the degree of profit-seeking of hospitals, which is based on the fact that all hospitals require economic sources, whether through government funding, through social donation or by self-operation, to support their normal operations. The service level and profit-seeking degree of hospitals determine the basic type of hospital culture. As shown in Figure 4.1, these cultures can be of the enterprise type, charity type, indifferent type, pirate type or discrete type.

All hospitals should set "patient-orientedness" as their core values, so that they regard the continuous pursuit of satisfaction of patients and their family members as the tenet. Also, the profit-seeking degree reveals whether hospitals hold the proper basic social responsibility. Non-profit hospitals should reflect the nature associated with their name, that is, show little profit-seeking

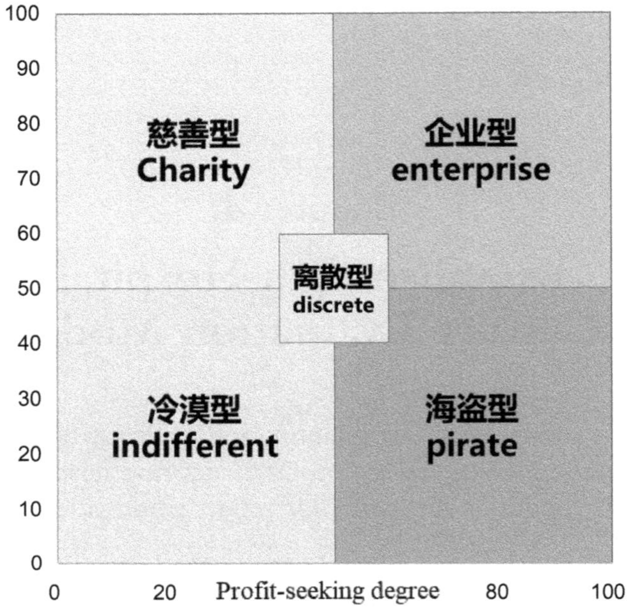

Figure 4.1 Hospital culture evaluation (S–P) model

intention; otherwise, their existence will become meaningless. Profit-making hospitals must make profits, but at a level that matches their medical service level. If they seek high profits but provide poor service, it is a violation against social morality and the hospital will then be spurned by the people.

Patient Experience Process — The Value Chain Delivering Warmth

Endowing hospital cultures with the "patient-oriented" core value generally means that core values cover all links of hospital service. Hospitals' scale and technology level should not be the targets of hospital culture evaluation. Whether in large or small hospitals, hospital culture is believed to be positive and healthy as long as it reflects the "patient-oriented" core value.

Figure 4.2 shows the basic service experience process of patients in hospitals. We have determined the experience indicators based on what the patients and their families see, hear, smell, taste, touch and feel at each service node and then concluded the indicators of convenience, environment, etiquette, service and management in the hospital operation (Figure 4.3) to form a schematic matrix diagram about patient experience and feeling in the hospital. Observing this expression longitudinally, we can identify the problems to be solved in convenience, environment, etiquette, service and management, in order to improve the visual feelings of patients and their family members. Horizontally, we can observe the hospital services and put forward measures to improve services from different sense aspects, in order to ensure convenience.

We have conducted significant research into the indicator system for such things as service level and profit-seeking degree and have come up with a relatively systematic indicator system to evaluate hospital culture types and measures to improve hospital culture construction. For the past five years, we have provided more than 100 hospitals with the special-subject consulting about "patient-oriented" hospital culture in China, and we will also improve the system according to unique customs and local regulations in different areas during the course of the implementation process.

Enterprise-type Hospital Culture

Enterprise-type hospital culture means that hospitals provide quality services while pursuing high profits. What needs attention is that "enterprise type" is a neutral description of hospitals. Just like enterprises, they must provide better products and services for more profits; otherwise, they cannot survive in the market. In many countries, some hospitals are funded by the government and belong to the public. These are the non-profit hospitals, and they need to stay true to their nature. It should be noted that not targeting profits does not mean making no profits at all. Problems will occur if they make too high profits, but they cannot survive if they suffer any

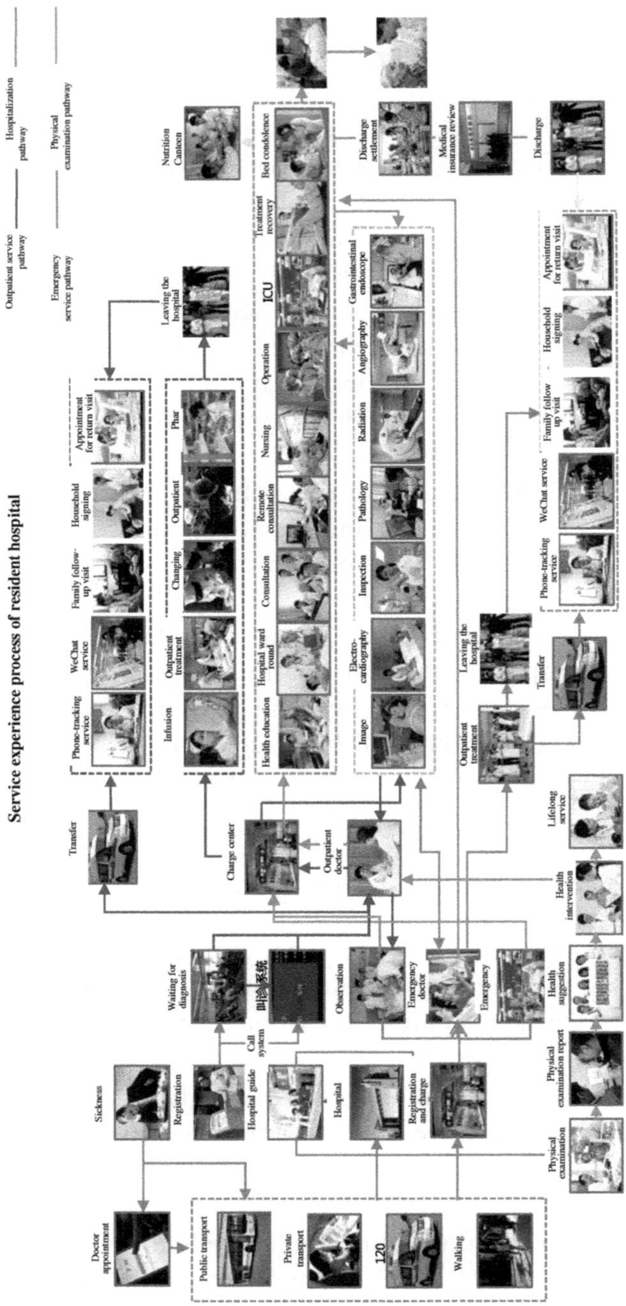

Figure 4.2 Flow chart of medical treatment experience of patients in the hospital

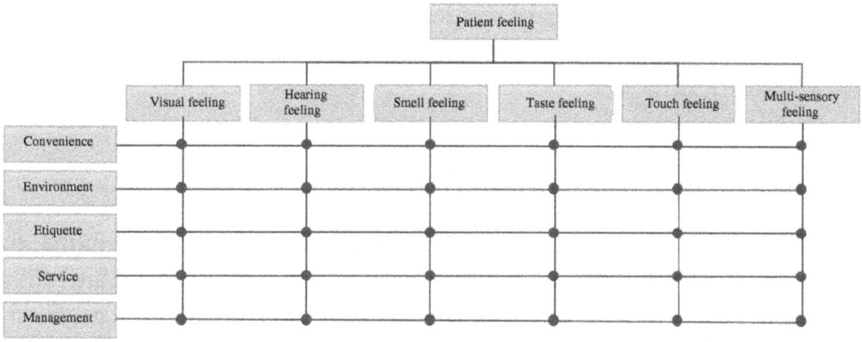

Figure 4.3 Schematic diagram of the patient experience and feeling in the hospital

losses. Especially for public-benefit hospitals with debts, they can make certain profits when the government picks up the tab, or they can repay the debts by themselves, which means they should make more profits to recover the debt. The profit-making private hospitals must make profits because they are fully exposed to the law of survival of the fittest.

Non-profit or profit-making hospitals are classified as the enterprise type as long as they show a relatively high profit-seeking degree.

Charitable Hospital Culture

Hospitals with a charitable hospital culture pay more attention to service quality, providing patients and their family members with relatively good healthcare services with a relatively low profit-seeking degree. Public or non-profit hospitals sponsored by public expenditure belong to this type.

Indifferent Hospital Culture

Hospitals with an indifferent hospital culture pay less attention to patient experience and have a relatively low service level and profit-seeking tendency as well. Obviously, this culture is not advocated for by society. Such hospitals have a low profit-seeking degree, but are still not liked by patients and residents, and they will be uncompetitive if they are located in cities or communities where medical resources are relatively sufficient.

Pirate-type Hospital Culture

Pirate-type hospitals use improper means to seek private gains or make exorbitant profits, with a strong profit-seeking degree, and they are indifferent to patients' feelings and provide poor services. Such hospitals will not be popular among the residents, and if public-benefit hospitals turn to the pirate-type, the regulatory departments should take the initiative to make changes and improve the overall service level. Private hospitals of this type cannot develop healthily, or last long.

Discrete Hospital Culture

Discrete hospital culture means that hospitals have a good general performance in both service and profit, without an obvious tendency towards either but with great uncertainty. If their profit-seeking degree increases or their service level declines, they will become indifferent or pirate-type. If their service level or profit-seeking degree increases, they will turn into a charity-type or an enterprise-type hospital.

Design and Evaluation of the Service Level Indicator System

In the book *Destruction and Reconstruction of the Hospital Culture* published in China in 2014, based on the status of hospital culture construction in China at that time, the indicator system was investigated and established in 22 hospitals, collecting a total of 410 indicators. The service level indicators in the hospital culture evaluation system were collected following several key principles. First was the principle of empathy; all that was difficult to be felt by patients are not included so as to guarantee that hospital culture construction will thoroughly reflect the "patient-oriented" core value. Second, the indicators can be experienced by most of the patients as one improvement measure is impossible of being experienced by all patients in a certain period. Third, the indicators must be empirical in nature. We cannot include an indicator that cannot be measured with statistics. If an indicator is maintained by perceptual judgment, it will be given with multiple results because people have different feelings towards even the same thing. Fourth, the proposed indicator system should comply with codes of practice. The design of the indicator system referred to the grading standard for hospitals at the secondary level and above in China at that time, as well as the specifications and requirements of the fourth edition of the American Joint Commission International (JCI) accreditation.

After following this practice for nearly four years, the evaluation indicator system for service levels provided in this book is comprised of 501 indicators, 410 more indicators than in 2014. Some of these indicators were modifications and improvements of the original ones. In addition, some new content was generated about medical services along with the rapid development and wide application of the Internet. Also, indicators such as online appointment, WeChat application and automatic examination report printing system became part of the hospital service indicator system. When designing the new indicator system, new details found in the fifth edition of the American JCI standards were also incorporated in the service-level indicator systems mentioned in this book.

Design and Evaluation of Profit-seeking Degree Indicators

Little research has been conducted on the profit-seeking behavior of hospitals in the current domestic and global literature. Through our research, we found that the degree to which hospitals seek profits is highly associated with whether some capital for their operation and infrastructures (including equipment) comes from donations given by charity organizations, especially government investments. The rule is simple and straightforward, requiring no more details. Seven indicators have been designed on the basis of this preliminary thought.

The first indicator is the proportion of the government's funds and donated and subsidized wage incomes in total personnel expenditures. This indicator mainly reflects how much of personnel expenditure in hospitals is from social donations or the government's fiscal subsidy. In China, non-profit hospitals are divided into two categories: those established by the government and those by public expenditure (including those held by individuals). Some hospitals established by the government get certain fiscal subsidies while the others get no subsidies due to the different regulations of the different governments having jurisdiction over these hospitals. So, how can hospitals getting little or no subsidies survive without making profits? The government fiscal subsidy system doesn't cover the non-profit hospitals sponsored by social capital; thus, they need to make profits cover the cost of their normal operations. If this indicator is rated higher than 50%, the hospital is judged as low profit-seeking, and given a score of 0; if it is rated lower than 50%, we shall deem it as profit-seeking, and give it a score of 100, especially for those without government funding or without donated and subsidized wage incomes. The degree will be scored according to the corresponding proportion.

The second indicator is the proportion of non-medical insurance incomes as part of the total income. This indicator reflects the degree of reliance of a hospital on medical insurance incomes for its operation. If the non-medical insurance income of a hospital occupies a relatively small proportion in its total medical income, this indicates that the hospital relies highly on the medical insurance institution and is controlled by the expenses of the same. Due to policy limit, its profit-seeking behavior will be weakened, as otherwise the insurance institution will not pay out. This will result in less profit-seeking behaviors because it may be punished by the insurance company. On the contrary, if non-medical insurance income occupies a relatively high proportion of its total incomes, this hospital relies on the medical insurance company to a lesser degree. Such institutions may be profit-making hospitals or non-profit hospitals carrying out more non-medical insurance reimbursement items, and their common characteristics are that they are rarely controlled by expenses of the medical insurance institution and hence they show relatively strong profit-seeking behaviors since they launch more items that the medical insurance will not cover. For a hospital, if the proportion of non-insurance medical income in the total income is less than 30%, a score of 0 shall be given, indicating a low profit-seeking nature; if it is more than 30%, it will be deemed as a profit-seeking hospital. The degree will be scored according to the corresponding proportion.

The third indicator is the asset–liability ratio. Hospitals need to repay the debts on the balance sheet step by step, relying on their own profits because the assets donated by the society and allocated by the government will be included in assets, instead of debts, as they need not be repaid. A higher asset–liability ratio shows that this hospital needs to repay more debts, so it must pursue profits to repay the debts on schedule. Therefore, we can conclude that the higher the asset–liability ratio, the higher the profit-seeking degree, and vice versa. An asset–liability ratio of less than 20% suggests low profit-seeking behavior, while a score above 20% indicates a profit-seeking nature. Hospitals with an asset–liability ratio which is higher than 75% will be given a full score. The scores for those hospitals that have ratios between 20% and 75% will be calculated according to proportion.

The fourth aspect is the ratio of performance to basic wages. This indicator shows the overall profit-seeking tendency of all hospital personnel. The value of this ratio at Mayo Clinic is basically zero because it does not follow a performance-based wage system. At present, hospitals in China implement the distribution system of "more pay for more work, and better pay for better service". This system itself encourages medical staff to pursue profits, which caters to the societal development of China. Actually, there is a system that encourages medical staff to "pursue profits" in many countries, including in many of the developed countries. At present, hospitals with ratios of performance to basic wages less than 3:7 are regarded as non-profit-seeking and given a score of 0. Those with a ratio over 3:7 show profit-seeking behaviors, and those with ratios higher than 7:3 show the highest profit-seeking degree and will be scored 100.

The fifth indicator is the proportion of fixed assets in government appropriation and donation payment. If donation or government funds make up a large proportion of the capital sources for fixed assets in a hospital, the profit-seeking degree will certainly be low because it bears no repayment pressure. Otherwise, the profit-seeking degree will certainly be higher, as in such a case the hospital will depend on its own capital. If the ratio of government appropriation and donation payment in the original value of fixed assets is more than 50%, the hospital will be given a score of 0, indicating a low profit-seeking degree; if it is less than 50%, the score should be calculated proportionally.

The sixth aspect is accessibility of the clinical pathway. The clinical pathway is a management method that specifically normalizes clinical medical behavior, reduces medical cost and improves medical quality, and this was first developed and introduced in the US at the beginning of the 1980s. It has been adopted in many countries since, including China. However, it is not smoothly running in China due to the following reasons. First, medical corruption runs rampant in China, due to the practice of "corrupting doctors with medicine" carried out by a large number of drug and equipment suppliers, replacing "supporting doctors with medicine". Quite a number of people are unwilling to execute the clinical pathway in its fundamental manner because such an action will cut off their "source of money". Second, the medical regulatory departments have never thought that executing the clinical pathway should be carried out by doctors and nurses; instead, they have taken that as an inflexible task to be delegated to the hospital. Therefore, the hospital bears the responsibility, which is not specifically undertaken by persons. As a consequence, the clinical pathway has not been really executed as most practices were taken just for examination. Third, many managers perceive the clinical pathway as a tool to control expenses, overlooking its function of normalizing medical behavior and improving medical quality. Actually, the clinical pathway has standardized the way specific diseases are treated. As long as the clinical pathway is executed, the profit-seeking behavior of doctors and nurses will be greatly weakened, and may even disappear. For this indicator, a full score should be given if the clinical pathway is used at a rate of more than 80%; a score of 0 will be given if clinical pathway utilization is less than 20%; the score should be calculated proportionally when between 20% and 80%.

The seventh aspect is the proportion of two-item expenses. We think that the six indicators above are universally applicable to judge the profit-seeking degree of hospitals. The seventh indicator was designed mainly for China, and it will be applicable only if other countries have situations similar to that seen in China. The so-called proportion of two-item expenses refers to the proportion of drug incomes and sanitary material expenditures in the total medical income of the hospital. This indicator has been designed based on the extensive corruption seen with the use of drugs and sanitary materials in Chinese hospitals at present. Corruption has led to serious profit-seeking behaviors among medical staff, and we can judge that serious medical corruption exists in all institutions with high proportion of two-item expenses. Therefore, reducing the proportion of two-item expenses is an important means of weakening "profit-seeking" due to corruption and is also one of the important indicators to measure the profit-seeking degree. Actually, in China, there is another strange phenomenon: governments have stipulated that hospitals established by the government can only purchase medical equipment through a government tender. It is through this link that the high government purchasing price appeared. The purchasing price of most equipment, especially large medical equipment, is generally 1–3 times that of private hospitals. Over the years, relevant management departments have turned a blind eye to this and done nothing. This is because of the inextricable interest relationship with the local management departments. At present, the proportion of two-item expenses is evaluated according to hospital type. For general hospitals and traditional Chinese medicine hospitals, if the proportion of two-item expenses is more than 65%, a score of 0 should be given; if it is less than 38%, full scores should be given, and the score should be calculated proportionally if it is between 38% and 65%. For maternal and child health hospitals, if the proportion of two-item expenses is more than 50%, a score of 0 should be given; if it is less than 28%, full scores should be given, and the score should be calculated proportionally if it is between 28% and 50%. For hospitals sponsored by social capital and individuals, the score should be calculated according to the details given earlier.

Evaluation of the Hospital Culture Type after Investigation

During the basic survey process, an investigation team should be established with a third party as the main party to develop a detailed survey plan, organize and implement the plan, and then summarize, sort out and analyze the investigation results. Then, the team should calculate the scores of hospital service level and profit-seeking degree, form the corresponding points accumulated after the evaluation of hospital culture types, establish the basic culture type of this hospital, and eventually issue evaluation and survey reports.

Evaluation Results

Values assigned to the service level (S) and profit-seeking degree (P) will be calculated separately through survey data and will be included in the S–P model, and the hospital culture type then corresponds to the quadrant where the coordinate point is located in. Figure 4.4 shows that when a hospital gets a score of 60 and 82, respectively, in service level and profit-seeking degree through evaluation, the coordinate point of this hospital will fall into the enterprise type, and it can also be seen from the evaluation results.

Improvement Direction in Hospital Culture Construction

The cultures of different types of hospitals will improve in different directions. Hospitals established by the government will certainly be the charity type. Non-profit hospitals sponsored by social capital

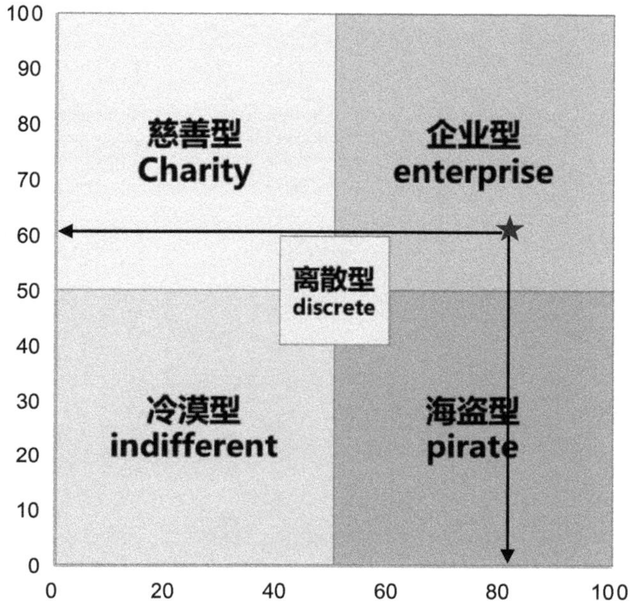

Figure 4.4 Improvement direction diagram of hospital culture of hospitals

should have the common property of charity and enterprise types, and the profit-making hospitals should be of the enterprise type, as shown in Figure 4.5.

The hospitals established by the government should certainly be of a charitable type, since the basic attribute of hospitals sponsored by the government is non-profitable as the Chinese government never levies tax on hospitals sponsored by itself (excluding the individual income tax). If these institutions aim to maximize their profits, there may be something wrong with the government itself. Insufficient government investment may drive these hospitals to seek profits for fear of shutting down. The second reason may be severe violation of economic laws in service pricing by the government, which makes it impossible for hospitals to embody their due social value. The third reason may be troubles in the design of top-level social system. As long as the "more pay for more work, and better pay for better

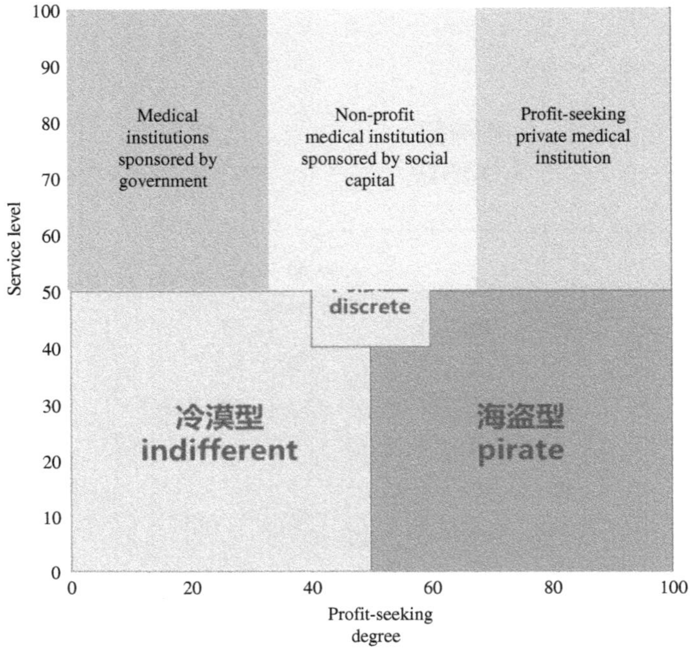

Figure 4.5 Schematic diagram of evaluation results of hospital culture types

service" principle is applied in a hospital, doctors will be busy running about for profits. Profit-seeking of doctors means profit-seeking of the hospitals as an outcome of the basic system. As is well known, profit-seeking behaviors of hospitals are the products of doctors' profit-seeking activities, since the majority of hospital income is achieved by the medications prescribed by doctors. Therefore, it is impossible to prevent doctors from seeking profits. The key lies in how to prevent doctors from seeking profits for themselves. As previously mentioned, Mayo Clinic has set a good example in this respect.

Non-profit hospitals sponsored by social capital should certainly aim to be profit-seeking, since with all investment coming from individuals, investors will recover costs and require return on investment. Second, non-profit hospitals sponsored by social capital never enjoy any government subsides. In order to make up the deficit, these institutions have to make profits. Furthermore, hospitals sponsored by social capital can only survive on higher human resource cost when there is competition with hospitals sponsored by the government. In conclusion, it is impractical to make hospitals sponsored by social capital develop a charitable culture, or at least it is impossible in China.

Profit-making hospitals sponsored by social capital should be improved towards being entrepreneurial and have features of sound technology and service level, which makes it justifiable regardless of profitability, since competing on the free market is critical to the survival of these profit-making hospitals.

During the process of constructing hospital culture, any kind of hospital should aim to reach the same objective — keep improving their services.

Part 2

The Experience of Patients and Their Family Members

Chapter 5
Catering to People's Visual Sense

We perceive the world through the five senses from eyes, ears, nose, mouth and skin, as well as the sense jointly formed by multiple organs, known as perception. This section is mainly based on the feelings of patients and their family members while seeking medical treatment. Studies have shown that 80% of a person's knowledge and memories are obtained through the eyes — the most important organ of human beings. Every year, there are tens of thousands, or hundreds of thousands, or even millions of patients and their family members visiting hospitals, which makes it impossible to hide anything — good or bad — from their visitors. What people see informs their feelings and even opinions about the hospitals. Anything improper will be observed and the news will be spread.

Reducing Visible Inconveniences

Lan Xiaofeng, Executive Director of JYWJ:

During the whole process in which patients and their family members see the doctor and receive medical service, most convenience indicators are visual, accounting for over 2/3 of the total number of indicators. Therefore, targeting the specific research object, we should carry out careful investigation on the current status of convenience indicators observed by patients and their family members, and then make plans to improve those aspects that are not good enough. This plays a significant role in effectively improving the experience of patients and their family members in seeking a doctor, receiving medical service and implementing the patient-oriented value.

Indicator 1. Rate of hospital publicity material possession in regional households

Meaning: It refers to the proportion of permanent residents in a certain area possessing the publicity materials of the hospital under investigation.

Purpose: In today's fiercely competitive, modern society, the marketing philosophy of "good wine needs no bush" should be reviewed. It requires long-run efforts to reach out to local residents and let more residents understand and recognize the medical services provided by the hospital. This indicator can directly reflect the achievements of one hospital during the process of implementing social publicity work.

Investigation method: Inquiry or field visit.

Evaluation method: Proportion*score.

Calculation method:

$$\textit{Rate of hospital publicity material possession in regional households} = \frac{n_h}{N} * 100\%$$

where

n_h = the number of households possessing hospital publicity materials; and
N = the total number of households investigated.

Improvement objective: The result should be combined with the current status in this aspect/historical survey data to prepare the improvement objectives for the next stage.

Indicator 2. Whether there are reserved parking spaces for bicycles and motorcycles in the parking lot

Meaning: The deployment of reserved parking spaces for bicycles and motorcycles in the parking lot.

Purpose: Parking spaces for bicycles and motorcycles should be set aside for patients' use. This will improve the patients' view of the hospital's service quality and prevent them from using the parking spaces of hospital employees.

Investigation method: Field observation.

Evaluation method: Full scores for available reserved parking spaces; a 0 score for unavailable parking space.

Improvement objective: Mark out reserved parking spaces for bicycles and motorcycles in the parking lot.

Liang Chenguang, Executive Director of Business Department of JYWJ:

Since the living standard of people is increasing day by day, vehicles have become a common mode of travel. Hence, it is especially important to set up signboards showing information regarding vehicle in/out and parking information in hospitals where people crowd every day. Signboards will show directions for patients and their family members or friends, thus supporting a tidy and orderly hospital environment.

Shunting signboards for different kinds of vehicles set in Laibin City Xingbin People's Hospital, Guangxi Zhuang Autonomous Region embodies a kind of considerate and well-thought-out service. After driving into the hospital, vehicles can proceed to their respective parking spaces following the driving/parking signs for ambulances, non-employee's vehicles, motorcycles, battery cars and non-motor vehicles.

The parking space located on the western side of the hospital front is reserved for non-motor vehicles. In front of the parking space for non-motor vehicles is the Emergency Department, and the parking space for ambulances is set at the southeast of the Emergency Department, which can ensure that the ambulance is available for first-aid at any time. Non-employee's vehicles will drive to the outpatient building or inpatient building via the western side of the front door, and drive out of the hospital via the eastern side if they will not stay. Otherwise, such vehicles should drive to the hospital parking lot via the eastern side, where there are landmarks for parking signs. Motorcycles and battery cars will drive into the hospital from the western side of the hospital, and drive towards the reserved parking space at the western side of corridor connecting the inpatient building and outpatient building after bypassing the outpatient building. The orderly access of all kinds of vehicles can ensure the separation of pedestrians and vehicles in the hospital, and prevent the mutual influence.

Indicator 3. Whether there are regional maps and bus routes posted in the hospital

Meaning: There should be city maps and bus schedules posted at important, easy to spot locations in the hospital, making it simple for patients to travel to and from the hospital.

Purpose: Posting regional maps in the hospital can help patients know their position and the regional layout comprehensively. Bus routes will help people to get to their desired destination easily. The maps and bus schedules will shorten the geographical distance between people and bridge thousands of households, thus bringing warmth to patients and their family members and reflecting the "patient-oriented" humanistic care offered by hospitals.

Investigation method: Field observation.

Evaluation method: Full score is given if regional maps and bus routes are made available, and a score of 0 is given otherwise.

Improvement objective: Regional maps and bus routes are posted where the patient flow is largest in the hospital, and such information is made available by doctors and other hospital employees.

Cheng Songlin, Executive Director of Business Department of JYWJ:

During the survey of cultural indicators, we once came across such a case: one family member of a patient anxiously inquired about the time of the last bus for going home, but neither our staff, patient's families nor fellow villagers could give an accurate answer after a long time. Luckily, a fellow villager who took the last bus in a similar case was able to give an approximate time. According to our investigation, the absence of regional maps and bus routes is common in almost all hospitals.

It may be weird since it is commonly believed that ordinary people should have a good idea of the bus schedule. However, that is not the

(Continued)

truth due to the following reasons: (1) Few people will catch the last bus posted on the schedule. (2) It's rare for ordinary people to remember the departure time of buses on purpose. (3) Hospital employees will not remember the departure time of buses from every county or bus station to any village and town/place. (4) There is no related information available in hospitals.

In conclusion, the absence of regional maps and bus routes will make it inconvenient for ordinary people to go home. After a quick discussion, the hospital agreed to take measures immediately. County maps and departure timetables of the first and last buses to all villages and towns were soon posted at noticeable positions, significantly freeing people from anxiety. They are no longer worried about missing the last bus home.

In fact, regional maps and bus routes should be publicized at easy-to-spot locations in all county-level hospitals, municipal hospitals and provincial hospitals so as to prevent ordinary people from worrying about missing the last bus.

Indicator 4. Presence of a meal delivery service

Meaning: Check whether the Food and Beverage Department actively provides meal delivery service.

Purpose: To make meals available for patients and their family members when difficulties are faced in dining out.

Investigation method: Observation and inquiry.

Evaluation method: Full score is given if meal delivery service is available, 0 otherwise.

Improvement objective: (A) Provide meal delivery services; (B) Provide meal delivery number at the nursing station or the hospital bedside; (C) Provide an online booking facility.

Lin Chang, Director of International Department of JYWJ:

I remembered that in the winter of 2015, one of my colleagues was hospitalized for an operation. Since he was alone in Beijing, he had no family members accompanying him for daily care. Though it was a small operation, he could take good care of himself before the operation. As he was going to undergo an operation, he had to stay in the ward according to the regulations of the hospital. When I came to visit him, I learned that he hadn't eaten anything for a whole day. No family members were around, no food had been sent, and he could not go out for meals by himself. Further, he did not want to bother the others, and he did not even tell us about it. At that moment, I felt quite sorry for failing to take care of him due to thoughtlessness, and was angry at the inaction of the hospital which failed to provide any food. Subconsciously, I thought that there should have been meal delivery services available for patients in need.

Taking Xinhuang County Hospital of Traditional Chinese Medicine that we use later as an example, we can see that it provided patients with nutritious food according to their physical conditions, and directly delivered food to their bed if necessary. This solved the problem of food and improved the hospital experience of patients.

Where Improvement is Needed According to the Patients

Zhang Shujun, Executive Director of Administrative Supervision Department of JYWJ:

Visual perception covers aspects of convenience, management, service, environment and etiquette. Environment-related visual feelings mainly come from the practical actions observed directly by patients during the process of visiting a doctor, including improvement in traffic

(Continued)

convenience and security, environmental cleanliness and degree of comfort, article configuration, privacy protection and other aspects. Various kinds of activities for improving hospital environment and patients' feeling are displayed through a series of detailed indicators, and efforts should be made to provide patients with the best doctor-seeing experience by satisfying and improving these indicators. One indicator is whether there is a map of the hospital, which will be seen by the patients upon their arrival. The setting of this indicator can make it easy for patients to determine their current location and identify where they need to go.

Indicator 5. Whether there are 'zebra stripes' on the roads accessing hospitals

Meaning: Carry out investigations on whether 'zebra stripes' demarcating pedestrian crossings are set on the roads accessing hospitals.

Purpose: To regulate the traffic and make it easy to cross the roads. Considering that there are a huge number of visitors and vehicles near the hospitals, traffic should be well-regulated, making it easy to cross the roads. Pedestrian crossings can ensure the safety and security of people crossing the road and ensure the free flow of vehicles, thus reducing traffic accidents. Constructing pedestrian crossings is an important measure that both protects the safety of patients and also is a measure of convenience for patients and their family members.

Investigation method: Field investigation.

Evaluation method: Full score when the pedestrian crossing is present, and 0 otherwise.

Improvement objective: Contact the Transport Agency to set up 'zebra stripes' in front of the hospital.

Cheng Songlin, Executive Director of Business Department of JYWJ:

'Zebra stripes' are also known as lifelines. 'Zebra stripes' should be available at every crossing, including at crossroads as well as on broad roads and small lanes and at T-shaped intersections.

When carrying out a cultural investigation through field observation at a hospital in Yunnan, no 'zebra stripes' were found on either sides of the road in front of a hospital near a T-junction. The other side of the road was the only way for students of a primary school to go home. Considering the relatively weak self-safety awareness of pupils, the high flow of traffic in the area, as well as the improperly parked taxis, there were a great number of safety hazards. Upon noticing this, the project team had a meeting with the hospital, and later, brand-new 'zebra stripes' were seen on the road.

Thanks to such an action, passengers and vehicles can travel on the road in front of the hospital in a more orderly manner. The principle of giving way to pedestrians at 'zebra stripes' has been well-observed, significantly reducing the safety hazards. This action shows the respect for life.

Indicator 6. Whether there are green channels for patients seeking emergency treatment

Meaning: Check whether there are green channels for patients seeking emergency treatment.

Purpose: Green channels refer to the rapid and efficient service system provided to critical patients. We should systematically regulate the whole medical service process, including admission, triage, examination, diagnosis and rescue of critically ill patients, and offer them timely, standard, efficient and thoughtful medical services. The establishment of green channels represents the most effective mechanism for rescuing critical patients, and such channels can be called as life protection channels. The presence of such channels will also make these hospitals popular among patients suffering from acute and severe diseases, benefiting the people and upholding and strengthening the reputation of the hospital.

Investigation method: Field observation.

Evaluation method: Full score if green channels are available; otherwise, 0 score.

Improvement objective: To ensure that patients in critical condition can get timely and effective medical treatment.

Indicator 7. Whether the waiting area is clean and tidy

Meaning: The waiting area of the Outpatient Hall should be clean and tidy, and the chairs set in the waiting area should be arranged in an orderly manner so as to provide patients with a clean and comfortable environment to see the doctor.

Purpose: As part of the service industry, hospitals should provide patients with a satisfactory waiting environment. On the other hand, as a special sector, hospitals should also prevent the spread of germs and disease; therefore, special attention should be paid to the environmental hygiene of the waiting area.

Investigation method: Field observation.

Evaluation method: Full scores should be given to those meeting the requirements; otherwise, a score of 0 is given.

Improvement objective: (A) Ground: clean and tidy, free from any sundries, with chairs in waiting areas being arranged in a neat and orderly manner; (B) Wall: clean and tidy, free from any sundries, with billboards set in a unified and orderly manner; (C) Air: well-ventilated, free from any unpleasant odor.

Li Qiming, Consulting Director of JYWJ:

Once, seven large pieces of luggage were found piled up in the waiting area of the Outpatient Hall at 10:30 a.m. during our department inspection. They turned out to belong to the patients who were scheduled to have an examination that day. Upon asking the hospital guide, we were told that the luggage had been there since she started her work shift at 8:00 a.m. "I had informed the security personnel. We have no choice but to leave them there as we didn't know who they belonged to," she said. She did not take any measures to deal with it in the following three hours. We also noticed that she was quite indifferent, paid no attention to the cleanliness of the surrounding area, did not approach patients and their family members, stood behind the hospital guide desk most of the time, and answered patients' questions in a really halfhearted way.

Later, with our help, the luggage was stored at the guidance desk. The hospital guide has to get out from the desk to do their tasks, such as helping people, providing answers to questions and addressing problems.

Indicator 8. Whether there are independent transfusion rooms for children

Meaning: It refers to the configuration of independent transfusion rooms for children in the hospital.

Purpose: This indicator should be set considering the following aspects. First, the transfusion room is one of the areas with high infection risks in the hospital. Since the immunity of children is much lower than that of adults, the setting of independent transfusion rooms for children can avoid cross-infection between adults and children. Second, children are easily affected by pain due to poor control over their emotions. Thus, they may reject or be afraid to have an injection. Infants and children can't explicitly express their feelings and may cry upon seeing needles. Therefore, setting aside independent transfusion rooms which are decorated with wall paintings, cartoons and other entertainment facilities for children can help create a good environment, distract them from the needles and ease their fear. Third, the influence of crying children on others should be prevented. This indicator encourages the hospital to set aside independent transfusion rooms for children, so that higher-quality, personalized and special services can be provided.

Investigation method: Field investigation should be adopted to check the configuration of independent transfusion rooms for children.

Evaluation method: Full scores should be given to those with independent transfusion rooms for children, while a score of 0 should be given to those without such a setting.

Improvement objective: (A) Set independent transfusion rooms for children; (B) Independent transfusion rooms for children should be equipped with cartoon murals on the walls.

Xu Juan, Director of Service Department of JYWJ:

There were no independent transfusion rooms set up for children in one county-level hospital; therefore, children and adults have to receive transfusions in the same space. The blood vessels in the hands and feet of young children are relatively thin, making it difficult to insert the needle. Furthermore, children cannot stay still for a long time, which causes the needle to dislodge easily, increasing the difficulty of transfusion. As a result, adult patients are usually the first to receive transfusion before children, and so younger patients and their family members have to wait much longer. Otherwise, due to huge difficulty in inserting needles in child patients, adult patients have to wait longer. After waiting for a long time, patients and their family members may have already been dissatisfied, and may be further aggravated by the noisy cries of children who may have been poked by the needle more than once, resulting in quarrels with the medical staff. If this happens, there will be more complaints from patients about the poor transfusion environment setting and the service attitude of medical staff. Complaints towards medical staff may result in poorer work performance. In order

(Continued)

(Continued)

to improve this circumstance and enhance patient satisfaction, independent transfusion rooms for children should be created, leaving a relatively quiet hospital environment. Independent transfusion rooms for children should be provided, with TVs broadcasting cartoons and precautions and instructions concerning transfusion, which can distract children's attention and at the same time inform the patients about transfusion precautions. As a consequence, the hospital environment is improved and complaints are reduced.

Indicator 9. Whether there are waiting areas for patients' family members in front of the ICU

Meaning: This indicator is used to check whether there are waiting areas for patients' family members in front of the ICU.

Purpose: Provide patients' family members with waiting areas in front of ICU wards. The family members of patients in the ICU would feel physically and mentally exhausted. The waiting areas would not only offer a temporary place for family members to have a rest but also shorten the distance between them and the patients and help them to be more aware of the patients' condition. Waiting areas for patients' family members should be comfortable, beautiful, tidy, and have health education materials, which will allow patients' family members to know more about the ICU patients or have a rest.

Investigation method: Field investigation should be adopted for ICU wards.

Evaluation method: Full score should be given when such waiting areas are available, 0 score otherwise.

Improvement objective: Create waiting areas for patients' family members in front of the ICU, which are comfortable, beautiful and tidy. There should be TVs and informational materials, helping family members have basic knowledge about precautions before and after surgery.

Zhao Ning, Director of Project Management Department of JYWJ:

In February 2015, my mom had a craniotomy in a third-level hospital — municipal central hospital — in my hometown, and was sent to the ICU after the procedure. At that time, my dad was quite worried when Mom was still in a coma and was anxious about whether the doctors and nurses would take good care of her. My dad, like many other patients' family members, had little medical knowledge. Since I have stayed in hospitals for several years during my career, I have good understanding that the ICU is a quiet and safe room where medical staff can supervise the changes in the health of patients and adopt requisite countermeasures in a timely manner; thus, I realized that the ICU is a good place for my mom's recovery. Therefore, I comforted my dad with my knowledge about ICU. At that time, the attending doctor told us that we could have a 15-minute video call with my mom in the ICU in the morning and afternoon, which really eased my dad's discomfort.

When it was time to have the video call, my dad came to the hospital early. He waited quietly in the waiting area where a TV screen, chairs and profiles of ICU departments and related medical staff are provided, allowing patients' family members to know more about the related medical staff in ICU. At each video call, there are many family members gathered here. Nurses will inform certain family members based on the bed number, and switch the video image to the corresponding bed. People usually leave the seats to have a clearer look of the patients inside, who may be eating food with the assistance of nurses or getting massages. This can assure those outside. Thanks to this video call, patients' family members can feel at ease and reassured!

Indicator 10. Whether there are recreational facilities in the Recovery Department

Meaning: There should be painting and calligraphy rooms, music entertainment and therapy rooms, and computer rooms in the Recovery Department, and these should be equipped with certain equipment and instruments, such as TVs, audio systems and fitness equipment.

Purpose: Patients who are following a recovery regimen, in addition to normal treatment, are supported with these other auxiliary facilities that can also ease the pressure, distract their attention and help cultivate sentiments. Such facilities as music therapy, painting and calligraphy and chess will promote recovery.

Investigation method: Field observation.

Evaluation method: Full scores should be given when such rooms are available; otherwise, a 0 score is given.

Improvement objective: There should be painting and calligraphy rooms, music entertainment and therapy rooms, and computer rooms set in the Recovery Department, all equipped with the corresponding equipment and instruments, such as TVs, audio systems and fitness equipment, which can serve as auxiliary facilities to enhance the effects of treatment and achieve the best results.

Services Needing to Be Improved for Patients

Ma Wufu, Executive Director of Consulting Service of JYWJ:

Patients can judge the service provided by hospitals based on the details they see in each link. People prefer to believe their first impressions and then reach a conclusion. For example, if a patient comes to a hospital and finds out that the clinic door is closed and there is no outpatient doctor available during work hours, he will jump to negative conclusions about the services provided by outpatient doctors, and even the overall hospital services. Visual service indicators can help us investigate the patients' first impression regarding service details at every link. Then we can prepare corresponding measures to change their impressions according to the foregoing investigation results. The first impression of others is essential to any unit or individual, especially for those in the service industry.

Indicator 11. Ratio of prompting the possible destination of staff in Medical Lab

Meaning: In the event that staff in Medical Lab are absent, their positions should be marked accurately, so that patients can reach them in a timely manner.

Purpose: Patients may feel anxious while waiting, and they and their families may become uncertain and have no idea about what to do. Generally speaking, patients have to queue for a long time in the Medical Lab. Thus, having warm prompts will not only reduce the inquiry of patients but also comfort them and enable them to wait patiently. Providing information about the whereabouts of the medical technician in the Medical Lab can reduce doctor–patient conflicts.

Investigation method: Random investigation should be carried out to check the setting of prompts on the whereabouts of workers in Medical Lab for 10–20 cases of staff absence.

Evaluation method: Proportion*score.

Calculation method:

$$\textit{Ratio of prompting the possible destination of staff in Medical Lab} = \frac{n_p}{N} * 100\%$$

where

n_p = Number of departments with prompts; and
N = Total number of departments in the Medical Lab.

Improvement objective: Set the prompt of possible destinations when they are absent.

Feng Yun, Consulting Director of JYWJ:

For a small maternal and child healthcare hospital at county level, there are relatively smaller daily outpatient and inpatient numbers. Therefore, the configuration and staff in Medical Lab are usually inadequate, especially doctors in charge of B-ultrasound examinations (there are a

(Continued)

(Continued)

total of 2 doctors there and they have to have a shift every 24 hours). During our investigation of cultural indicators, we found that some staff were late, absent from work, or had left their stations to go to the toilet, and under such conditions, patients have to anxiously wait for even longer, without seeing any form of "notice". Even when there is not much workload, it is still necessary for staff to work normally, to ensure that patients can get timely service. If a medical service is unavailable due to a special reason, the hospital should "communicate" with patients and their family members by using a billboard, which can ease anxiety, lower the potential for "touch-and-go" doctor-patient conflicts, and better show the "humanistic care" of hospital to patients.

Indicator 12. Ratio of the same doctor for return-visit patients

Meaning: Whether patients returning for a follow-up appointment receive further consultation from the same doctor as with whom they had their initial diagnosis.

Purpose: If patients are received by the same doctor, they don't need to repeatedly describe their illness and the doctor can also check if they have made a proper judgement and improve their medical skills. Meanwhile, patients usually show strong dependency and trust on their chief physician, and this good impression of their own chief physician will be significantly improved with each recovery. This will support the establishment and also improve the doctor's reputation.

Investigation method: Random telephone follow-up or field investigation on 20–30 return-visit patients to check whether they are diagnosed and treated by the same doctor, and finally summing up the results.

Evaluation method: Proportion*score. Patients who are diagnosed and treated by the same doctor shall be counted.

Calculation method:

$$Ratio\, of\, same\, doctor\, for\, return\text{-}visit\, patients = \frac{n_s}{N} * 100\%$$

where

n_s = Number of patients being treated by the same doctor they saw in their first appointment; and

N = Total number of return-visit patients investigated.

Improvement objective: Establish the "same doctor for one patient" system, and allow return-visit patients to get diagnosis and treatment from the same doctor as the initial diagnosing physician.

Guo Ran, Director of General Office of JYWJ:

One of my friends suffered a bruised pelvis after playing basketball, and the CT showed that it was pelvis displacement. Later, his doctor suggested an MRI examination for correct diagnosis, proper therapeutic regimen and early recovery. The MRI appointment was scheduled for the following month. My friend asked the doctor if he could make another appointment with him the next time. The doctor answered yes, and told him his name for direct registration. At that time, even though he was physically uncomfortable due to his injury, my friend was reassured since he did not need to repeat his case history during his next visit to the same doctor.

Indicator 13. Rate of patients being accompanied by medical staff when being transferred

Meaning: This indicator reflects whether patients are accompanied and guided by medical staff during a transfer.

Purpose: During a transfer, the state of patients may change from time to time, and can even turn unfavorable. Therefore, it is essential to arrange for medical staff to accompany patients during the transfer. They should record the changing state of patients and carry out emergency treatment when necessary, which can prevent the patients' condition from worsening during the transfer, effectively saving their lives, avoiding medical disputes, demonstrating the due attention and care of the hospital to patients and enhancing patient satisfaction.

Investigation method: Carry out field observations and inquire about transfer records.

Calculation method:

$$\textit{Rate of patients accompanied by medical staff when transferred} = \frac{n_a}{N} * 100\%$$

where

n_a = the number of patients accompanied by medical staff when transferred; and

N = the total number of patients investigated.

Improvement objective: When transferring patients, especially those in a critical condition, medical staff should be dispatched to accompany them, which can prevent further deterioration.

Wu Aixian, Consulting Director of JYWJ:

When investigating this indicator in one hospital, field observation and inquiry of the transfer records were carried out by the personnel of the project team. During the investigation, we found that not every patient being transferred was accompanied by medical staff. The overall rate of patients being accompanied by medical staff during a transfer was low. For example, some high-risk pregnant women in the Gynecology and Obstetrics Department were accompanied to another hospital only by their family members, without any medical staff overseeing the whole process. When we investigated this event further, reasons such as no requirement from patient's family members and little time to dispatch any spare medical staff were given. The project team immediately told the Gynecology and Obstetrics Department that this was irresponsible behavior. Even though it was not required by the patient's family members, medical staff should be dispatched proactively to prevent medical risks.

Thirty transferred patients were investigated, and among them 75% of patients were accompanied by medical staff, leaving 25% unattended during transfer. Meanwhile, the absence of any accompanying attendant

(Continued)

was seen more commonly when pregnant women from the Gynecology and Obstetrics Department were transferred, which not only failed to meet the "patient-oriented" culture of hospitals, but also led to potential medical risks. As a result, it is necessary for hospitals to enhance the management of an accompanying attendant for transferring patients.

Indicator 14. Examination-accompanying rate for patients who need critical or Grade I care

Meaning: Patients in critical or Grade I care should be accompanied by medical staff for the related medical examinations, so this indicates the examination-accompanying state and rate for the patients.

Purpose: According to the severity of their illness, critical or Grade I patients should be accompanied by medical staff for related medical or special examinations. Nursing staff who accompany patients can observe the patients' condition at each moment and can thus prevent or handle unexpected incidents during the examination, thus ensuring safety.

This can not only ensure patients' safety and save on examination time but can also make the patients' family members feel relieved, which is beneficial to the improvement of general service quality.

Investigation method: Combining information about the patients in critical care, field investigation is performed to inspect whether nursing staff are accompanying patients.

Evaluation method: Proportion*score.

Calculation method:

$$\textit{Examination-accompanying rate} = \frac{n_a}{N} * 100\%$$

where

n_a = Number of patients in need of critical care being accompanied by nurses; and

N = Total number of patients investigated.

Improvement objective: (A) Appoint nursing staff to accompany patients who need critical or Grade I care for outing examination; (B) Nursing Department should check this activity regularly or irregularly.

In a hospital, compared with other medical staff, nurses are most frequently exposed to inpatients. Especially under grading nursing management, nurses for critical and Grade I care need to give more supervision and care to patients.

Liang Chenguang, Executive Director of Business Department of JYWJ:

Since Xingbin People's Hospital, Guangxi, implemented grading nursing management, the Department of Cardiology has paid more attention to details, making patients and their family members feel cared for and loved. The head nurse of the Department of Cardiology requested all nursing staff in the department to live up to the standard of grading nursing management and provide more careful nursing for patients needing critical or Grade I care. When these patients need examinations, the nursing staff must accompany them and notify the necessity of examinations to them and their family members. After examination, the nursing staff should accompany them back to the ward. During the process, nursing staff talked with patients and their family members about the recent condition updates and informed them about the diet and timetable while in hospital, all of which led to patients and their family members praising them for this.

Management Issues Noticed by Patients

Wang Zhiqiang, Executive Director of Business Department of JYWJ:

As the saying goes, "The eyes are the windows to the soul"; therefore, visual inputs can directly affect people's feelings about the medical procedures. Everyone wants to leave a good first impression on others since the first impression is key in interpersonal communication. This also applies to the hospital, which aspires to leave a good first impression on patients.

(Continued)

Patients' first impression of the hospital depends on what they see and perceive. Hence, we must create a visual environment that is both comfortable and soothing to patients.

The hospital can create a better visual feeling for patients from such aspects as environment, procedures, professionalism and quality of employees, all of which can be realized through management. Modern hospital management is more about reflecting the professionalism and humanistic care of the hospital. Any management system should be based on the patient's medical experience and will bring patients a warm and comfortable visual feeling as long as empathy is fully achieved. Consequently, the hospital can have a good first impression on the patients and improve their medical experience.

Indicator 15. Punctuality rate in the morning

Meaning: The rate of hospital staff coming to work on time in the morning.

Purpose: First of all, the medical staff can make the rounds and talk to patients regularly if they come to work on time. This not only allows the doctors to know more about the patients' conditions but also gives patients strong psychological comfort, which could help patients to understand their condition better and have more confidence in recovery. Second, if the medical staff come to work on time, they can find any safety hazards in a timely manner and provide corresponding medical services for patients, thus avoiding any medical risks, reducing medical accidents and lowering the aggravation rate and mortality rate of patients. Third, if a doctor, especially an outpatient doctor, does not come to work on time, patients will have to suffer in pain for a longer time, which will greatly and adversely affect the medical experience of patients and their family members. This indicator reflects the working attitude and punctuality of the hospital staff. The higher the indicator, the more employees are coming to work on time. They can then offer corresponding services to patients, and this will be deemed as good service quality. A lower indicator suggests that many people are late and so are unable to provide the needed services for patients on time, and this will be deemed as poor service quality.

Investigation method: Field observation and recording shall be carried out to record the number of latecomers in the morning.

Evaluation method: Proportion*score.

Calculation method:

$$\textit{Punctuality rate in the morning} = \frac{n_e}{N * d} * 100\%$$

where

n_e = Number of employees coming to work on time in the morning;
N = Total number of hospital staff; and
d = The number of days investigated.

Improvement objective: (A) Staff of the Administrative Department should come to the Hospital Office for sign-in/clock-in first; (B) Develop an attendance system to check the attendance of employees, and penalize those who are late.

Chang Xu, Director of JYWJ Data Center:

I once had a cold and went to a hospital to see a doctor at 7:00 a.m. I queued up and registered for an specialist appointment. I reached the Internal Medicine Department at around 8:00 a.m. and the queue was already longer than the corridor. I regretted that I hadn't come earlier. The doctor who was supposed to diagnose us didn't show up at 8:15 a.m. Patients in the queue started to complain, making my headache worse. Finally, a 40–50-year-old doctor walked into the consulting room unhurriedly, when it was 8:40 a.m. according to my phone. The

(Continued)

hospital's working hours start at 8:00 a.m. but the doctor was 40 minutes late.

A doctor was late for work for 40 minutes without giving any explanation. This shows the negligence of the hospital as well as the disrespect of the doctor towards patients. It was said that the doctor was one of the few doctors with a secondary senior title in that hospital and was also the director of the department. How could an intermediate leader of the hospital manage his subordinates if he himself is a rule-breaker? If such cases aren't punished and restricted, the subordinates in the hospital will surely follow him, and the hospital's rules and regulations will become nothing but hollow words.

Indicator 16. Average age of the hospital guides

Meaning: Average age of all hospital guides.

Purpose: This indicator is set to ensure professional guidance services for the patients in the long run. If the average age of hospital guides is too young, patients will assume that the hospital guides lack experience and in turn lose confidence in them. If the average age of hospital guides is too old, they may not provide services for patients actively and it will be hard to change their conventional modes of thinking. Therefore, the average age of the hospital guides is assessed to ensure the allocation and recruitment of hospital guides is more effective.

Investigation method: Look up data. Search employee information in the Human Resources Department of the hospital and perform data analysis and calculation.

Evaluation method: The average age of the hospital guides should be 20–30 years. Full score shall be given if the hospital guides are aged between 20 and 30, 50% of the score is given if they are aged between 30 and 35, and a 0 score is given otherwise.

Calculation method:

$$Average\ age\ of\ hospital\ guides = \frac{a}{N_H}$$

where

a = Total age of hospital guides; and

N_H = Total number of hospital guides employed at the hospital.

Improvement method: Deploy or recruit personnel of a suitable age to take this post; people without a nursing background can also be hired as long as standard hospital guide training is given.

Wang Shuang, Director of the JYWJ Business Department:

We have to make clear the position of hospital guides before we talk about their age. The hospital guide is the first window to the hospital's services, is the organizer and manager of the hospital's order, the lubricant for the medical activities of the entire hospital and the image representative of the hospital. Therefore, the image of the hospital guides is very important. Age matters due to the importance of their public image. For instance, in one hospital, if all hospital guides are older nurses retired from the Clinical Department who sit by the guide desk all day long without any makeup and are indifferent to patients, negative impacts on the service quality and brand image of the hospital will be produced. From the managerial point of view, older hospital guides are rarely blamed considering their age, which further affects their service quality. In conclusion, hospital guides should be between 20 and 30 years old on average, in view of the importance of their images to a hospital and the management difficulty.

Indicator 17. Whether there is an informatory sign or isolation strip for queuing in the registration area

Meaning: It refers to the presence of an informatory sign or isolation strip for queuing that should be set in the hospital's registration office.

Purpose: There should be good orderliness in the hospital. However, during peak hours when the registration office is normally quite busy, crowded and noisy, unfavorable situations will not only affect the work efficiency of the hospital staff but also increase the waiting time for the patients. Sometimes line jumping and even disputes can occur. Hence, setting up an informatory sign or isolation strip for queuing will remind patients to line up and avoid line jumping, supporting a good registration order. A good sense of order can imperceptibly improve the work efficiency of the registration staff, reduce the waiting time, reduce the odds of disputes occuring and increase the satisfaction of patients.

Investigation method: Adopt field investigation and observe the situations in the hospital's registration office; check if there is any informatory sign or isolation strip for queuing; check the queuing of patients during peak hours.

Evaluation method: Full scores should be given if the hospital's registration office has an informatory sign or isolation strip for queuing and helps patients queue in order; 0 score should be given if the hospital doesn't set any informatory sign or the isolation strip for queuing at the registration office, or if there is an informatory sign or isolation strip and yet patients do not queue in an orderly manner for registration.

Improvement objective: (A) Set the informatory sign of "Please Queue in an Orderly Manner" in a visible position in the registration office; (B) Set an isolation strip for queuing at the registration office; (C) The registration staff should remind patients to queue in an orderly manner.

Sun Longqing, Executive Director of Business Department of JYWJ:

When I provided management consulting services for a hospital in Guizhou on the construction of a "patient-oriented" hospital culture, the project team noticed something when they investigated the registration indicator on-site; many people were gathered around the charging window and quarrels were heard from the crowd. It was then

(Continued)

(Continued)

found that someone had jumped the queue in front of a middle-aged woman who had been queuing in the line for a long time. So she couldn't get registered, which made her anxious, and this developed into a quarrel. The dispute was settled when the toll collector registered her. We noted down this problem and talked to the president. The hospital installed an isolation strip immediately and hung a sign which reminded people to queue in an orderly manner. Later, when the project team conducted another investigation, patients said that the orderliness of the hospital was greatly improved and the toll collectors could focus on their work, which further reduced waiting time and increased patient satisfaction.

Indicator 18. Is the outpatient surrounded by other patients when receiving diagnosis or treatment?

Meaning: The doctor can diagnose the patient without being distracted and the patients can be protected from exposure.

Purpose: The one-to-one diagnosis can ensure that the clinic is quiet and undisturbed and can also ensure privacy of patients, especially in the Gynecology Department and the Andrology Department. In addition, this also creates an undisturbed and peaceful environment for the doctor to enable them to conduct a comprehensive and concentrated conversation with the patient regarding their condition. This can guarantee medical service quality, while making patients feel relaxed and comfortable.

Investigation method: Field observation and personal experience.

Evaluation method: Full scores should be given if the patient is alone when diagnosed by the doctor without being surrounded by a crowd; otherwise, 0 score should be given.

Improvement requirements: Perform triage through hospital guides, reasonably control the outpatient number in each outpatient clinic; well-equipped hospitals shall install an electronic queue management system to facilitate patient entry into the clinic in an orderly manner.

Liu Taiyong, Consulting Director of JYWJ:

Speaking of this indicator, I remember what happened when I took one of my colleagues to a hospital. There wasn't any registration or queuing system in the hospital, patients would all gather around the doctor. When my colleague was diagnosed, the doctor asked several quite private questions. He was too shy to answer because of the strangers around him. However, patients and their family members seemed to enjoy this very much and listened to him carefully. I felt embarrassed myself, not to mention my colleague. Worst of all, the doctor wanted to perform a physical examination on the spot. The entire diagnosis wasn't pleasant at all, and it was even disrupted by some other patients. The scene was quite chaotic. Personally, that was a pretty bad experience. When it finally wrapped up, we went to the pharmacy with the doctor's prescription, and we saw the doctor was surrounded by other people again, regardless of the chairs provided in front of the clinic for them to sit on.

At that very moment, I felt that this kind of diagnostic reality — which pays no attention to personal privacy — immediately needs to be improved. Of course, this seemingly trifling task requires the hospital to create certain conditions and provide correct guidance. It should initiate a registration system and register patients in an orderly manner. Human guidance is also needed to facilitate older patients' doctor visits; by strengthening the diagnostic process, patients would better understand the hospital and feel respected.

Indicator 19. On-the-job rate of staff working in Admission Office

Meaning: Whether the Admission Office staff take off during their duty hours, are absent from their post or leave their post and visit others during work with no reason.

Purpose: The Admission Office is a place where patients handle admission procedures. Patients and their family members are anxious about the disease, and if the staff working in Admission Office are often absent from their post, patients will have to wait, which will impact the timeliness of medical treatment, and cause emotional problems to patients and their family members. This will result in a negative evaluation on the overall service quality of the hospital.

Investigation method: Carry out field observation to confirm whether staff working in Admission Office are on duty for several consecutive days.

Calculation method:

$$\text{On-the-job rate of staff in the Admission Office} = \frac{n_d}{N} * 100\%$$

where

n_d = Number of staff members actually on duty; and
N = Number of staff members supposed to be on duty.

Improvement objective: Staff working in the Admission Office should be on duty at any time, and there should be a whereabouts card if they go to the toilet at night.

Ma Xinxin, Director of Consulting Quality Management Department of JYWJ:

I have been engaged in hospital management consulting for a long time. I was often invited by some hospitals for investigation. In addition, I would arrive at the hospital at night many times due to the long distance. Once, I visited a hospital in Guizhou after 11:00 p.m. I importuned the hospital accompanying personnel to take me to have a look around as I wanted to learn the basic information about the hospital. When we passed the Admission Office, a staff member immediately handed me a cup of tea, and it surprised me very much because in many other hospitals the staff would sleep in the Duty Office at night and wake up reluctantly once a patient comes. Then, I asked: "Do you have rest rooms in the Duty Office?" However, he was surprised and replied: "We cannot rest. If a patient comes and cannot find us immediately, he will be anxious." I saw a deeply rooted "patient-oriented" hospital culture from this simple answer.

Indicator 20. Rate of making ward rounds by the director of the department

Meaning: The ward round of the department directors is one of the important jobs in hospitals and an important procedure to ensure medical quality and safety and to improve the quality of young medical staff. The directors of departments should take an active part seriously. The indicator refers to the implementation of ward rounds by the department directors.

Purpose: The department directors can find potential hidden hazards neglected by young physicians during a ward round in a timely manner, which can not only reduce the possibilities of missed diagnosis and misdiagnosis, but also contribute to the growth of young physicians. In addition, the core of hospital culture is patient experience, and all activities shall reflect the humanistic care of the hospital to patients. Conducting ward rounds helps the hospital set up a service image of "excellent skills and first-class service", enhance the patients' trust in the hospital and build better credibility for the hospital.

Investigation method: Investigate ward during the round every day and make statistics about the attendance of the department directors when other doctors make the ward round.

Evaluation method: Proportion*score.

Calculation method:

$$Rate\ of\ Director's\ ward\ rounds = \frac{n_r}{N_r} * 100\%$$

where

n_r = Total number of ward rounds made by the director of the department during investigations; and
N_r = Total number of investigations conducted.

Improvement objective: The department directors must lead other doctors in the department to make a ward round every week.

Wang Youcui, Consulting Director of JYWJ:

When we carried out the management consulting program of hospital cultures in Hunan Xinhuang Traditional Chinese Medicine Hospital and investigated relevant hospitalization indicators, we entered the ward and greeted a patient in her fifties, a thin and dark-skinned rural woman of an ethnic minority. We did not see her family members in the ward. We asked her if she knew her chief physician and nurse, if she was well treated by doctors and nurses, if it was convenient to have meals and dry clothes, and if she had family members to accompany her. She burst into tears. We did not ask her why she was crying, we just comforted and told her that if she needed something, she could turn to the doctors and nurses in the department or the Social Service Department for help. People are very vulnerable when they are ill, and it can be seen that she needs to be cared for by her family members. The common scenario in rural areas is that women stay at home, men work outside, and their children may study or work outside. When the women are ill, no one will care for them and accompany them during their time of need. Therefore, patients will feel warm if care and good services are provided during each procedure in the hospital.

Etiquette — The First Impression of Patients and Their Family Members

Wang Zhifen, Executive Director of Business Department of JYWJ:

Uniform dress, neat appearance, exquisite makeup and polite greetings will surely form a beautiful landscape. About 55% of people's first impressions come from vision. During the course of service, if the patient receives a smile, eye-contact and guidance from hospital guides, registration and charging personnel, medical staff, inspection personnel, pharmacy staff and even the driver, cleaner and security staff, and sense

(Continued)

their good mental outlook at any time, this hospital indicates a good visual etiquette culture. This indicator runs through 13 processes, involving 28 specific indicators and is aimed to guide hospitals to examine their own operation and improve the service level.

Indicator 21. Rate of greeting patients

Meaning: It refers to the rate of staff in the hospital taking the initiative to nod and smile if encountering patients.

Purpose: "Constructing a harmonious doctor–patient relationship and a civilized hospital" is the pursuit of every hospital. But in recent years, the doctor–patient relationship is quite tense, and patients extort, abuse and beat up medical staff, besiege the hospital, or even deliberately cripple and beat medical staff to death. All these violent and malignant events mainly result from distrust between doctors and patients. From the perspective of the hospital, medical staff are obliged to improve this situation. Actively greeting patients is one of the measures for medical staff to take the initiative to improve the doctor–patient relationship.

If patients find that medical staff take the initiative to greet them, they will feel respected, which will greatly narrow the distance between the medical staff and patients and enhance the trust the patients have in the hospital.

Investigation method: Field observation should be randomly applied to 100 medical staff in different departments to check if they take the initiative to nod and smile when encountering patients.

Evaluation method: Proportion*score.

Calculation method:

$$Rate\,of\ greeting\ patients = \frac{n_g}{N} * 100\%$$

where

n_g = Total number of people taking the initiative to greet patients; and

N = Total number of people investigated.

Improvement objective: (A) Strengthen training on service etiquette and code of conduct for medical staff, enable them to raise awareness and enhance training; (B) Medical staff shall nod and smile to each other, which will become a habit later.

Liu Lu, Director of Service Department of JYWJ:

People who have been to Liuyang Maternal and Child Health Care Hospital will be impressed by its nursing staff. As soon as you enter the hospital, the nursing staff, no matter from which department, will smile and nod to you. If you stop at the nursing station for a moment, you will be offered a cup of hot tea immediately.

The survey of cultural indicators is conducted in secret, and to investigate the hardware equipment of the hospital, personnel of the project team usually do it in the evening. During the course of the investigation, we checked every corner of the hospital, and also took photos with our cell phones. We met medical staff from various departments in the hospital. As we were new in the hospital, nurses usually thought we were family members of patients. Each medical staff we met fervently asked about our needs and was eager to help us with the direction, and some even offered us a cup of tea. After careful observation for a while, we found that this is the way they work. We can feel the "patient-oriented" service philosophy. We often hear the words, "I will come here again when I give birth to a child, because the hospital has good skill, favorable environment and better service".

Indicator 22. Smiling rate of hospital guides

Meaning: Whether hospital guides smile when accepting patients and their family members, and the smile ratio.

Purpose: A smile is not only a simple body language but also an expression of self-confidence, positive work and life attitudes, and even a style of etiquette. If hospital guides greet patients with a smile, it can effectively narrow the distance between the two sides and have a good impression on patients and their family members, and it will become easy to develop a harmonious atmosphere of seeking medical advice. During the daily interpersonal interaction, a greeting with a smile also reflects good personal accomplishment and sincerity. Examination of the smiling rate of hospital guides is suitable for all hospitals. If a hospital has no hospital guides, the position shall be set. The higher the smiling rate of hospital guides, the more sincere the feelings to patients and their family members. These kinsfolk-like guides will impress the patients and their family members and enhance the image of the hospital. In addition, patients and their family members will be comfortable during the doctor-seeing process, the probability of doctor–patient disputes will be reduced, the satisfaction of patients will be improved and the service level of the hospital will be further improved.

Investigation method: One-week field observation according to actual situations of the hospital. Carry out field observation on whether hospital guides accept patients and their family members with smiles by specially assigned person at a fixed time every day under the premise that hospital guides know anything about it. Twenty hospital guides are recorded every day. Observe whether hospital guides accept patients and their family members with a smile, and make records.

Evaluation method: Proportion*score.

Calculation method:

$$Smiling\ rate\ of\ hospital\ guides = \frac{n_{sm}}{N}$$

where

n_{sm} = Number of hospital guides who smile while greeting patients; and

N = Total number of hospital guides investigated.

Improvement objective: Hospital guides consciously develop the habit of service with smile, and they always wear a smile.

> Wang Ce, Executive Director of Business Department of JYWJ:
>
> One day, I went to Medical Department for work, and on the way, I met an old woman in her sixties, asking very angrily where she could file a complaint. I took her to the Medical Department and found that there was no one there. She insisted on seeing the president, but the President was not there. Hearing this, the Vice-president came out to investigate, and the old woman said that she has been seeking medical advice in the Traditional Chinese Medicine Hospital for about 20–30 years. She comes to take medicine every week and has her blood pressure checked by the hospital guides. However, when she asked for help from the hospital guide, who may have been a new employee, she did not respond and did not smile, but was just playing with her cell phone. Later, the patient was angry and banged the table, shouting to get her blood pressure taken. The staff raised her head and said impatiently: "Roll up your sleeves, why shout?". So, the old woman was very angry and came to complain, asking the hospital to discipline her. Otherwise she won't come to the hospital anymore. Later, the Vice-president asked for the director of the Outpatient Department. He said sorry with a smile, and explained that the hospital guide was fresh here, and must be disciplined and educated. After some comforting words, the old woman left to get her medicine.

Indicator 23. Rate of charging window personnel accepting professional training on service with smile

Meaning: It refers to the ratio of charging window personnel who accept the professional training on service with smile.

Purpose: Any skill must be learned and trained before being mastered, including smiling. It seems simple, but in fact, training and guidance by professional personnel through professional courses is required.

A proper smile can add extra points to the medical service institution, while an improper smile may be counterproductive, or even cause unnecessary troubles and contradictions. The charging window receives many patients and their family members; therefore, they need to take professional training on providing service with a smile.

Investigation method: Check training records.

Evaluation method: Proportion*score.

Calculation method (based on year-end data):

$$\textit{Rate of personnel accepting professional training} = \frac{n_p}{N} * 100\%$$

where

n_p = The number of personnel manning the charging window who accept professional training on providing service with a smile; and
N = The total number of people.

Improvement objective: The hospital regularly organizes training on service with smile for window service personnel, and training on service with smile is carried out during shift handover every morning within the department.

He Xulong, Director of Contract Department of JYWJ:

"Morning, Please, Hello, Sorry, Please wait a moment, I am so sorry to keep you waiting, Thank you, Thanks for coming". You can hear these words read clearly and loudly in the hall of the Charging Department in Sixth People's Hospital of Nanning. What is it? It turns out that the staff are practicing "seven major civilized terms" every day.

Since November 2017, Sixth People's Hospital of Nanning and Beijing Jingyi Wanjia Technology Co Ltd have worked together to advance the "patient-oriented" hospital culture construction, diagnose

(Continued)

(Continued)

every medical advice-seeking procedure in the hospital, give etiquette trainings and enhance cultural level.

The Charging Department has carried out a series of activities and measures after referring to company training and indicator improvement measures. First of all, under the guidance of the project team, 5S management in the department is carried out, which has improved the environment in the area. As the environment changes, the working attitudes of the employee change. Through the daily etiquette training practice, each staff also applies the civilized etiquette learned during their work. Serving with a smile, voicing the amount in receiving and paying, and politely seeing people off have become the habits of Sixth People's Hospital of Nanning. Summer comes, and staff in the Charging Department make uniform and beautiful clothes dedicated to the department.

With better environment, improved attitude and enhanced efficiency, the hospital has won constant praise from patients, and the service in the Charging Department of Sixth People's Hospital of Nanning has greatly changed.

Chapter 6
Using Warm and Pleasant Words

Ears play an extremely important role in the development of feelings. People get bored or may even panic in a loud or noisy environment, especially patients who need to rest and recover in a quiet environment. When people hear words that they don't like, they feel disgusted. Doctors need to diagnose illnesses through questioning patients, nurses need to take care of patients and patients will go through several stages during their stay in the hospital. At each stage, they will hear a variety of expressions from hospital staff, and which can influence their feelings about the hospital. Hearing has a major role in the formation of feelings; some people are fine when some words are used while others are not. Therefore, doctors and nurses must observe patients, understand their interests and hobbies and say things that they like. As the Chinese saying goes: A sentence may have numerous results, it just depends on the way you say it.

Cui Guotao, Executive Director of Business Department of JYWJ:

When patients are seeking medical advice, the lack of information often leads to confusion, which makes it impossible for them to receive efficient diagnosis and treatment services. From the perspective of the patient, in order to facilitate quick diagnosis and treatment and ensure their safety, patients need to know where the corresponding diseases are going to be treated, where the corresponding consulting rooms and wards are, how to call medical staff when they feel uncomfortable, etc.

(Continued)

(Continued)

The rapid and successful transmission of such information needs to be realized through "hearing". For example, learning about the disease through telephone counseling, finding the department where they can get treated by asking staff at the hospital and calling medical staff through the call system.

Therefore, "hearing-convenience" means that when patients are seeking medical advice, audible information related to diagnosis and treatment will help them to get diagnosis and treatment services quickly.

Creating a Quiet Environment for Patients

Cui Baohui, Executive Director of Business Department of JYWJ:

Tension and anxiety are inevitable for patients. It is also very important for patients to feel the environment when they are under the pressure of diagnosis and treatment. The auditory satisfaction of patients and their family members with the hospital environment comes from the following: Whether the hospital environment is quiet, whether the clinic and the examination area are noisy or disorderly, whether the ward is quiet or whether different types of light music are played according to the diseases of patients in different departments. All of these are the key factors affecting the auditory satisfaction of patients.

When patients seek medical advice in the hospital or are hospitalized, they already feel uncomfortable and can easily become anxious and impatient. Patients are very sensitive to the external factors they hear. A good and quiet environment in the hospital can ease the anxiety of patients, who will then actively cooperate with doctors for treatment and recovery. At the same time, this situation is also conducive to the medical staff as it aids in their diagnosis and treatment of the patients (most diagnoses and treatments need to be conducted in very quiet conditions). The hospital should comprehensively consider the hearing satisfaction of the patients and their family members in each service process to improve the satisfaction and sense of gain felt by patients and their family members.

Indicator 24. Noise decibel in the ward

Meaning: According to the requirements of the current national standard on the degree of quietness in the city in *National Environmental Standard for Noise*, the daytime noise level in hospital wards and rest rooms for medical staff shall not exceed the standard of 50dB, and the nighttime noise level shall not exceed the standard of 40dB.

Purpose: Keeping the ward environment quiet is the most basic service that the hospital provides to the patients. In an environment where the noise level is higher than the standard value, patients cannot rest or recover calmly, which is not conducive to the recovery of the body.

Investigation method: Carry out field measurement (download the decibel measurement software with a mobile phone), randomly select a place in each floor of the inpatient ward in the hospital, measure the noise level for one consecutive one week in the morning, afternoon and evening, and calculate the average as the noise level of the ward.

Evaluation method: The noise decibel by day and at night in the ward should not exceed 50dB and 40dB, respectively (50% by day and at night accordingly).

Calculation method:

$$\textit{Average noise level in the ward } (dB) = \frac{TNL}{N}$$

where

TNL = Total noise level recorded in decibels (dB); and
N = Total number of investigations conducted.

Improvement objective: Medical staff should set an example and try to lower their voice during work. When helping to admit patients into the ward, patients and their family members should be notified to keep quiet, and the medical examination routine of nurses should be strengthened.

Liu Taiyong, Consulting Director of JYWJ:

In recent years, wards are usually transformed during the development of hospitals. I experienced this in several hospitals. Because of renovation work, patients in the ward cannot rest well, and medical staff are terribly upset during work. The project team proposed to the hospitals that they adjust the time that decoration and renovation work was carried out to avoid any disturbance. When old wards in a certain health center of Guizhou were under renovation, two departments were combined, so the staff had to work in one department. Although there were many people, the environment in the ward in the evening was very quiet. Basically, every patient was satisfied, and the number of people increased. The main reason for this is that nursing staff had explained to and guided the hospitalized patients, notified them of the combination of two departments into one and asked everyone to be quiet and not to disturb the others in the ward in the evening. In addition, the hospital also had instituted requirements for the decoration time, and it had finally avoided the problems of patient dissatisfaction or decrease in the number of patients due to loud noise during renovation.

Satisfaction from Clear and Pleasant Words

Yang Dongdong, Executive Director of Business Department of JYWJ:

When patients are at service windows, whether it is in the charging department, pharmacy or Admission Office, they will hear polite greetings. When patients are seeking medical advice, the outpatient doctors or the resident physicians will listen to them patiently. Before patients leave the hospital, the doctor or the nurse in charge of hospitalization will exhort patients repeatedly on precautions after they are discharged. After patients leave the hospital, medical staff will carry out telephone follow-up and ask patients about their recovery. Only if patients and their family members hear pleasant words and things that they understand can the satisfactory effect be produced.

Indicator 25. Follow-up rate of emergency call patients

Meaning: Carry out a telephone follow-up randomly on 20% of the patients calling for help, find flaws in the work and understand what patients are dissatisfied with first before they are accepted into the hospital.

Purpose: Improve the service procedures, attitude and level in the Emergency Department gradually through telephone follow-up.

Investigation method: Randomly call 30 to 50 patients calling for help.

Evaluation method: Proportion*score.

Calculation method:

$$\text{Follow-up rate of emergency call patients} = \frac{n_{ec}}{N_e} * 100\%$$

where

n_{ec} = Number of follow-up calls made; and
N_e = Total number of emergency calls received.

Improvement objective: Improve the construction of Emergency Department in the following aspects: (A) Whether the operator's actual combat drill is in place and whether it can be arranged as a whole; (B) Whether the visit is prompt and timely; (C) Whether the rescue is timely and effective; (D) Whether the service attitudes are good.

Xu Juan, Director of Service Department of JYWJ:

An emergency call often happens when patients or their family members are in a critical condition. And at this time, professional medical staff are needed to simply deal with the condition when the medical equipment is simple and crude and send them to the hospital for further treatment as soon as possible. Due to the state of emergency and the simple and poor equipment, pre-hospital first aid treatment is often not as good as that in the hospital. And since patients or their

(Continued)

(Continued)

family members are very anxious at this time, it may lead to dissatisfaction if they are not handled properly. The Emergency Center of a certain hospital is often the point of complaint for patients. In order to reduce complaints and improve service, the hospital has set up a follow-up center and found many problems in the process of following up with patients who called for help, some of which included such issues as slow driving by the driver, the driver being unfamiliar with the road, the stiff tone of the emergency personnel, bad service attitudes, unskilled operations, etc. Through the follow-up of patients who called for help, the hospital has understood the reasons for complaints, and then worked on improving management, assessment and training, etc. So, complaints about pre-hospital first aid are obviously reduced, and patient satisfaction is improved. Setting up the emergency patient follow-up system and ensuring a certain follow-up rate helps the hospital understand the ideas and opinions of patients in time, and thus rectifies issues in a timely manner to improve patient satisfaction.

Indicator 26. Notice rate of family members of patients before consultation

Meaning: Whether the chief physician explains the purpose, procedure and other things that shall be notified to the patient's family members before a consultation.

Purpose: Before consultation, the doctor in charge of initial diagnosis should do the following tasks: (A) Standardize the writing of outpatient medical records, and make clear the department to visit and the purpose for consultation; (B) Necessary auxiliary examination; (C) Explain to patients and their family members clearly, inform them of the consultation procedure and obtain their understanding and cooperation; (D) If the patient's situation is not so bad and they are generally in good condition, they can go to other departments for consultation on their own; (E) If the patient is not an emergency case but is in bad general condition, they can be escorted to the relevant departments for consultation by hospital guides; (F) If the patient is undergoing any emergency treatment and can be transferred, they should be escorted to the Emergency Department and return after the doctor who is going to be seeing them clearly knows the patient's condition; (G) If the patient is critically ill and is not suited for immediate transfer, the relevant specialist physicians should be invited for consultation and treatment, and after the patient is in a stable condition, they should be transferred to the relevant specialist physicians.

Before consultation, the doctor in charge of the initial diagnosis must communicate well with family members about the responsible department as well as the cause and benefits of consultation, so that patients and their family members can understand the significance of consultation and cooperate actively.

Investigation method: Patients and their family members who have been consulted on the spot are required.

Evaluation method: Proportion*score.

Calculation method:

$$\textit{Notice rate of patients' family members before consultation} = \frac{n_n}{N} * 100\%$$

where

n_n = Total number of people following the notification procedures; and

N = Total number of people investigated.

Improvement objective: All patients and their family members can clearly understand the purpose and procedures of consultation.

Feng Yun, Consulting Director of JYWJ:

One day, a township health center received a patient in a bad state, and this led to admission to the internal medicine ward for further observation and treatment after a preliminary diagnosis and treatment by the outpatient doctor. After the patient was hospitalized in the internal medicine ward for three days, his condition showed no signs

(Continued)

(Continued)

of improvement. The family members were already dissatisfied. After the attending doctor reflected on this specific situation to the director of the department, the person in charge of the department decided to seek consultation from outside the hospital, considering that the technical strength in the hospital was relatively weak. Four days after hospitalization, a hospital at a higher level was requested to provide technical support, and after consulting experts outside the hospital, the diagnosis and therapeutic regimen of the patient were determined. When the new therapeutic regimen was applied, the patient's condition stabilized and improved. However, when the patient was discharged from the hospital, the family members had doubts about the consultation fee, but after the hospital explained, they understood and paid the fee. This case reflects that the doctor must communicate with the patient's family members when changing a specific therapeutic regimen and must obtain their consent. Although consultation is a normal medical practice, it is still necessary to inform the patient's family members in advance to avoid unnecessary troubles and disputes.

Indicator 27. Telephone follow-up rate of discharged patients

Meaning: When the patient is discharged from hospital, whether staff carry out telephone follow-up on each patient within a specified time.

Purpose: Urge the hospital staff to call every patient within a certain time frame after they have been discharged from the hospital. Telephone follow-ups cover the evaluation of medical staff by the patient, the effect of treatment and recovery and also serves as a reminder asking the patient for a return visit. Telephone follow-ups are an important service tracing measure. The hospital should not only pay attention to curing the hospitalized patient but also consider healthcare tracking after discharge to help the patients recover quickly and allow them to feel continued care from the hospital.

Investigation method: By means of spot check, randomly follow up with 50–100 discharged patients by phone, and check the actual follow-up rate; any follow-up records can be referred to.

Liu Taiyong, Consulting Director of JYWJ:

"Hello, this is the follow-up center of the county hospital. How are you feeling recently? Has the wound recovered?" Recently, Wang Bi, a staff member at the follow-up center of Xishui County People's Hospital was following up with patients that had been discharged three days ago. While tracking their recovery, a synchronous survey on hospital satisfaction was also carried out.

In June 2014, the county hospital set up the patient follow-up center taking the Party's mass line education and practice as the opportunity and following the "patient-oriented" service tenet. According to department responsibilities, the patients are divided into discharged, in-patient and transferred patients. 100% follow-up services are provided to the discharged patients to keep up with their recovery. They also carried out field investigations on patients who were hospitalized for 3 and 7 days, and improved any measures that the patients complained about as being unsatisfactory. Further follow-up on transferred patients and supervising whether doctors in the hospital have guided the transfer, i.e. explained their condition to the new doctor and assisted the transfer process, were also assessed. During the process of follow-up, the hospital also announces the follow-up results of each department through the PA system, and makes public the addressing of problems that have been identified in the last month.

"Patient satisfaction is an important standard for assessing medical staff." Before the follow-up center was set up, there were more than 10 complaints from patients on average each month. The doctor–patient relationship was relatively tense. With the system of "follow-up for patients" advancing, there are only two or three complaints every month, and the satisfaction of patients has greatly improved. Wang Jun, president of the hospital, said that the hospital found a "key" to change the work style of the medical staff by its mass education activities, i.e. to "customize" a set of complete and systematic mechanisms based on the needs of patients, and combine the improvement of hospital business and management level with the prominent problems proposed by patients through strict systems and measures. Medical staff further enhance service awareness, and this became a powerful solution in the "last step" of patient service.

Evaluation method: Proportion*score.

Calculation

$$\textit{Telephone follow-up rate of discharged patients} = \frac{n_{dc}}{N} * 100\%$$

where

n_{dc} = Number of discharged patients who are called; and
N = Total number of people investigated.

Improvement objective: Set up a doctor–patient office and appoint specially assigned persons for follow-up of discharged patients, realize 100% telephone follow-up rate for discharged patients and record the follow-up of every discharged patient.

Patients' Auditory Feelings Needing to Be Managed

Gu Lili, Executive Director of Business Department of JYWJ:

The construction of a "patient-oriented" hospital culture is closely related to the experience of patients in the hospital. Patients are usually influenced by what they hear. During interpersonal interaction, the power of language is strong, especially when there is communication between the medical staff and the patients.

Hearing management indicators include following up with transferred patients, phone answering by a chief physician, phone answering by the director of a clinical department at night, communication with patients in terms of bedside handover, whether to actively inform operation status in real time during the operation, whether to deny the diagnosis and treatment of other medical staff in front of patients or not, etc. All of these can be enhanced through hospital management. But this is not only a process for strengthening the management within the hospital, but also one requiring medical staff to help and care for patients and provide more comprehensive and higher-quality services for them when needed. It can enhance the patient's opinion of the hospital and reflect the level of care the hospital provides.

Indicator 28. Follow-up rate of transferred patients

Meaning: Medical staff in a department should contact the transferred patients to check whether they get better (Telephone follow-up, SMS follow-up or home follow-up).

Purpose: The follow-up rate of transferred patients is an indicator to evaluate the follow-up of transferred patients. The higher the rate is, the more effective the follow-up system of the hospital is, and the higher the hospital's service level is. At the same time, the hospital's care for transferred patients can be indirectly judged. Paying attention to the diagnosis and recovery of transferred patients should be the basic responsibility of the corresponding departments, which can simultaneously lead to improvement of treatment and positive recognition from family members. The lower the indicator is, the more the hospital's service awareness needs to be improved.

Investigation method: Investigate the data of transferred patients and inquire their status from patients or family members (20–30).

Evaluation method: Proportion*score.

Calculation method:

$$Follow\text{-}up\, rate\, of\, transferred\, patients = \frac{n_{tv}}{N} * 100\%$$

where

n_{tv} = Number of visits to transferred patients made; and
N = Total number of patients investigated.

Improvement objective: The hospital should set up the follow-up system for transferred patients: Telephone follow-up, SMS follow-up or home follow-up to meet the standard.

Wu Aixian, Consulting Director of JYWJ:

The survey of this indicator was completed by personnel of the project team together with the head of Hospital Cultural Management Department. During the course of collecting basic information on

(Continued)

(Continued)

transferred patients in various departments, unexpected problems were found. It turned out that the hospital did not strictly enforce the system that transferred patients need to fill out referral forms since 2016. As a result, departments have paid increasingly less attention to following up with transferred patients. Except for the Pediatric Department and the Gynecology and Obstetrics Department, other departments have not recorded the basic information about transferred patients or carried out telephone follow-up for transferred patients.

Although it was found in the investigation that the Gynecology and Obstetrics Department and Pediatric Department had basic information about transferred patients, this was limited to information concerning only a small number of transferred patients, and the follow-up work became a mere formality. Only the follow-up time is registered in the follow-up book, and there is basically no patient feedback. When the personnel of the project team and Hospital Cultural Management Department reached out to patients again, it was found that many patients or their family members had not been contacted by the hospital. In order to ensure the objectivity of the investigation results, the target patients were transferred within half a month, but the results are unsatisfactory. This investigation thus received no score.

The investigation results show that the hospital basically does not follow up with their transferred patients, and thus does not meet the requirements of the "patient-oriented" hospital culture.

Standards Existing in Hearing Etiquettes

Zhang Hongtao, Executive Director of Business Department of JYWJ:

The construction of the "patient-oriented" hospital culture is closely related to the sensory experiences of the patients. With regards to hearing, the hospital should provide a professional and comfortable auditory

(Continued)

environment for patients. When patients are seeking medical advice, the medical staff's behavior will demonstrate the culture at that hospital.

For auditory etiquette indicators, such as the rate of polite expressions used by 120 operators, control rate of polite expressions used by staff in Medical Lab, rate of pharmacy staff seeing people off politely, usage rate of civilized expressions of staff working in Admission Office, etc., standardized etiquette rules can be developed in every service procedure, so that patients can be more comfortable and assured, and less anxious. The improvement of auditory etiquette indicators is not only the external manifestation of the whole connotation of the hospital, but also a process of requiring medical staff to take the initiative to provide better service when the patients need it. In this way, patients feel that the hospital is professional and they are respected.

Indicator 29. Rate of pharmacy staff seeing people off politely

Meaning: Whether pharmacy staff say "please take care" and other polite expressions after patients collect their medicine.

Purpose: As hospitals form a special service sector, proper polite expressions will enable anxious patients to feel warm, and the rate of pharmacy staff seeing people off politely reflects on whether the service provided by staff in the Pharmacy is satisfactory to patients. The etiquette shown by the medical staff when they see patients off reflects the service philosophy of the hospital, which is related to the image of the entire hospital.

Investigation method: Through field observation, randomly observe 50–100 patients taking medicine and see whether the pharmacy staff see them off politely.

Evaluation method: Proportion*score.

Calculation method:

$$\textit{Rate of pharmacy staff seeing patients off politely} = \frac{n_{pf}}{N} * 100\%$$

where

n_{pf} = Number of polite 'farewells' observed; and
N = Total number of 'farewells' observed.

Improvement objective: Improve the service awareness of staff by means of training and field guidance and practice, so that staff in the Pharmacy know how to see patients off politely.

Indicator 30. Usage rate of civilized expressions of staff working in Admission Office

Meaning: Whether staff working in the Admission Office use "Hello", "Thank you", "Thank you for coming", "Pay attention to your information" and other expressions, and whether they are impatient and wage tit-for-tat actions against patients and their family members.

Purpose: As the saying goes, "A positive expression warms people like a fire in the cold winter, while a bad one hurts seriously like snow in the summer".

Use common, polite, comforting and encouraging language during work; avoid simple, rude, sarcastic, insulting, and abusive language; and often use phrases like "hello, please, I'm sorry, thank you, you're welcome, and thank you for coming" to make people feel friendly, harmonious and free. Civilized expressions allow people to communicate more smoothly, which helps achieve the goals of both sides.

Investigation method: Carry out weekly field observation around the Admission Office and conduct two surveys on civilized language of staff working in the Admission Office on Monday and Wednesday or on Tuesday and Thursday. The survey lasts for two weeks and 50–100 people are involved.

Evaluation method: Proportion*score.

Calculation method:

$$Usage\ rate\ of\ civilised\ expressions\left(Admission\ Office\right) = \frac{n_{ce}}{N} * 100\%$$

where

n_{ce} = Number of people using polite expressions; and
N = Total number of people investigated.

Improvement objective: (A) Set up the Hospital Cultural Department. Hospital culture specialists should regularly go to departments to check whether the staff working in Admission Office use polite expressions; (B) The hospital should conduct regular smile etiquette trainings or smile etiquette competitions and other activities for window departments; (C) Usage rate of civilized expressions by the staff working in the Admission Office should reach over 90%.

Standard expressions of staff working in the Admission Office:

(1) Hello, we have a lot of patients today. Please do not worry and line up in order.
(2) It's a total of RMB **. We charge you RMB **, and here is the change. Please keep it well.
(3) Are you insured? Please give me your medical insurance card.
(4) Please pay the advance hospitalization fee of RMB **.
(5) We charge you RMB **, please keep the receipt well, and give it back to the settlement office when you are discharged from hospital.
(6) Your admission procedure is done, and please go to the** Department in the ** floor of the ** building in Admission Office.
(7) Hello, please give me the receipt for the advance payment. Which department did you visit and what's your name?
(8) Your hospitalization expense is a total of RMB **, and you have paid RMB **. Please pay another RMB ** (return RMB **).
(9) Here is your settlement document. Please keep it well.
(10) I'm sorry for the trouble. I'll correct it right away. A moment, please.

The following aspects should be done well and with the proper use of civilized expressions:

(1) Language should be accurate and appropriate. Pay attention to the art of language, and strive for integrity of the semantic meaning of speech.
(2) Word usage should be well coordinated and connected, so that words can convey the expected meaning.

Liu Lu, Director of Service Department of JYWJ:

The hospital is always busy in the morning, especially the areas for payment, discharge and hospitalization. The project team once found in the investigation of cultural indicators that there was a long queue at the cashier desk in the Admission Office. In this case, a staff member at the charging window left for 25 minutes, causing repeated complaints from the waiting patients. Most of the patients went to another window after waiting for more than 10 minutes, while some patients waited at the same window for half an hour. There was still no explanation from any cash collector. When patients asked about it at another payment window, "Just wait!" was the indifferent answer. Soon after that, another surprising thing happened. When a patient was paying the discharge fee, the cashier gave them an extra RMB 20 in change. When the patient came to return it, the cashier, instead of thanking them, urged the patient's family members to not stand in the way.

This example shows that cashiers in the hospital treat patients badly, but our patients do not treat them with the same attitudes in return. Put yourself in others' shoes: What would the cashier do if she was the patient? "Patient-oriented" hospital culture is reflected in the small details of the hospital. By improving the use of polite expressions by staff working in the Admission Office, patients can really feel the changes in the cultural environment of the hospital.

(3) When you use civilized expressions, face the patients, wear a smile and look into the patient's eyes; do not be absent-minded. Speak clearly with a sweet voice.
(4) In terms of language selection, try to use Mandarin.

Indicator 31. Rate of using polite expressions to see people off

Meaning: When a patient is discharged from hospital, staff should see the patient off politely: "Please come here for re-examination in time", "please take care", "remember to take medicine on time", etc.

Purpose: The humanistic care provided by the hospital for patients should not only include that given to in-hospital patients but also that given to patients being discharged. It is the eternal goal for medical staff to treat patients as their kinsfolk and to treat and cure the patients. It is the direction and goal of hospital staff to create a good hospital image and improve the reputation and popularity of the hospital.

Investigation method: Observe whether 30–50 patients are seen off properly during the discharge.

Evaluation method: Proportion*score.

Calculation method:

$$Rate\ of\ polite\ farewells = \frac{n_{pf}}{N} * 100\%$$

where

n_{pf} = Number of patients who are seen off politely; and
N = Total number of patients investigated.

Improvement objective: The medical staff can use polite expressions to see patients off when they are discharged once they have undergone etiquette training so as to improve patients' satisfaction with the medical staff.

Lin Chang, Director of International Department of JYWJ:

Once I went to Tianjin United Family Hospital to look for my friend and saw the following scene while I was waiting at the door:

A nurse walked a pregnant woman to the door of the hospital and, while waiting for the cab, kept telling the pregnant woman something, such as the time of the next antenatal care, how to eat when you go home, do not always lie down during pregnancy, exercise moderately, etc. Because the pregnant woman came to the hospital alone, the nurse also took the initiative to help the pregnant woman call a taxi.

By this whole process, we can see that the nurse not only treated the person coming to the hospital politely but also told the pregnant woman precautions as she saw her as her kinsfolk. The intimate

(Continued)

(Continued)

inquiry and warm atmosphere make the patient feel at home, comfortable and free.

Later, I told my friend about this, and she said that in United Family, such cases are frequent every day. The hospital tries to provide every patient who visits the hospital their best service. At the same time, my friend strongly recommended me to come to United Family when I'm pregnant.

Chapter 7
Providing Fresh Air for Patients

Different smells lead to different feelings. Certain fragrances make people comfortable, while unpleasant odors make them feel oppressed. If the air is mixed with various smells, it causes chest tightness and shortness of breath, and if serious, even sickness. This is what we know as smell. Hospitals are often filled with the smell of disinfectants, which is not popular among the public. Everyone likes to breathe in fresh air; however, it's not easy for the hospital to maintain fresh air.

Yang Shuanping, Executive Director of Business Department of JYWJ:

Smell is one of the most important senses. Different smells may give different impressions to patients or residents about the hospital.

Generally speaking, unpleasant odor in the toilet is relatively obvious, which can be easily perceived by patients or residents through the sense of smell. If the hospital toilet is not cleaned in time and the deodorant is not placed, it may attract insects, mosquitoes and flies, which represents an unhygienic environment and affects the patient's impression of the hospital. This will further lead to a lower overall evaluation of the hospital by patients or residents. If the toilet of the hospital can be cleaned in time and a deodorizer or air freshener is placed, patients or residents will feel better about the hospital's environmental sanitation and develop a good impression of the hospital.

Indicator 32. Whether there is an unpleasant odor in toilets

Meaning: Toilets here refer to the public ones, and this indicator refers to the whether the public toilets within the jurisdiction of the hospital smell bad.

Purpose: The unpleasant smell from the public toilets in the hospital can be easily smelled by the patients, which affects their experience of seeking medical advice. In addition, particularly in a hospital environment, odor may cause respiratory infection if not removed in time. In order to build a good hospital environment for patients and their family members, enhance patients' recognition of the hospital and improve patient satisfaction and image of the hospital, it is critical to carry out a study on whether there is an unpleasant odor in public toilets of the hospital.

Investigation method: Field observation and personal experience. Number the public hospital toilets, and carry out the investigation on the unpleasant odor of public toilets in the hospital during the following three periods of time: 9:00 a.m.–10:00 a.m., 3:00 p.m.–4:00 p.m. and 7:00–8:00 p.m., and create a 30-day toilet record on unpleasant odor.

Calculation method:

$$\textit{Rate of toilets with no unpleasant odor} = \frac{n_t}{N} * 100\%$$

where

n_t = Number of toilets meeting the cleanliness standard; and
N = Total number of toilets investigated.

Improvement objective: (A) Cleaners are required to wash the toilet at least 3 times every day and clean the toilet in time; (B) After spraying the disinfectant, keep the toilet ventilated; (C) Light sandalwood and Indian incense in the toilet to remove unpleasant odors.

Qiu Yanpeng, Consulting Director of JYWJ:

When I visited a hospital in Guizhou, I could smell an unpleasant odor at the end of the corridor of the Outpatient Department on the first

(Continued)

floor. The toilet was also very wet and filled with foul water. Patients had to tiptoe very carefully. When you opened the door, there was dirt in the urinal, and the garbage can was "filled to capacity" with rubbish overflowing on the ground.

Seeing this, we have to ponder: What's the reason for this? Obviously, the hospital administrator does not pay enough attention to the cleaning and management of the hospital toilets, and cleaners work in a haphazard manner. In addition, when the toilet is clogged, no one has been sent to dredge it.

It can be found from chatting with patients that their overall impression on the hospital is that the technical level of this hospital is good, but the service is poor. In addition, the hospital toilet is dirty, messy and poorly equipped. If other hospitals can treat my disease, I will never choose XX hospital.

Chapter 8
Pleasant Smells and Palatable Food

People need food and water, especially hospitalized patients. Whether the water is odorless or the food is delicious are what we call taste in physiology. Taste is extremely important to people. A simple truth is that no one wants to eat what they don't like. It is not easy for patients, especially inpatients, to get food with a satisfying taste. In China, people from different regions may have different tastes in food. Therefore, it is difficult to cater to all the different preferences.

Xie Zhichang, Executive Director, School of Management of JYWJ:

Taste is a kind of feeling produced when the human taste organ is stimulated by food. It is also an important sense for humans. The most basic tastes are sweet, sour, bitter and salty. All kinds of tastes are made up of a mixture of these four tastes. While assessing the hospital experience, a small part is also contributed by "taste" perception, mainly focusing on service such as, for example, whether the food provided by the Catering Department is balanced in nutrition or delicious. Many hospitals pay attention to the dining service of the Catering Department, and some also set up a nutrition department to provide patients with "customized" nutritional therapeutic regimens, which not only provides patients and their family members with quality food but also reflects the service philosophy of humanistic care.

Indicator 33. Satisfaction with food taste in the Catering Department

Meaning: Whether patients and their family members are satisfied with food in the Catering Department.

Purpose: "Hunger breeds discontentment", and the taste of food not only affects the mood of the patients but also the recovery rate and satisfaction of the patients. Hospitals need to improve the taste of food in order to improve the dining experience of patients and their satisfaction with the Catering Department.

Investigation methods: Survey, ask 50–100 patients and their family members.

Evaluation method: Proportion*score.

Calculation method:

$$\textit{Food satisfaction rate} = \frac{n_{sf}}{N} * 100\%$$

where

n_t = Number of patients and/or family members satisfied with food provided by the Catering Department; and

N = Total number of patients and/or family members investigated.

Improvement objective: (A) Train cooks about nutritious diets and teach them to prepare nutritious and delicious meals; (B) The hospital negotiates with the Catering Department to improve the food quality and reduce the price; (C) Questionnaire should be given to patients regularly and reasonable suggestions should be heard; (D) Carry out health publicity and explain to patients about the importance of a balanced diet, so that they will understand the limited-tastes meals for patients; (E) Add a "small pot dish" properly to meet the needs of different people.

Liu Taiyong, Consulting Director of JYWJ:

Three ultimate problems in life: What to eat in the morning? What to eat at noon? What to eat at night? This applies to doctors and patients, too. For inpatients, diet in the hospital is not only a daily necessity but also a part of holistic treatment. However, at present, the diet provided by most hospitals is not ideal, and patients are not satisfied with it. There are many reasons for this, such as presence of only a single variety of food, diet for the elderly not being different from that for the young, eating too early, dishes getting cold, etc. Patient dissatisfaction with food in the hospital also affects their overall satisfaction with the hospital. Therefore, if the food is delicious, fresh, affordable and healthy, the hospitalized patients will enjoy a "nutrition station", which is also an important part of the "patient-oriented" hospital culture construction. Guizhou Provincial People's Hospital is one of the positive examples. During the Mid-Autumn Festival, hundreds of people will "fly" to the Provincial People's Hospital to queue up for moon cakes, which has been reported by many news media. It is obvious that if the best diet is provided for patients, the hospital's overall reputation will greatly improve.

Chapter 9
Warmth and Comfort

Coldness, warmth and other feelings of the skin are transmitted to the brain and create a general comfortable or uncomfortable experience in people. If a hospital is too hot in summer or too cold in winter, patients and their family members will certainly feel uncomfortable. Allowing patients and their family members to enjoy a pleasant and satisfactory temperature is indispensable for improving services.

Convenient Facilities Required to Get Satisfactory Temperature

Guo Ran, Director of General Office of JYWJ:

One winter, when I was in Kunming, my colleague suddenly felt stomach discomfort and went back to his room. Then, it got worse, and we went to a local hospital to seek medical advice. My colleague was diagnosed as having gastritis and needed to undergo transfusion all night in the hospital. When I tried to get hot water for my colleague, I did not find any place to get water around the hospital ward, let alone hot water! After asking the nurse, I was told that there was no place in the hospital to get hot water. I was stunned that a hospital of such a large scale had no drinking water for patients and their family members! This made me extremely upset and perplexed.

Then I bought a vacuum cup in a 24-hour convenience store nearby and asked the clerk for some hot water. I was greatly touched by this. Everyone needs water, and who ever will come to the hospital again if it does not even provide water?

Indicator 34. Ownership rate of bath equipment in ward toilets

Meaning: The proportion of wards with bath equipment in the toilet of all wards of the hospital.

Purpose: This indicator examines whether the hospital provides a more convenient environment for patients who may need to be warded a few days or even longer. Because of the limited facilities, it will inevitably be inconvenient for patients to live in the ward. For example, taking no bath for a long time will not only bring discomfort to the patients and affect their emotions but will also create an environment for bacteria to breed and even lead to infections. Therefore, providing bath equipment in ward toilets can not only make the patients more comfortable but also prevent infections.

Investigation method: Carry out field statistics of the number of wards with bath equipment in the toilet.

Evaluation method: Proportion*score.

Calculation method:

$$Rate\ of\ ward\ toilets\ with\ bath\ equipment = \frac{n_b}{N} * 100\%$$

where

n_b = Number of ward toilets equipped with bath equipment; and
N = Total number of ward toilets investigated.

Improvement objective: Every toilet in all of the all wards should have bath equipment.

Indicator 35. Rate of 24-hour supply of hot water for daily use in each ward

Meaning: Whether hot water is available for 24 hours in each ward.

Purpose: Patients are special people who need a lot of hot water to wash, clean, etc., in their daily life. As many hospitals do not supply 24-hour hot water, patients have to use kettles to boil water on their own after the stored hot water runs out. This greatly increases safety hazards, and also brings a lot of trouble to the hospital management. Therefore, hospitals should ensure that every ward can supply hot water for 24 hours a day, especially in winter.

Investigation method: Checking each ward or surveying patients.

Evaluation method: Proportion*score.

Calculation method:

$$Rate\ of\ hot\ water\ supply\ in\ wards = \frac{n_w}{N} * 100\%$$

where

n_w = Number of wards which supply 24-hours hot water; and
N = Total number of wards investigated.

Improvement objective: Every ward must have 24-hour supply of hot water.

Never Ignore Impacts of Environment on Touch

Xie Zhichang, Executive Director, School of Management of JYWJ:

Tactile sense is an important sense of humans and an important perceptive part in the medical experience of patients. At the same time, it is closely related to the environment in which we live. In different environments, our feelings also vary. When entering a tropical rainforest environment, you can obviously feel the "sauna-like" dampness and sultriness, while when wandering about in a desert under the scorching sun, you will feel the heat wave. When patients are undergoing different medical procedures, they will unconsciously feel the service experience through tactile sense.

Indicator 36. Rate of air-conditioners present in the transfusion and observing rooms

Meaning: Air-conditioners should be present in the transfusion and observing rooms.

Purpose: Air-conditioners are set up to adjust and control the temperature, humidity, cleanliness, flow and other parameters of ambient air in the building/structure by manual means. The temperature in transfusion and observing rooms can affect patients' feeling about seeking medical advice. Therefore, it is necessary to equip the rooms with air-conditioners so that the patients no longer need to suffer from heat or coldness. With air-conditioners, the humidity and cleanliness of air can also be guaranteed. Whether in spring, summer, autumn or winter, patients can feel that they receive good attention from the hospital.

Investigation method: Field observation.

Evaluation method: Proportion*score.

Calculation method:

$$\begin{aligned}&\textit{Rate of air-conditioners in transfusion}\\&\qquad\textit{and observation rooms} = \frac{n_{ac}}{N} * 100\%\end{aligned}$$

where

n_{ac} = Number of wards which supply 24-hours hot water; and
N = Total number of wards investigated.

Improvement objective: Air-conditioners need to be equipped in the transfusion and observing rooms.

Indicator 37. Whether there are skid-resistant carpets on the floor of the Recovery Department

Meaning: In order to better serve patients and reduce the possibility of secondary damage to patients during the recovery process, skid-resistant carpets need to be placed on the floor.

Purpose: Whether an object is smooth or not can be felt by people, and a smooth floor will lead to falls, which is a common unsafe factor in the hospital. Approximately 5%–15% of falls will cause brain injury, soft tissue contusion, fracture, dislocation and other injuries. As a result of illness, patients suffer from body balance issues, motor dysfunction, sensory disorder, body weakness, etc. They are more vulnerable to falls than normal people. After falling, patients may suffer from fracture, stroke recurrence and even death, which not only increases pain and delays their recovery process but also leads to medical disputes.

Therefore, it is important to strengthen health education, ensure good safety management of patients and their family members, lay skid-resistant carpets and take other measures to reduce the occurrence of falls by patients and their family members.

Investigation method: Field observation.

Evaluation method: Full scores should be given when skid-resistant carpets are available; otherwise a score of 0 is given.

Improvement objective: Lay down skid-resistant carpets or indoor plastic floors on the ground, and paste anti-skid tapes in key areas to prevent patients from falling down and hurting themselves; the carpets should also be regularly cleaned.

Let Patients Feel Warm During Contact

Wang Tianqi, Executive Director of JYWJ Service Department:

Doctors and nursing staff are bound to have physical contact with patients. Physical contact is ubiquitous in services, such as during guidance, treatment, in the inpatient ward and during operation. Change the behavior of medical staff to optimize customer experience and impact the satisfaction of the customers. This indicator will help to set the tone of hospital culture from the perspective of system and,

(Continued)

(Continued)

at the same time, influence the behavior of employees step by step with a feasible training system. The improvement of this kind of behavior is definitely possible. By constantly inculcating the "patient-oriented" cultural philosophy in the hospital, promoting the active service awareness of staff and making "ideological preparations" for the implementation of the system and the process, patients can see how things develop from the very beginning.

Indicator 38. Rate of support for patients unable to move freely

Meaning: During the investigation, the proportion of patients unable to move freely must be supported by hospital guides.

Purpose: The so-called "patient-oriented" spirit should not simply be a slogan, and furthermore, it should be reflected in what kind of services we have provided for patients in the process of diagnosis and treatment, especially in what we have done for patients unable to move freely.

Disease itself will cause anxiety and fear, especially to patients who are unable to move freely. At this time, even the slightest help will provide them with great encouragement and support.

Investigation method: Field observation and random inquiry. Field observation is used to randomly observe and record that hospital guides take the initiative to support patients unable to move freely. Also, random questioning of patients unable to move freely can be

Zhang Yunpeng, Consulting Director of JYWJ:

On the afternoon of August 24, a middle-aged man with a bitter face in Outpatient Hall of the People's Hospital of Jianhe County drew the attention of Jiang Zhiyan, director of Social Development Department of the hospital. After an inquiry, she learned that the man came to our

(Continued)

hospital because of pain in his waist and leg in recent days, and he had difficulty in walking. After a further conversation, she learned that the man, with a surname Wang, in his fifties, was from Censong of Jianhe and had joined the army in 1983 where he had served for more than 10 years. He was unfortunately wounded during that time. He now worked in a factory for a living. His mother was in her eighties and was living at home. His three children were not around, so he had to come to the hospital for medical advice alone.

At the end of the conversation, Director Jiang and her colleagues transferred Mr. Wang to a wheelchair and accompanied him through the processes of registration, billing, payment and CT via the green channel. While waiting for the examination results, Mr. Wang was invited to rest in an office and was encouraged to confront the disease. He believed in the diagnosis and treatment of the hospital and remained optimistic. After the examination results were provided, the doctor suggested hospitalization based on his condition. After handling hospitalization registration, Director Jiang and her colleagues used a wheelchair and sent Mr. Wang to the bone surgery department for hospitalization and treatment. After learning about Mr. Wang, medical staff in the departments showed sympathy and concern, saying that during hospitalization they would provide as much assistance as possible.

When Director Jiang accompanied him during the visit, Mr. Wang was so excited that he was choked with sobs several times and his eyes were filled with tears. A small act of kindness allowed Mr. Wang to feel warm! Afterwards, Director Jiang admitted that she was deeply moved: Mr. Wang's illness originated in the army, but he never regretted joining the army and bore the pain by himself. His only worry was that he might not be able to stand up and would be a burden on his family and children. After being on active service for more than 10 years, where he dedicated his youth to the barracks and to his motherland, after he was demobilized, he became the backbone of his family, working hard, taking care of the elderly and raising children.

done to assess whether they are actively supported by hospital guides when passing by the information area during the investigation and making records.

Evaluation method: Proportion*score.

Calculation formula:

$$\textit{Rate of support for patients unable to move freely} = \frac{n_{su}}{N} * 100\%$$

where

n_{su} = Number of people who actively support patients who cannot move freely; and

N = Total number of people investigated.

Improvement method: Through training, assessment and clear job responsibilities, improve the awareness of support and assistance provided by hospital guides for patients unable to move freely.

Indicator 39. Warmth retention rate of stethoscopes in winter

Meaning: Warmth retention of stethoscopes in winter, such as warming the stethoscope with hands in advance.

Purpose: The shell of the head of an ordinary stethoscope is usually made of metal. In winter, the cold metal will cause discomfort, aggravate the physiological and psychological burden of the subject and even affect the examination result.

If the doctor can warm the stethoscope with his/her hands (or other insulation equipment) before auscultation, the unnecessary stress reaction of the patient can be reduced to a certain extent. This small action reflects the care and is a silent kind of communication. The sincerity of the service of the hospital reflected in these minor details is one of the basic embodiments of the "patient-oriented" and "all for patients" principles.

Investigation method: Random observation. The survey cannot be carried out in summer. So, the scores must be equally divided among the other indicators then.

Calculation method:

$$Warmth\,retention\,rate = \frac{n_{ws}}{N} * 100\%$$

where

n_w = Number of warm stethoscopes in winter; and
N = Total number investigated.

Improvement objective: Proceed step by step, start from the middle level, and improve gradually. The ultimate goal is that all outpatient doctors warm their stethoscopes in winter before they see patients.

Sun Longqing, Executive Director of Business Department of JYWJ:

When I carried out the management consulting program of hospital cultures in a hospital in Guizhou one winter, I went to the outpatient department to check on this indicator. At that time, the warmth retention rate of stethoscopes of doctors was very low. Later, after the hospital culture diagnostic report was released, the department made significant improvement. On one occasion, a grandmother brought her grandchild to the pediatric department to see the doctor, and the pediatrician warmed the stethoscope with his/her hands before auscultation. At that time, the kid's grandmother was very moved, saying directly to the doctor: "You are so careful and considerate." In fact, warming the stethoscope with ones hands is only a small action, but helps people feel particularly warm during the cold winter.

Patients' Touch Needing to Be Managed

Wang Shanshan, Director of Brand Development Department of JYWJ:

The sense of touch can be directly felt by patients through body contact. Whether the patient is receiving service or diagnosis and treatment,

(Continued)

(Continued)

medical staff shall try to avoid discomfort caused to the patient's body. If pain is inevitable, they shall inform the patients in advance.

The management system or methods can, to a certain extent, reduce the discomfort directly felt by the patient. For example, if there is secondary anesthesia during operation, it will bring certain risks to the patient and affect the patient's body to a certain extent. With the management system, the anesthesiologist can make a complete assessment and be prepared in advance, before the operation starts, to avoid the occurrence of secondary anesthesia, which can thus help reduce discomfort or negative influence on the patient's body.

Indicator 40. Rate of secondary anesthesia of operative patients

Meaning: Whether the patient is under secondary anesthesia during the operation.

Purpose: Secondary anesthesia threatens the life of patients and increases their economic burden. To avoid secondary anesthesia, the technical level of doctors needs to be improved, in order to effectively make them well prepared for the operation and aid in selecting the appropriate anesthetic method and reducing unnecessary drug waste so as to improve medical quality.

Investigation method: Checking medical records and operation records.

Evaluation method: Proportion*score.

Calculation method:

$$Rate\ of\ secondary\ anesthesia = \frac{n_{sa}}{N} * 100\%$$

where

n_{sa} = Number of patients undergoing secondary anesthesia during operations; and

N = Total number of operations conducted.

Improvement objective: (A) Reduce the rate of secondary anesthesia to below 3%; (B) The hospitals set up a management group and establish a corresponding assessment system to punish unqualified doctors and reward doctors realizing low rate of secondary anesthesia.

Li Qiming, Consulting Director of JYWJ:

In a certain hospital, a post-operative patient complained about the Department of Anesthesiology, mainly because of "intraoperative awareness": In the operating room, after the anesthesiologist anesthetized the patient with an oxygen mask, the patient was in a coma, but suddenly woke up during the operation. The patient remembered that after waking up, he was very sober, felt that he was lying on the operating table and that when the scalpel scratched his back, he felt severe pain. The patient realized that he had to tell the doctor that he was awake, but he could not open his eyes or move. Later, he heard an alarm (from the anesthesia machine). Although the anesthesiologist gave him secondary anesthesia immediately, the strong feeling of drowning and impending death during the operation cast a serious psychological shadow on him.

Upon investigation by the Medical Department, it was found that the anesthesiologist did not accurately assess the patient and the dosage of narcotics administered was improper. The patient was compensated accordingly. However, as the patient described the bad experience of intraoperative awareness to other patients many times, some patients lost trust in the anesthetic technology of the hospital and requested transfer to other hospitals, which damaged the reputation of the hospital.

Chapter 10
Leaving a Good Impression on Patients

Touched patient gave the "secret prescription"

— A warm doctor–patient story happening in Tanzhong People's Hospital of Liuzhou City

"Thanks so much!" On April 18, Mr. Ouyang Shusen, 66 years old, lying on a hemodialysis bed at Tanzhong People's Hospital of Liuzhou City, took a piece of paper with "secret folk medical prescription" written on it from his clothes pocket and handed it to Jiang Zongshun, president of the hospital, and repeatedly expressed his gratitude. As he spoke, he cried excitedly, and tears flowed down the wrinkles around his eyes.

So, what's the story? Ouyang Shusen was diagnosed with uremia 4 years ago and needed regular hemodialysis. On January 25 this year, he was transferred to Tanzhong People's Hospital of Liuzhou City to continue hemodialysis. "The doctors and nurses are so nice to me!" Ouyang Shusen said. Every time he entered the hemodialysis room, he was warmly greeted. During hemodialysis, doctors and nurses always paid more attention to him, helping him with his bedpan and other things. On New Year and other holidays, they boiled eggs for him to supplement his protein intake. "I never experienced such good service in other hospitals." Ouyang Shusen said with tears gleaming in his eyes. He used to feel that he was just a patient in the hospital. After going to the Tanzhong People's Hospital of Liuzhou City, he felt that he was a relative of the doctors and nurses there. "We get along with each other very well, which makes very happy and moved."

(Continued)

(Continued)

"Because he has no children, he is always alone and lonely." He Qi, Ouyang Shusen's attending doctor, said that most of the other patients in the hemodialysis room were accompanied by their family members, but Ouyang Shusen was not, and he suffered from various diseases and was unable to move around, "so it is our duty to take care of him." Ouyang Shusen had to undergo dialysis twice a week, for three and a half hours each time, and during these time periods, doctors and nurses in the hemodialysis room always took special care of him, and called him Uncle Ouyang kindly. Ouyang Shusen was in low spirits when he first came to the hospital for dialysis; however, "Now, he smiles whenever he comes, and his spirit is getting better and better," said He Qi in relief.

"The doctors and nurses are so kind, so I should do something to show my gratitude!" Ouyang Shusen thought repeatedly and decided to hand over a recipe for a secret folk remedy passed down from his ancestors to the hospital. Upon receiving it, the doctors said, "We will keep your 'treasure' well." President Jiang Zongshun received the gift given by Mr. Ouyang on behalf of the hospital, and he expressed that they would conduct relevant research on the "secret recipe" and expected that it could really serve the patients.

This true story tells that patients' good impression of the hospital or the medical staff comes from the feelings in multiple aspects.

People may form a direct judgment on something through a single sense or a mixture of senses. We call this integral cognition perception. Perception is psychological, but direct judgment is physiological. A certain opinion on the hospital formed by the patients will lead to mixed perception. The hospitals need to take great efforts in multiple aspects to give patients and residents a good impression of the institution. It is important to note that people's satisfaction is not based on a comprehensive evaluation of a hospital in multiple aspects. Patients are not a consulting institution, and their satisfactory or unsatisfactory impression merely comes from their attention to details. For example, a patient may be very grateful or resentful towards a doctor due to one small action.

Resident Awareness and Timeliness — Approach to Convenience

Wang Shanshan, Director of Brand Development Department of JYWJ:

People can get help from medical staff rapidly and even reach the right ones to regain their health based on relevant information received earlier. This can reduce their panic and helplessness and make them feel psychologically safe.

When patients suffer from illness and their family members are anxious and worried, the hospital administrator must consider the following aspects: How to make patients feel the smooth flow and convenience of the whole medical procedure based on their overall cognition and how to make the patients feel peaceful subconsciously, instead of more irritable.

Indicator 41. Awareness rate of registration appointment

Meaning: Awareness rate of registration appointment means the degree of knowing the online registration appointment in the investigated hospital by patients.

Purpose: Registration appointments can free patients from queuing, so that they can go to the hospital at the appointed time. Meanwhile, improving the awareness rate of registration appointments is in favor of improving the hospital's influence so that more residents will know the departments and experts in the hospital and the patient service radius will be expanded.

Investigation method: Random investigation and on-site patient inquiry.

Evaluation method: Randomly investigate 50–100 patients, and if there is no reservation registration system, a score of 0 should be given.

Calculation method:

$$\text{Awareness rate of registration appointments} = \frac{n_{ra}}{N} * 100\%$$

where

n_{ra} = Number of people aware of the existence of online registration systems; and

N = Total number of people investigated.

Improvement objective: (A) Provide online reservation and registration; (B) Strengthen the hospital publicity and ensure the awareness rate of the hospital's online registration appointment is above 95%.

> Xu Xin, Consulting Director of JYWJ:
>
> A female employee wanted to go to the county hospital of traditional Chinese medicine to cure the pimples on her face. However, she worked from Monday to 12:00 a.m. on Saturday, and those were the working hours of the Dermatology Department, so she had no way but to visit a doctor during the one-hour break at noon. However, in general, there were so many people that she had to wait for a long time several times, and sometimes she had to go back to work without seeing the doctor. It made her miserable, and it was also time- and money-consuming. Later, she heard that the hospital had an online registration appointment service, and the validity period for the registration form was 7 days. This was quite convenient and time-saving for her.

Indicator 42. Whether the hospital decocts traditional Chinese medicine?

Meaning: Whether the hospital decocts traditional Chinese medicine.

Purpose: Since Chinese medicine is special and has certain requirements for decocting time and methods, it's not convenient for most people to decoct the medicine at home. If the hospital can decoct traditional Chinese medicine, it will be helpful. Decocting traditional Chinese medicine is also one of the requirements in the latest grade evaluation standard for hospitals of traditional Chinese medicine.

Investigation method: Field observation and inquiry about the hospital.

Evaluation method: Full scores should be given when such an indicator is available, 0 score otherwise.

Improvement objective: According to actual situation in the hospital, introduce the decocting of traditional Chinese medicine at the proper time.

Wang Shuang, Director of the JYWJ Business Department:

Decoction of traditional Chinese medicine in the hospital is an important measure that makes it easy for patients to use, and also a necessity for the development of traditional Chinese medicine in hospitals. In the new era, China begins to advocate the development of Chinese medicine strongly from the government, makes great efforts in revitalization and development of Chinese medicine, gives equal importance to traditional Chinese and Western medicines, and strives for mutual complementation and coordinated development between them and the creative transformation and innovative development of the health-preserving culture of traditional Chinese medicine. From the national policy level, the development of traditional Chinese medicine is an irresistible trend. But as a patient, efficacy and convenience are the most important. Once, as a sub-healthy patient, I went to a hospital of traditional Chinese medicine and was prescribed Chinese medicine. I took the Chinese medicine home. However, since I was quite busy, the medicine was only taken once, and the rest got wasted.

(Continued)

(Continued)

If the hospital could decoct traditional Chinese medicine and provide me with the 5-day dosage of medicine which can be directly taken, I could have consumed the medicine after heating it up. This would have saved me more time and avoided wastage. The medicine will only show obvious efficacy if it is taken continuously. If there was no service of decocting traditional Chinese medicine, I would choose Western medicine instead next time. This directly affects the business of traditional Chinese medicine in hospitals. Therefore, the service for decocting traditional Chinese medicine is essential for the development of Chinese medicine.

Impact on Patients' Mood Even from Slight Changes in the Environment

Ma Wufu, Executive Director of Consulting Service of JYWJ:

When people go to a new place, most of them would first notice the atmosphere surrounding them. Patients would judge a hospital's environment with their senses and have a kind of perception about it. For example, if a patient finds cigarette butts on the floor and dirty windows, he or she would develop bad feelings about the hospital. By designing a perception-environment indicator and investigating patients' feelings about the environment, the hospital could identify the problems in its environment.

Indicator 43. Filter-cleaning rate when using air-conditioners

Meaning: By investigating whether air-conditioners in the inpatient ward are maintained and cleaned monthly. This indicator could reflect whether cleaning and maintenance of air-conditioners (electric fans) qualify for the total score.

Purpose: Air-conditioners may develop a great deal of dust and bacteria during use if the filters are not cleaned over a long period. So, the filters should be taken out and cleaned once every week, which is beneficial for keeping the air inside fresh and can protect patients' physical health. Cleaning the filter of air-conditioners (or electric fans) in inpatient wards can reflect the quality of the hospitalization environment, and it is one of the important factors that can affect hospital service quality and patient satisfaction. When the hospital has developed to a certain level, to further improve its environment and technical level, it has to pay more attention to the small details and promote the general image of the hospital better. If the filter of air-conditioners in inpatient wards is not cleaned for a long time, the dust accumulated would easily be a breeding ground for bacteria and lead to poor air quality, which is bad for the recovery of patients. Hospitals should clean and maintain the air-conditioners in inpatient wards regularly to ensure the cleanliness and clarity of the filters and even the outer appearance of air-conditioners. The service quality needs to be improved by focusing on the small details and minor matters.

Investigation method: Check cleaning records and inquire about the cleaning frequency.

Calculation method:

$$Filter\text{-}cleaning\ rate = \frac{acf}{pcf} * 100\%$$

where

acf = Actual cleaning frequency of air-conditioning filters; and
pcf = Planned cleaning frequency of air-conditioning filters.

Improvement objective: The filters in air-conditioners should be cleaned by specially assigned persons. During use, the filters should be taken out and cleaned once a month.

Indicator 44. Whether the hospital has a hall or area for recovering patients to exercise?

Meaning: Since the intensive training of recovering patients is less, halls or areas are needed for them to exercise or spend their leisure time.

Purpose: Recovering patients have special needs, may be elderly or may find it inconvenient to move. It is necessary to set up a specific hall, area, or activity room to let patients perform their recovery activities more conveniently. In some smaller hospitals, we can often see some patients doing their recovery training exercises in corridors, wards and other public areas. Because they have difficulty in moving, they could cause trouble to others and affect other patients and disturb the hospital order. Therefore, setting up a rehabilitation area is convenient for both the recovering patients and the others. It will also support the medical staff to take care of them.

Investigation method: Field observation.

Evaluation method: Full scores should be given when such an indicator is available, 0 score otherwise.

Improvement objective: Hospitals should provide a hall or activity area especially for recovering patients.

Zhang Xiaolong, Consulting Director of JYWJ:

Among the hospitals we have worked with, with the improvement of service ability and service level as well as the increase in number of outpatients and those being hospitalized, many are faced with insufficient rooms in the Medical Department. Take Hechi Yizhou Maternal and Child Health Care Hospital as an example. Since 2013, this hospital has continuously promoted the specialized development of childcare and recovery. In this regard, it specially renovated an old building into a health care and recovery building for children with a full-floor sports recovery center on the top floor. A variety of recovery and leisure facilities were set up in the spacious and bright recovery center, allowing every child who came here to enjoy a happy childhood. They received not only one-to-one treatment with a rehabilitative therapist but also a safe, warm and exclusive amusement park under the care of nurses. We believe that these lovely children can grow and develop faster and better and have a healthy life in such an environment.

The Essence: Willing and Active Service

Lan Xiaofeng, Executive Director of JYWJ:

There are 66 perception indicators for multi-sensory feelings towards service, including self-driving, 120, arrival, guidance, medical technology, outpatient treatment, transfer, hospitalization, consultation, doctor, nursing, operation, ICU, recovery, discharge, patient's death, physical examination and other aspects. These indicators reflect whether patients and their family members are well served by medical staff based on their perceptions and feelings about the doctor-seeing process. For example, whether the medical staff have given good psychological guidance to patients before and after the operation, or whether the medical staff have comforted patients' family members when patients were not well, or whether "120 ambulance" can reach patients within the shortest time as possible? Such service indicators can directly affect the multi-sensory feelings of patients and their family members, so such work must be done well and keep pace with the times.

Indicator 45. Active greeting rate of gatekeepers

Meaning: Whether the gatekeepers nod or use polite expressions such as "Hello" when someone visits the hospital.

Purpose: Gatekeepers are set in many hospitals in China. They are specifically responsible for the safety and safeguarding of the institutions. A gatekeeper is the first person seen by patients when they enter a hospital, although some gatekeepers are employed by social security companies. Whether the gatekeepers can kindly interact with patients would give patients and their family members a very important first impression.

Investigation method: Field observation.

Evaluation method: Proportion*score.

Calculation method:

$$Active\ greeting\ rate\ of\ gatekeepers = \frac{n_g}{N} * 100\%$$

where

n_g = Number of gatekeepers who greet visitors proactively; and
N = Total number of gatekeepers investigated.

Improvement objective: Gatekeepers should be trained on service etiquette, and the training should be put into practice and supervised by the relevant departments.

Indicator 46. Rate of emergency first-aid personnel comforting patients and their family members

Meaning: Whether emergency first-aid personnel have comforted patients and their family members during an emergency when they showed tension, anxiety or other emotions.

Purpose: When an emergency happens, patients and their family members would often have negative feelings of tension and anxiety due to the physical discomfort or due to not knowing what's happening. At this time, if emergency first-aid personnel can give some comfort, it will make patients and their family members feel warm instead of helpless.

Investigation method: Field observation.

Evaluation method: Proportion*score.

Calculation method:

$$Rate\ of\ emergency\ first\text{-}aid\ personnel\ offering\ comfort = \frac{n_e}{N} * 100\%$$

where

n_e = Number of emergency first-aid personnel comforting patients and family members; and
N = Total number of cases observed.

Improvement objective: During each emergency, the emergency personnel shall comfort patients and their family members with words or body movements.

Indicator 47. The number of annual medical disputes

Meaning: Medical disputes happen when there are differences between hospitals and patients in the results of or reasons for diagnosis, treatment or nursing, and the people involved claim for accountability or financial compensation. It can only be settled through administrative or legal mediation and adjudication. It can be simply understood as an event that patients require for compensation, and no matter whether the compensation has been fulfilled or not, it is still considered as medical disputes.

This indicator refers to the number of medical disputes in the hospital in a year.

Purpose: Medical disputes and accidents are the extreme manifestations of medical risks. But they represent only the tip of the iceberg, and the whole iceberg represents all the hospital risks.

In most cases, medical disputes are caused by medical quality and service attitude, and solving medical disputes may involve great difficulties, multiple links, heavy workload and more skills. Doctor–patient disputes could prompt the hospitals to deeply investigate and correct the problems existing in the process of medical treatment and service, and improve technical ability, quality and service. However, a hospital needs to put a large amount of manpower and financial resources to solve the medical disputes, but they would often achieve half the result with twice the effort. For patients, disputes could lead to a negative impression about the hospital and lead to questions about the hospital's technical services. At the same time, the negative emotions can easily be carried over to the medical staff, who are suffering the work pressure and headache-inducing disputes, especially when these medical disputes are not the unilateral responsibility of the hospital.

Medical disputes could have a significant negative impact on both doctors and patients, no matter what causes them, what types they are or how they are eventually resolved.

Beijing Jingyi Wanjia Technology Co Ltd began to study the prevention and control model of medical risks and a series of implementation measures in 2017. At present, the model and measures have been applied in many hospitals with good results.

Investigation method: By checking data and considering the number of beds, the medical disputes of the hospital are counted and analyzed.

Evaluation method: If the number of beds is less than 200, then the number of annual disputes should be ≤4; if the number of beds is between 200 and 300, the number of annual disputes should be ≤6; if the number of beds is between 300 and 400, the number of annual disputes should be ≤7; if the number of beds is between 400 and 500, the number of annual disputes should be ≤8; if the number of beds is more than 500, the number of annual disputes should be ≤10; full scores should be given for hospitals without medical disputes, while a score of 0 should be given for those with ≤0; the score shall be calculated proportionally for the interval values.

Calculation method:

$$Control\ of\ annual\ medical\ disputes = \left(1 - \frac{n_{amd}}{N_b}\right) * 100\%$$

where

n_{amd} = Actual number of annual medical disputes; and
N_b = Upper limit of the standard according to the number of beds in the hospital.

If there is no medical dispute, the hospital receives full scores; if the result is negative, it gets a score of 0.

Improvement objective: (A) The hospital should standardize the behavior of diagnosis and treatment, improve the technical level of medical staff and reduce the occurrence of medical accidents; (B) Strengthen the construction of medical ethics and establish a good image; (C) Establish and improve each rule and regulation, and standardize every operation instruction; (D) Medical staff should improve their service awareness and establish a good doctor–patient relationship; (E) After medical disputes occur, medical staff should deal with them calmly, report to hospital's leadership immediately and communicate with and explain to patients and their family members; (F) If the disputes cannot be mediated, the hospital should apply for arbitration. If the arbitration is invalid, the dispute should be appealed at court.

Indicator 48. Active inquiry rate of hospital guides

Meaning: During the investigation, the proportion and number of patients helped by hospital guides proactively when compared to the total number of patients helped should be assessed.

Purpose: Active inquiry should be one of the basic responsibilities of hospital guides. Active service awareness is one of the main objectives of the "patient-oriented" hospital culture. Active inquiry can support the establishment of the relationship between the doctor and the patient. In this regard, this could guide patients to express their illness more accurately and make the guidance service more targeted. Passionate and active guidance services can also reduce the potential risk during the subsequent medical treatment and reduce the chance of doctor–patient conflicts.

Investigation method: Field observation and random inquiry. Record whether the hospital guides proactively talk to patients who enter the hospital hall by on-site random observation.

Evaluation method: Proportion*score.

Calculation method:

$$Active\,inquiry\,rate\,of\,hospital\,guides = \frac{n_{hp}}{N} * 100\%$$

where

n_{hp} = Number of hospital guides actively approaching and helping patients; and

N = Total number of people investigated.

Improvement objective: The initiative for active inquiry of hospital guides should be improved through training, assessment and clarifying job responsibilities. Active inquiry rate of hospital guides should reach 100%.

Indicator 49. Rate of "looking, listening, questioning and feeling the pulse" used in clinics of traditional Chinese medicine

Meaning: This indicator inspects how the outpatient doctors of traditional Chinese medicine used the "looking, listening, questioning and feeling the pulse" methodology. The four diagnostic methods of traditional Chinese medicine refer to looking, listening, questioning and feeling the pulse. "Looking" is a purposeful view of the patient's mental state, skin color, gesture, posture, tongue color and nature, and so on, in order to detect visceral lesions.

Purpose: In recent years, with the improvement of medical technology, advanced examination instruments have been widely used in the clinic. However, they cannot completely replace such physical examinations and diagnosis method as "looking, listening, questioning and feeling the pulse".

By careful looking, listening, questioning and feeling the pulse, traditional Chinese medicine doctors make the patients feel respected and valued, and makes it easier to build a relationship of trust. At the same time, it reflects the professional level of the doctors and their humanistic care for patients. It is the basis of accurate diagnosis of the disease, which is conducive to establishing a good image for the doctors and the hospital.

Investigation method: Observe the diagnostic process of 30–50 patients randomly to inspect whether the doctors have used the traditional diagnosis methods in traditional Chinese medicine, and a record of the results should be made.

Evaluation method: Proportion*score.

Calculation method:

$$Rate\ of\ TCM\ methodology\ usage = \frac{n_D}{N} * 100\%$$

where

n_D = Number of patients treated using the four traditional diagnostic methods; and

N = Total number of people investigated.

Improvement objective: The rate should be over 95% after training doctors and standardizing the process of diagnosis and treatment.

Indicator 50. Proactive helping rate of nurses in the transfusion room

Meaning: Whether the nurses in the transfusion room help patients proactively is an important aspect reflecting the service quality of hospitals.

Purpose: Active help provided by nurses in the transfusion room to patients and their family members is key to establish a good relationship between nurses and patients. If there is a patient in difficulty and needing help, a helping hand from the nurses would leave him or her with a good impression and enhance their good feeling about the hospital.

Investigation method: Field observation.

Evaluation method: Proportion*score.

Calculation method:

$$Proactive\ helping\ rate\ of\ nurses\ in\ the\ transfusion\ room = \frac{n_{nhp}}{N} * 100\%$$

where

n_{nhp} = Number of nurses helping people proactively; and

N = Total number of nurses investigated.

Improvement objective: (A) The hospital should specify the job responsibilities of nurses in the transfusion room; (B) The hospital should carry out trainings for nurses on a regular basis, requiring those in the transfusion room to help patients proactively with water or any other assistance they may need; (C) Spot checks and outpatient satisfaction surveys should be conducted regularly, and the investigation results should be considered during management assessment.

Li Jiuhe, Director of Human Resource Department of JYWJ:

From October 2016 to December 2017, I worked as a special consultant on hospital culture management for the Maternal and Child Health Care Hospital of Rong'an, Guangxi, and investigated the "proactive helping rate of nurses in the transfusion room". I found the nurses in transfusion room showed poor performance. Perhaps because there were more children patients due to the abnormal temperature changes, the nurses were very busy. But there was one thing which impressed me deeply: A mother came to see the doctor with two boys. The sick one was around one-year-old and on his mother's back and the older one holding her hand was about five years of age. In the transfusion room, the younger brother was in his mother's arm and crying, while the older one was running around the room and not listening to his mother. Soon, a nurse came over and squatted down, saying to the child, "Stop running, and if you stay here, I will give you this candy and this toy." The nurse reached out two hands, with a sweet in one hand, and a cheerful little doll in the other. The boy picked up the candy and the doll and sat down quietly with his mother. The mother showed her gratitude and thanked the nurse. The nurse replied, "You're welcome," and took the hand of the little boy in the mother's arms, saying "What lovely babies they are," and then she returned to the infusion solution preparation room. At that time, I felt warm, as if the place was not a hospital, but a warm kindergarten environment.

Indicator 51. Whether there are heating equipment in Outpatient Treatment Room

Meaning: There should be heating equipment in Outpatient Treatment Room, such as air-conditioners, heaters or electric fans.

Purpose: Some physical examinations or treatments need to be performed in the Outpatient Treatment Room. Because of the cold weather and lower body resistance, patients could catch a cold or develop a fever during treatment. If there is heating equipment in Outpatient Treatment Room, patients would feel comfortable during the treatment, which would increase patient satisfaction with hospital service quality.

Investigation method: Field investigation.

Evaluation method: Full scores should be given when such an indicator is available; otherwise a score of 0 is given.

Improvement objective: Ensure the outpatient transfusion room is cool in summer and warm in winter.

Indicator 52. Whether there is equipment for warming hands in the outpatient transfusion room

Meaning: Outpatient transfusion rooms should be equipped with hand-warming equipment to avoid uncomfortable feelings experienced by patients during transfusion in winter.

Purpose: Some patients, especially females and children, would feel cold in winter, which is not suitable for puncture with needles. Providing hand-warming equipment in outpatient transfusion rooms can make patients feel better during the treatment, increase their satisfaction with hospital service quality and show how much the hospital cares for the patients.

Investigation method: Field investigation.

Evaluation method: Full scores should be given when such an indicator is available; otherwise, 0 score.

Improvement objective: (A) Ensure the air-conditioners work normally; (B) Install hand-warming equipment in winter, such as

Li Jiuhe, Director of Human Resource Department of JYWJ:

When I provided consultancy support for XX People's Hospital in January 2016, I investigated cultural indicators, and the investigation result and improvement plan had not been issued yet. One day, my stomach hurt and I got a fever after eating some hard rice and hot vegetables. After sleeping for more than an hour in the hotel, I got up and vomited. At about 8:00 p.m., I went to the Emergency Department. Due to an accident, most emergency doctors were busy dealing with the wounded; therefore, I had to go to the Pediatric Department (it is near the Emergency Department and I knew the doctor there), and the physician put me on a drip in the transfusion room.

I remembered it was a very cold winter, especially in the evening since it had snowed in January in most parts of Yunnan. The transfusion room of the Pediatric Department was a boardroom built behind the outpatient building with no air-conditioner or stove, or anything else to keep hands warm, such as a hand warmer or a hot-water bag. A kettle was provided, but patients had to get hot water themselves, and no disposable paper cups were provided. The children in the room were all wrapped in an overcoat or blanket and were being held in their parents' arms; I wore little, just a pair of pants and a thin coat. I felt colder and colder with chills all over my body while undergoing transfusion at night. After the transfusion, my hands and feet were very cold, and my legs were numb. I did not get back to normal body temperature until I covered myself with two thick quilts and had drunk a few cups of hot water when I returned to the hotel. To cap it all off, I caught a cold the next morning.

hot-water bags and a warming pad; (C) Provide patients who feel cold in the puncture position with heater or hot-water bag to warm their hands before puncture.

Indicator 53. Rate of introducing the basic information of the to-be-transferred hospital

Meaning: It refers to the proportion of introducing the basic information of the to-be-transferred hospital (such as address, bus route, doctor, department and other information) to patients who need to visit another hospital for further treatment.

Purpose: When patients need to be transferred, they usually do not know why it is better for them, and doctors should give them some advice. Any hospital may advise patients to transfer to another hospital for treatment; however, that is not the end of their duty. It is one of the basic responsibilities of the hospital to continue to pay attention to transferred patients. The hospital should introduce basic information about the hospital they are being transferred to patients, which can reduce patient's fear about the unknown state and improve their confidence in the hospital.

Investigation method: Field observation; investigate the record of transferred patients, and inquire regarding this to 10–20 patients by phone. Carry out field observation to know whether the doctors introduced the basic situation of the to-be-transferred hospital to patients. Also, some records of transferred patients can be selected and they can be asked via phone about whether the doctor has introduced the basic situation of the to-be-transferred hospital.

Evaluation method: Proportion*score.

Calculation method:

$$\textit{Rate of introducing basic information} = \frac{n_{bi}}{N} * 100\%$$

where

n_{bi} = Number of patients who have been given basic information about the hospital they are being transferred to; and

N = Total number of people investigated.

Jia Ning, Consulting Director of JYWJ:

Hospital of Traditional Chinese Medicine of Baojing County strengthened their service and followed up patients after the improvement of their hospital culture. On March 6, 2016, the

(Continued)

(Continued)

Emergency Department of the hospital received a critically ill patient, and after the emergency treatment, doctors found that they could only do some simple therapy and that the patient needed to be transferred due to his complicated condition. The family members were anxious because they had never been to Guangxi Xiangzhou Hospital of Traditional Chinese Medicine and they were worried that the patient would not be treated in time. While arranging the ambulance for transfer, the Director of Emergency Department introduced the patient and the family members to some basic details regarding Guangxi Xiangzhou Hospital of Traditional Chinese Medicine, and also informed the Director of Emergency Department of that hospital about the patient's condition. These two tasks reassured the patient and family members. Afterwards, the patient and family members came to the hospital to express their thanks. The hospital did pre-treatment in a timely manner, and also arranged a relevant transfer and treatment process in Guangxi Xiangzhou Hospital of Traditional Chinese Medicine enthusiastically, which ensured that the patient received the treatment in time and had a chance for better recovery. The Director of Emergency Department said to patients: "Our service will not terminate when patients leave the hospital. We will continue to serve them until they are well enough to live a normal life."

Improvement objective: (A) Hospitals should formulate a template for introducing details of the to-be-transferred hospital and train the departments in this regard; (B) Hospitals should test the medical staff regularly and do spot checks randomly to assess whether they have provided relevant information to the patient in this regard.

Indicator 54. Proportion of VIP wards configured in hospital

Meaning: The hospital should have VIP wards for high-end service to meet the needs of different patients.

Purpose: With the improvement of people's living standards, ordinary people have higher demands for medical treatment. They not only long for higher technical standards but also a higher level of hospital service and continuous improvement of hospital environment. Therefore, the setting of VIP wards is not only needed to meet the higher level of patients' medical needs but is also an important measure for hospitals to provide high-end and personalized services.

Investigation method: Check the number of VIP wards in the hospital and compare with the total number of hospital wards.

Evaluation method: If the presence of VIP wards configured in the hospital is less than 5%, a score of 0 should be given; full score otherwise.

Calculation method:

$$Proportion\ of\ VIP\ wards = \frac{n_{VIP}}{N} * 100\%$$

where

n_{VIP} = Number of VIP wards; and
N = Total number of wards.

Improvement objective: The hospital should set up different types of VIP wards according to the nature of different departments, and the basic configuration includes a senior bed, wardrobe, a chaperonage bed, TV and sofa. There should be certain prerequisites such as a water heater, toilet, towel rack, wash table, disposable toilet necessities, etc., in the bathroom. A microwave oven, refrigerator or other facilities can be provided according to the actual conditions. VIP wards in the hospital should make up about or higher than 5% of the total number of wards in the hospital.

Indicator 55. Frequency of broadcasting videos about health knowledge

Meaning: Hospitals should arrange for hospital experts to record health education videos about different diseases by themselves or through cooperation with television stations and broadcast these videos in different areas of the hospital at different time periods.

Purpose: Looping a video of hospital health knowledge can help patients quickly learn about the hospital, perceive its status, and promote the image and popularity of the hospital. Short videos about health knowledge are a very good way to enhance publicity and promote education. Short videos, composed of text, sound, images and color, could attract the attention of patients and their family members if carefully selected and professional photography is used and creative post-production is done. This would greatly increase the significance and effect of health education. As long as the hospitals care about patients, the short video will be made wonderfully well.

Investigation method: Check prominent and visible locations in different areas of the hospital one by one by field investigation and record how many times health knowledge lectures are broadcast.

Evaluation method: Full score should be given if the calculated value ≥1, and a score of 0 should be given for hospitals that do not broadcast videos about health knowledge; this should be calculated proportionally for the interval values.

Calculation method:

$$\textit{Frequency of broadcasting health education videos} = \frac{n_{hev}}{PA * 10} * 100\%$$

where

n_{hev} = Number of times videos are played daily; and
PA = Number of public areas in the hospital.

Improvement objective: LED display screens should be installed at prominent positions in public areas of the hospital to play short videos on health education recorded by the hospital. These should be played on a loop ten consecutive times in all public areas every day.

Indicator 56. Rate of interaction on important holidays and festivals

Meaning: Heads of departments or hospitals should comfort patients during important holidays and festivals (New Year's Day, Spring Festival, Lantern Festival, Women's Day, Labor Day, Mother's Day, Children's Day, Dragon Boat Festival, Father's Day, Mid-Autumn Festival, Teacher's Day and National Day).

Purpose: Important festivals are supposed to be a day of reunion and celebration; however, because of their physical condition, patients have to stay in the hospital for medical treatment, so the medical staff should treat them as their family members. Celebrating the festival with patients is not only a reflection of the "patient-oriented" culture but also a reflection of the hospital's humanistic care. This can enhance the hospital's reputation and image as well as increase the patient's cohesion and satisfaction.

Investigation method: Check hospital records and summarize the condition of comforting patients on important holidays within a year.

Evaluation method: Around 9–12 times a year, full scores should be given; 5–8 times a year, half scores should be given; 1–4 times a year, quarter scores should be given; otherwise, a score of 0 is given.

Calculation method:

$$\textit{Rate of interaction during important holidays} = \frac{n_i}{N_h} * 100\%$$

where

n_i = Number of times patients are comforted and interacted with; and
N_h = Number of important holidays in that year.

Improvement objective: The hospital should give holiday greetings to the inpatients on different festivals, at least on New Year's Day, Spring Festival, Lantern Festival, Women's Day, Children's Day, Dragon Boat Festival, Mid-Autumn Festival, Teachers' Day, National

Day and other festivals, which could improve patient's trust in and gratitude to the hospital.

Ma Xinxin, Director of Consulting Quality Management Department of JYWJ:

On March 8, 2014, Women's Day, I was working in Zhengxing Hospital of Zhenxiong County, Yunnan Province, China. In the morning, as soon as I entered the outpatient building, President Luan sent me a rose and greeted me, saying, "Ms. Ma, thank you for your hard work, Happy Women's Day." Then, I realized that all the leaders of Zhengxing Hospital were wearing formal dress and standing at the entrance of the outpatient building and the inpatient building to greet patients and staff, giving every lady a rose, which is the most representative gift and the most gentlemanly blessing one can receive on Women's Day. Surprised and joyful ladies holding roses could be seen all over the hospital. I thought that they were surprised because it was the first time they enjoyed such a treatment in the hospital, and they were happy because this gave them the feeling of being respected and appreciated.

Indicator 57. Rate of patients' family members knowing the therapeutic regimen

Meaning: This indicator assesses whether chief physicians communicated with patients' family members and listened to their advice when making therapeutic regimens.

Purpose: Due to the lack of medical knowledge, patients and their family members are always in a passive role during the treatment and diagnosis. They often complain about disorder prescriptions and examinations. If doctors clearly tell them about the type and stage of the disease and seek their input regarding the therapeutic regimen, this would increase their sense of involvement and enhance the interactivity and cooperation between physicians and patients.

Zhang Xiaolong, Consulting Director of JYWJ:

Zhang Jingliu, Director of Tanzhong People's Hospital of Liuzhou City/Traditional Chinese Medicine Department of Liuzhou Maternal and Child Hospital, was cleaning his desk after treating a patient. This habit was something that had been developed since he was a college student. At this time, a "patient" came to his door, and then drew back. Director Zhang saw him and said, "Hi, who are you looking for?" The "patient" heard him, went into his office, and said "Doctor, nice to meet you, I want the doctor who treated my wife the day before yesterday. The nurse in the inpatient ward told us to leave the hospital because of insufficient beds; however, the doctor said we needed to stay in hospital for about five to seven days." Director Zhang opened the computer and found the correct medical record. After reading, he explained to the family member: "According to your wife's medical condition, she needs to continue the treatment and this normally requires five to seven days. After this stage of treatment, whether she can be discharged should be decided according to her recovery. I don't know why the nurse allowed you to leave the hospital, but don't worry, I will check on this right now." And then, Director Zhang called the Inpatient Ward Office and learned the truth — the family member misunderstood the nurse who just wanted to move the patient to another bed. After the explanation, the family member knew more clearly not only about his wife's medical condition but also the therapeutic regimen, and thus had a greater trust in the doctor. Finally, he felt relieved and left Director Zhang's office. Such cases happen every day among medical staff in Tanzhong People's Hospital of Liuzhou City (Liuzhou Maternal and Child Hospital). If the medical staff could show more concern, communicate more clearly and help proactively, they will receive trust and high scores from patients and their family members.

Investigation method: Investigate 50–100 patients' family members randomly and ask them about therapeutic regimens.

Evaluation method: Proportion*score.

Calculation method:

$$\text{Rate of patients' family members knowing the therapeutic regime} = \frac{n_{ftr}}{N} * 100\%$$

where

n_{ftr} = Number of patients who knew the therapeutic regimen; and
N = Total number of people investigated.

Improvement objective: The hospital or department should make sure that every patient and their family member knows about the therapeutic regimen before the treatment to improve their sense of involvement and agreement.

Indicator 58. Rate of calling to remind pregnant women of physical examination 42 days after delivery

Meaning: The hospital should call pregnant women for physical examination 42 days after delivery.

Purpose: Due to the delivery of the fetus and the exfoliation of the placenta, a wound is formed on the surface of the endometrium, which would completely heal in 6 weeks (42 days) after delivery, and the uterus can then basically recover to the former state. During this period, the pregnant women would gradually recover and have basically returned to the normal state after pregnancy and delivery. However, how well their organs have recovered still needs to be examined thoroughly in the hospital. Reminding new mothers of the physical examination 42 days after delivery can effectively help in the supervision of their physical conditions, guarantee healthy growth of the baby, improve the health indicator of new mothers and babies, increase patient satisfaction and improve service quality.

Investigation method: Questionnaire. Investigate 50 pregnant women who gave birth 42 days ago and ask about whether they have received a phone call regarding physical examination.

Evaluation method: Proportion*score.

Calculation method:

$$\textit{Rate of reminding pregnant women of physical examinations} = \frac{n_{pr}}{N} * 100\%$$

where

n_{pr} = Number of patients reminded; and
N = Total number of people investigated.

Improvement objective: The hospital should improve the quality of service and give a phone call a week ahead to alert the new mother who needs physical examination 42 days after delivery. Doctors should make a form to record the time of delivery, remind pregnant women to attend a physical examination 42 days after delivery and formulate corresponding assessment plans.

Patient Satisfaction Comes from Efforts in Many Aspects

Zhang Shujun, Executive Director of Administrative Supervision Department of JYWJ:

In addition to the most visual environment and service, the normativity and scientificity of the hospital's internal management will also affect the feelings of the patients, and even the effective control of medical risks. With the establishment and improvement of the internal system, the hospital strives to make the patient comfortable and confident before, during and after the hospitalization. For the average visit time of outpatients, doctors should not spend too short a time in patient inquiry. The hospital must first regulate the problem through a system to ensure that each patient receives the same time for inquiry from the physician, which is helpful to promote the improvement of doctor–patient relationship and can also enable patients to get more comprehensive and in-depth inquiry. This indicator belongs to the class of perception in management.

Indicator 59. Frequency of patient consultations held by the hospital

Meaning: The hospital should regularly hold all forms of patient symposium or exchange to listen to and know the opinions and ideas of patients so as to improve the service level of the hospital.

Purpose: The hospital, by holding a patient symposium or exchange, can collect objective opinions and suggestions of patients and their family members. By sorting out and analyzing these opinions and suggestions, the problems in various service processes can be found out and rectified. Therefore, the hospital services and medical experience of the patients will be enhanced in a comprehensive manner.

Investigation method: Record query.

Evaluation method: Full scores should be given if the frequency of patient consultations held by the hospital is ≥4; a score of 0 should be given to those hospitals that do not perform consultations, and it should be calculated proportionally for the interval values.

Calculation method:

$$Frequency\ of\ patient\ consultations = \frac{n_{pc}}{N} * 100\%$$

where

n_{pc} = Number of consultations held annually; and
N = Total number of departments.

Improvement objective: Through institutional constraints, each department should hold a patient symposium or exchange meeting at least once every quarter.

Indicator 60. Average waiting time of a patient during peak hours

Meaning: This indicator refers to average waiting time of a patient in Outpatient Hall from 8:00 a.m. to 11:00 a.m.

Qiu Lixue, Supervisor, Teaching and Researching Office, School of Management of JYWJ:

At 10 a.m., there were still long queues at the entrance of the Ultrasound Department in Zheng'an People's Hospital of Guizhou, China. There were pregnant women waiting with an empty stomach, gloomy old people, children in the arms of their parents, etc. However, there was a strange phenomenon: The queue was very long, but everyone was waiting quietly and silently.

After careful look, you could spot a nurse coming out to communicate with everyone from time to time. She kept comforting everyone with a smile and kind words, and said, "Sorry, now it is No. 35's turn. Please wait patiently. Here are some publicity materials of our department and some magazines, and if you are thirsty, there is a water dispenser." She was actively interacting with every patient, and patiently gave answers to questions raised by every patient, so that every patient was calm.

We are constantly upgrading our equipment and improving our services. However, there are still patients who need to wait for examination; therefore, the nurse has played an important role in calming the patients.

Purpose: "Difficulty and high cost to receive medical treatment" have become the major problems faced by regional residents, while the difficulty in receiving medical treatment is mainly manifested in difficulty in registering an expert's attention, long waiting time, numerous patients waiting to be seen, etc. On one hand, it shows that the hospital, department and experts are very welcomed and highly trusted by ordinary people. On the other hand, it reflects that resource allocation of the hospital fails to meet patient requirements.

The waiting time of the patients indicates the popularity of a specialist doctor and the allocation of experts and specialists of a hospital. This indirectly reflects the degree of importance given to meticulous and convenient services. If the waiting time is too long, it may aggravate physical discomfort of the patients and also make patients and their family members uncomfortable, anxious and may even lead to complaints. To adopt effective measures for shortening the waiting time is conducive to improving the hospital service quality, building a good image and increasing social and economic benefits of the hospital.

Investigation method: Adopt field investigation, select suitable time periods from 8:00 a.m. to 11:00 a.m. after assessing the actual situation for some days, observe 30–50 waiting patients randomly, and record the time from seeing the doctor to accepting the treatment.

Evaluation method: A score of 0 should be given if the average waiting time is more than 30 minutes, full scores should be given if waiting time is less than 1 minute, and it should be calculated proportionally for the interval value.

Calculation method:

$$\textit{Average waiting time during peak hours} = \frac{TWT}{N}$$

where

TWT = Sum of waiting time of all patients investigated; and
N = Total number of patients investigated.

Improvement objective: Control the waiting time of the patient at peak hours within 30 minutes, and add expert clinics based on needs or assign more outpatient doctors during peak hours; also, provide appointment service. Patients who have an appointment are treated during non-peak hours, and the reservation registration system is organically connected with the on-site registration system; the hospital can be equipped with an electronic queue management system so as to decentralize patients in a timely and effective manner.

Part 3

Hospital Culture Construction

Chapter 11
Diagnosis of Hospital Culture

It is not easy to rapidly, relatively and accurately judge the culture construction of a hospital. For over 500 indicators to be investigated objectively, accurately and quickly, it is vital to objectively evaluate culture types of the hospital and propose feasible improvement measures and overall solutions.

An Objective, Accurate and Quick Investigation Plan

To investigate over 500 indicators with regard to every aspect of the hospital, it is necessary to walk around all corners of the hospital. Since hospitals are varied in terms of size, it is especially important to make scientific investigation plans.

As regards the indicators, some need long-term investigation, some need enough samples and still others require wide investigation. Therefore, scientific arrangements are needed to ensure speediness and accuracy of functioning.

Table 11.1 shows how the indicators are sorted according to the investigation days, so as to enable selection of the most time-consuming and important indicators of the investigation and making an appropriate investigation plan based on difficulty and complexity. For example, the most number of indicators need to be investigated in inpatient wards, which takes the longest time. Therefore, the investigation of such indicators should be emphasized. From further analysis, we can see that in investigating the indicators of the inpatient

Table 11.1 Investigation and analysis of hospital culture indicators

		Days investigated		Survey form		Experience category					Sensory category						
S.N.	Investigation location	Number of days	%	Walking	Non-walking	Convenience	Service	Management	Environment	Etiquette	Touch	Vision	Hearing	Taste	Smell	Perception	Total
1	Inpatient ward	460	21.9	73	3	14	18	16	28		4	59	1	3	2	7	76
2	Doctor	189	9.0	33	6		17	21		1	3	16	3			17	39
3	In treatment	151	7.2	3	28	1	20	9		1	3	19	4			5	31
4	Medical technician	128	6.1	11	15	12	7	2	1	4		13	2			11	26
5	Nursing	123	5.9	17	4		10	8		3	3	12				6	21
6	Discharge	120	5.7	11	2	1	9	2		1		7				6	13
7	Before admission	104	4.9	10	12	13	2	7				13	1			8	22
8	Arriving at the hospital	84	4.0	43	4	5	14	4	20	4		37	3		1	6	47
9	120	78	3.7	14	1		5	6	2	2		8	2			5	15
10	Payment of fees	67	3.2	10	9	8	5	3		3		15	3			1	19
11	Physical examination	67	3.2	4	14	4	11	2		1		5	2			11	18
12	Hospital guidance	64	3.0	2	14		4	6	2	4	1	12				3	16
13	Operation	62	2.9	11	3	3	6	3	2		1	7	1			5	14
14	Consultation	59	2.8	10	1		8	3				6	1			4	11
15	Recovery	59	2.8	17			9	4	3	1	1	12	1			3	17
16	Taking medicine	39	1.9	4	5	4	2	1	1	2		5	2			3	10
17	Self-driving	34	1.6	8		6	2					7				1	8

18	Registration	29	1.4	2	15	6	3	6		2		15	1			1	17
19	Outpatient treatment	29	1.4	8	3	1	7	2	1			7	1			3	11
20	Handling of admission procedures	28	1.3		4		1			3		2	1			1	4
21	Admission Office	24	1.1	3	3		3	1	2			4	2				6
22	Reservation	22	1.0	7	2	5	4					8				1	9
23	Emergency	20	1.0	6	8	4	3	4	3		1	12				1	14
24	Waiting for diagnosis	16	0.8		10	5	2	1	2			8	1			1	10
25	ICU	14	0.7	8		1	3	3	1			7				1	8
26	Patient death	14	0.7	1			1									1	1
27	Emergency transfer	6	0.3		6		2	4				2	3			1	6
28	Walking	3	0.1	3					3			3					3
29	Transfer	3	0.1		3		2	1				1	1			1	3
30	Return visit	2	0.1		2		1	1				2					2
31	Bus	2	0.1	2		2						2					2
32	Home	2	0.1	2		1	1					2					2
33	Total	2102	100	324	177	96	182	120	71	32	17	328	36	3	3	114	501

ward, the maximum number is seen in environment-related indicators in the experience category and visual-related indicators in the sensory category. For these indicators, a larger number of investigators and much more division of labor are needed, and the environment should be carefully investigated with patient's visual feeling as the main aspect.

In a similar manner, the investigation plan should be well prepared, and hospital personnel should be encouraged to participate in the investigation for indicators needing more intervention. However, objectivity should be ensured. The numerous benefits seen when hospital staff participate in the investigation are as follows: First, it reflects that the hospital leader attaches great importance to hospital personnel; second, it allows personnel concerned in the hospital to carry out inspections according to the investigation standards and to truly feel their service levels; third, medical staff can better understand the hospital culture construction system and methods as a whole, thus laying a good foundation for the overall improvement of hospital culture in the future.

Objectivity — The Soul of Hospital Culture Survey

In 2015, the first management consulting program on hospital culture construction was carried out in Tanzhong People's Hospital of Liuzhou City, Guangxi, China. President Jiang Zongshun, an extremely rigorous and realistic leader, kept the investigation confidential. The project team was stationed in the hospital for the course of the investigation to maintain objectivity. Since hospital employees knew nothing about the investigation, while they were in the Department of Neonates, the hospital security personnel observed this attention and thought that these people's observations in the ward every day were aimed at the newborns. Therefore, the hospital security personnel brought the investigators to the Safety Management Department. After communication, the hospital employees knew that they were members of the management consulting project team invited by the hospital.

Actually, most hospitals have their own standard for patient satisfaction surveys, but it is usually difficult to expose their scars by themselves, and the survey results are usually quite different from that of a third party. For example, we carried out one survey about how much medical staff in a hospital smiled. To our surprise, the smiling rate was only 15% compared with that obtained through the original survey (95%). This is a true story. When releasing the diagnostic report, we mentioned this and pointed out that the medical staff of this hospital basically did not smile, which greatly shocked the hospital administrator.

In fact, it is really tough to completely maintain high objectivity. When the survey was initially carried out, the investigators could basically reflect on the original situation; however, when more employees in the hospital learnt that such a survey about hospital cultures was being conducted by a third party, the hospital's service level would suddenly increase. In 2014, we conducted experiments as regards the management consulting project for hospital culture construction in Linwu County Traditional Chinese Medicine Hospital in Hunan, China. As many indicators were involved in the investigation, all aspects of the hospital were surveyed. As a result, the investigations went deep into all aspects of the hospital service. When many departments of the hospital knew that a third party was conducting a cultural survey, they would unconsciously and actively find out their own service problems, which greatly affected the objectivity of the survey. The president of the hospital said very emotionally, "I really didn't realize that hospital culture construction plays such an important role. The investigation has not ended yet and it has already shown effects." Later, the service level of this hospital underwent tremendous changes, and local residents thought highly of services provided in this hospital. Even now, President Zhou Xianjing can still recall the amazing scene at the time.

There were also unpleasant incidents. When we carried out the management consulting program for hospital culture in 2015, an investigator found that a pharmacist working in the pharmacy was smoking in the hospital, which was a serious violation of the rules. Therefore, the investigator immediately took photos using a phone;

unfortunately, the pharmacist discovered this and unreasonably attacked this investigator. The project team argued; unfortunately, the main leader of the hospital took the side of the pharmacist, which deeply puzzled us. As a third party, we strictly insisted on the principle of objectiveness and fairness, and so we decided to suspend serving this hospital and immediately withdrew the project team. Later, the main leader of the institution recognized the mistake and apologized to the company and the project team, and then the services were again continuously provided by the project team.

Evaluating Hospital Culture Type Objectively

After investigating hospital cultural indicators, the culture type of this hospital will be shown in the chart after the scores of the indicator are matched with corresponding weights, and the results are input into the pre-compiled procedure. Over the past five years, special consultation on hospital culture construction has been carried out by JYWJ for more than 100 hospitals in China. Figure 11.1 summarizes the hospital culture type of more than 100 hospitals, which has already resulted in highly relevant knowledge about hospital culture construction.

When issuing the diagnostic report, it should be ensured that the results are not spread to the society since some hospitals show an indifferent hospital culture, and this may be influenced by the result. Furthermore, the culture type of very few hospitals belongs to the pirate-type. Such results are objective, but cannot be issued faithfully. Once this is known to the public, it may have a serious negative impact on the hospitals. We must make it known to the top leaders of the hospital that we will slightly move the coordinate point up when it is issued, so that the culture type will change. When releasing the diagnostic report, we will testily say that service levels of the hospital couldn't be any worse. Therefore, immediate measures should be taken to improve the satisfaction of patients and their family members, as otherwise some hospitals will fall into the pirate category — the president will become the captain of the pirate ship and employees

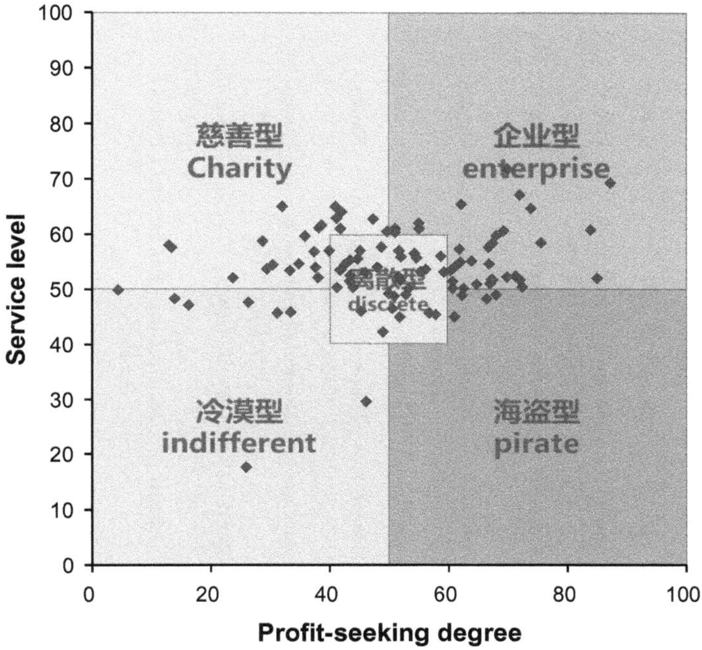

Figure 11.1 Schematic diagram of hospital culture evaluation types of many hospitals

will become the crew! Those hospitals should notice their problems and understand the necessity and urgency of hospital culture construction through the above humorous warning.

Show the Gaps to Prepare for Systematic Improvement Measures

The released diagnostic report must be comprehensive and complete, so that all employees of the hospital clearly know their problems and are well prepared for the next systematic improvement measure and action.

The diagnostic report should be clear with accurate data, abundant pictures and texts, and diverse forms.

S.N.	Province	Hospital type	County	S.N.	Province	Hospital type	County
1	Yunnan	General hospital	Fengqing	14	Guangxi	Maternal and Child Health Hospital	Liuerfu
2	Guangxi	General hospital	Pingguo Aluminum	15	Yunnan	General hospital	Shiping
3	Guizhou	General hospital	Tianzhu	16	Hunan	Hospital of Traditional Chinese Medicine	Linwu
4	Guizhou	General hospital	Suiyang	17	Guangxi	Hospital of Traditional Chinese Medicine	Long'an
5	Henan	Hospital of Traditional Chinese Medicine	Gushi	18	Hunan	Maternal and Child Health Hospital	Liuyang
6	Guizhou	General hospital	Xishui	19	Yunnan	General hospital	Jingdong
7	Chongqing	Maternal and Child Health Hospital	Jiangjin	20	Hunan	Hospital of Traditional Chinese Medicine	Baojing
8	Guangxi	Maternal and Child Health Hospital	Binyang	21	Guizhou	Hospital of Traditional Chinese Medicine	Jianhe
9	Guangxi	Hospital of Traditional Chinese Medicine	Tiandong	22	Guizhou	General hospital	Cengong
10	Xinjiang	Maternal and Child Health Hospital	Aksu	23	Guangxi	Maternal and Child Health Hospital	Debao
11	Guangxi	General hospital	Xijiang	24	Guangxi	General hospital	Xincheng
12	Guizhou	General hospital	Qianxi	25	Guangxi	Maternal and Child Health Hospital	Yangshuo
13	Guangxi	General hospital	Liuerkong	26	Chongqing	Maternal and Child Health Hospital	Xiushan

27	Hunan	Hospital of Traditional Chinese Medicine	Xinhuang	40	Guangxi	General hospital	Rong'an
28	Guizhou	Hospital of Traditional Chinese Medicine	Xiangzhou	41	Hunan	Hospital of Traditional Chinese Medicine	Anxiang
29	Guangxi	Maternal and Child Health Hospital	Tianyang	42	Guangxi	Hospital of Traditional Chinese Medicine	Wuming
30	Guangxi	General hospital	Tanzhong	43	Yunnan	General hospital	Binchuan
31	Guizhou	General hospital	Songtao	44	Xinjiang	Hospital of Traditional Chinese Medicine	Wusu
32	Yunnan	General hospital	Shuangjiang	45	Yunnan	General hospital	Ning'er
33	Chongqing	Hospital of Traditional Chinese Medicine	Rongchang	46	Guizhou	General hospital	Yanhe
34	Guizhou	Hospital of Traditional Chinese Medicine	Sansui	47	Jiangsu	General hospital	Kunshan Rehabilitation
35	Yunnan	Hospital of Traditional Chinese Medicine	Fengqing	48	Guizhou	Hospital of Traditional Chinese Medicine	Weng'an
36	Guangxi	Hospital of Traditional Chinese Medicine	Debao	49	Hunan	Maternal and Child Health Hospital	Nanxian County
37	Guangxi	Hospital of Traditional Chinese Medicine	Lingchuan	50	Guangxi	Maternal and Child Health Hospital	Wuming
38	Guangxi	General hospital	Honghui, Liuzhou	51	Hunan	Hospital of Traditional Chinese Medicine	Nanxian County
39	Yunnan	General hospital	Wuding	52	Guangxi	Maternal and Child Health Hospital	Yizhou

(*Continued*)

(Continued)

S.N.	Province	Hospital type	County	S.N.	Province	Hospital type	County
53	Guizhou	General hospital	Xiazi	67	Fujian	Maternal and Child Health Hospital	Changting
54	Guizhou	Hospital of Traditional Chinese Medicine	Jiangkou	68	Yunnan	General hospital	Chenggong
55	Guizhou	General hospital	Zhijin	69	Yunnan	Others	Baoshan Anli
56	Hunan	Hospital of Traditional Chinese Medicine	Qiyang	70	Guizhou	Maternal and Child Health Hospital	Zheng'an
57	Guizhou	General hospital	Chishui	71	Yunnan	Maternal and Child Health Hospital	Yanshan
58	Shaanxi	General hospital	Shenmu	72	Guizhou	Hospital of Traditional Chinese Medicine	Dejiang
59	Yunnan	Maternal and Child Health Hospital	Gejiu	73	Guizhou	Hospital of Traditional Chinese Medicine	Liping
60	Yunnan	General hospital	Xinping	74	Yunnan	General hospital	Yanshan
61	Guizhou	Hospital of Traditional Chinese Medicine	Libo	75	Guangxi	Hospital of Traditional Chinese Medicine	Hezhou
62	Yunnan	General hospital	Yongping	76	Guizhou	General hospital	Dejiang
63	Guangxi	General hospital	Guiping	77	Henan	Maternal and Child Health Hospital	Wen County
64	Guangxi	General hospital	Xingbin	78	Yunnan	General hospital	Weixin
65	Guangxi	Maternal and Child Health Hospital	Rong'an	79	Guizhou	General hospital	Pingba
66	Guizhou	General hospital	Zhenning	80	Yunnan	General hospital	Menghai

81	Guangxi	Maternal and Child Health Hospital	Guiping	93	Guizhou	General hospital	Yinjiang
82	Guizhou	Hospital of Traditional Chinese Medicine	Dushan	94	Guangxi	General hospital	Sixth People's Hospital of Nanning
83	Chongqing	Maternal and Child Health Hospital	Pengshui	95	Yunnan	General hospital	Mojiang
84	Yunnan	General hospital	Tonghai	96	Guangxi	General hospital	Tanzhong2
85	Guizhou	General hospital	Meitan	97	Yunnan	Maternal and Child Health Hospital	Banna
86	Guizhou	General hospital	Zheng'an	99	Yunnan	General hospital	Lianghe
87	Yunnan	Maternal and Child Health Hospital	Weixin	100	Guangxi	Maternal and Child Health Hospital	Pingle
88	Guizhou	General hospital	Xixiu	101	Guizhou	General hospital	Jinsha
89	Guizhou	General hospital	Pingtang	102	Guangxi	Maternal and Child Health Hospital	Tianyang
90	Guizhou	General hospital	Cengong2	103	Yunnan	Private hospital	Qiubei Renji
91	Guizhou	General hospital	Sansui	104	Guizhou	General hospital	Taijiang
92	Guizhou	Hospital of Traditional Chinese Medicine	Jinsha	105	Guizhou	General hospital	Jianhe

Table 11.2 shows a very important document in the diagnostic report. Based on the control rate in each process (link) of the hospital's culture diagnosis, it shows aspects that the hospital needs to improve according to the patients' feelings. In terms of the patient's visual feeling, the control rate of this hospital (Cengong County People's Hospital) is only 46.9% (less than 50%), showing a big gap in having satisfactory patients' visual feeling. Therefore, numerous complaints would be raised since many patients and their family members were not satisfied. This is the major shortcoming in the hospital's service level because the visual feeling accounts for 65.5% of the total score of all the factors with which the patients are satisfied. In a similar manner, the gaps in other terms can be directly analyzed.

According to patients' feeling, the overall control rate of this hospital is as low as 49%. According to the results of the process analysis, the control rates of 20 processes is less than 50%, including discharge, medical treatment, medical skill, arrival at the hospital, 120 emergency, pre-arrival at the hospital, guidance treatment, payment, medicine taking, physical examination, registration, patient self-driving, transfer, appointment, recovery, ICU, emergency transfer, waiting for treatment, patient returning home and return visit. In this regard, the hospital can clearly know that the service level in certain processes need to be improved.

From Table 11.3, we can clearly know the specific problems from the perspectives of patient experience. This table reflects the problems encountered by the hospital in patient convenience, service, management, environment and etiquette. In terms of convenience, the control rate of this institution only reaches 44.7%, and so much more efforts are needed to improve convenience. The control rate of the service is 52%, indicating a need for urgent improvement. The control rate of management is 56.3%. In this regard, immediate measures should be taken to continuously improve the service level. The environmental control rate is 48.3%, and improvement plans should be formulated immediately. Serious problems are seen in etiquette, with a control rate of only 25.4%. Therefore, serious measures should be taken in terms of the civility and politeness of employees, in order to improve employee quality as early as possible.

Table 11.2 Culture control rate in all links of Cengong county people's hospital according to the patients' feeling (%)

S.N.	Procedure	Vision	Hearing	Smell	Taste	Touch	Perception	Up to standard
1	Bus	100.0						100.0
2	Walking	100.0						100.0
3	Patient death						100.0	100.0
4	Admission Office	75.4	84.3					78.0
5	Emergency	83.4				100.0	0.0	78.0
6	Consultation	86.4	66.7				54.2	73.0
7	Operation	58.9	89.7			0.0	99.3	71.0
8	Doctor	78.4	67.2			80.0	63.1	71.0
9	Nursing	70.5				35.6	64.4	64.0
10	Handling of admission procedures	62.5	23.1				100.0	61.0
11	Inpatient ward	57.4	96.2	53.7	53.7	26.5	44.4	55.0
12	Outpatient treatment	45.3	47.4				67.9	51.0
13	Discharge	29.9					62.4	45.0
14	In treatment	49.5	50.6			16.9	29.9	43.0
15	Medical technician	35.9	0.0				56.8	43.0
16	Arriving at the hospital	37.6	46.2	0.0	0.0		67.1	41.0
17	120	35.6	0.0				55.0	38.0
18	Before admission	25.9	0.0				52.4	36.0

(*Continued*)

Table 11.2 (*Continued*)

S.N.	Procedure	Vision	Hearing	Smell	Taste	Touch	Perception	Up to standard
19	Hospital guidance	25.3				6.3	100.0	34.0
20	Payment of fees	30.8	31.3				64.3	33.0
21	Taking medicine	0.0	27.5				85.0	31.0
22	Physical examination	44.4	0.0				29.0	30.0
23	Registration	21.4	78.6				66.7	29.0
24	Self-driving	31.1					0.0	28.0
25	Transfer	24.0	12.0				60.0	27.0
26	Reservation	32.5					0.0	26.0
27	Recovery	27.1	0.0			0.0	41.2	26.0
28	ICU	13.8					100.0	25.0
29	Emergency transfer	0.0	35.1				0.0	19.0
30	Waiting for diagnosis	17.1	0.0				40.0	18.0
31	Home	0.0						0.0
32	Return visit	0.0						0.0
33	Total	46.9	43.0	33.7	33.7	35.2	60.1	49.0

Table 11.3 Culture control rate in all links of Cengong county people's hospital according to the patients' experience (%)

S.N.	Link	Convenience	Service	Management	Environment	Etiquette	Control rate
1	Bus	100.0					100
2	Walking				100.0		100
3	Patient death		100.0				100
4	Admission Office		89.2	100.0	50.0		78
5	Emergency	100.0	63.6	51.7	100.0		78
6	Consultation		65.8	92.6			73
7	Operation	7.1	80.6	96.5	100.0		71
8	Doctor		78.7	68.2		0.0	71
9	Nursing		58.2	78.4		44.0	64
10	Handling of admission procedures		100.0			48.6	61
11	Inpatient ward	59.5	37.2	55.5	63.4		55
12	Outpatient treatment	100.0	51.2	53.8	0.0		51
13	Discharge	40.0	37.0	71.0		68.8	45
14	In treatment	0.0	42.1	53.3		18.2	43
15	Medical technician	50.6	31.5	57.1	100.0	16.3	43
16	Arriving at the hospital	0.0	70.5	66.7	23.5	45.2	41

(*Continued*)

Table 11.3 (*Continued*)

S.N.	Link	Convenience	Service	Management	Environment	Etiquette	Control rate
17	120		35.9	52.9	54.5	0.0	38
18	Before admission	44.4	0.0	22.2			36
19	Hospital guidance		28.3	33.8	100.0	2.2	34
20	Payment of fees	46.1	38.0	26.5		6.9	33
21	Taking medicine	63.8	22.5	0.0	0.0	5.0	31
22	Physical examination	23.8	19.7	100.0		16.7	30
23	Registration	35.7	40.0	31.5		3.1	29
24	Self-driving	40.0	0.0				28
25	Transfer		42.0	12.0			27
26	Reservation	44.8	0.0				26
27	Recovery		39.1	0.0	0.0	83.3	26
28	ICU	76.9	34.2	6.8	0.0		25
29	Emergency transfer		0.0	28.3			19
30	Waiting for diagnosis	10.9	0.0	40.0	46.2		18
31	Home		0.0				0
32	Return visit		0.0	0.0			0
33	Total	44.7	52.0	56.3	48.3	25.4	49

Plotting the Radar Map to Show the Current Status of Hospital Culture

A highly aggregated gap radar map is particularly important to let hospitals clearly identify their problems and gaps at a glance. In addition to directly reflecting on the current status of hospital culture construction, it also provides basic references to measure hospital culture improvement results in the future.

Figures 11.2 and 11.3 show the diagnostic report radar chart of Tanzhong People's Hospital of Liuzhou City, Guangxi, China, and this diagnostic report was issued on January 23, 2018.

Plotting the Schematic Diagram of Hospital Culture Type

After inputting the investigation results of all indicators into a preset program, a schematic diagram of the hospital culture type will be obtained automatically. This diagram shows the current hospital

Feeling classification of culture investigation indicator

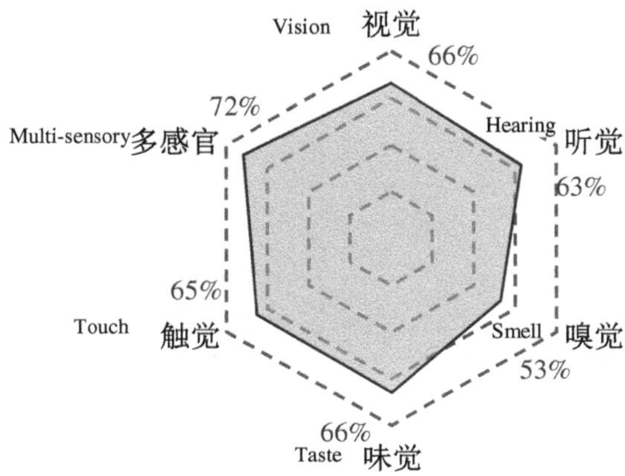

Figure 11.2 Classification gap of Tanzhong people's hospital of Liuzhou city based on patients' feeling

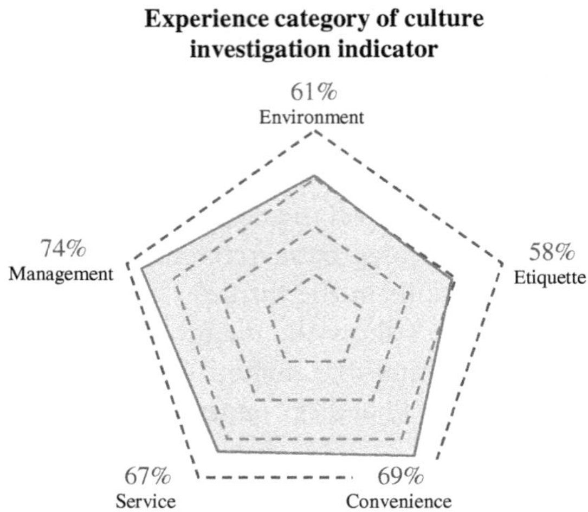

Figure 11.3 Classification gap of Tanzhong People's Hospital of Liuzhou City based on patient experience

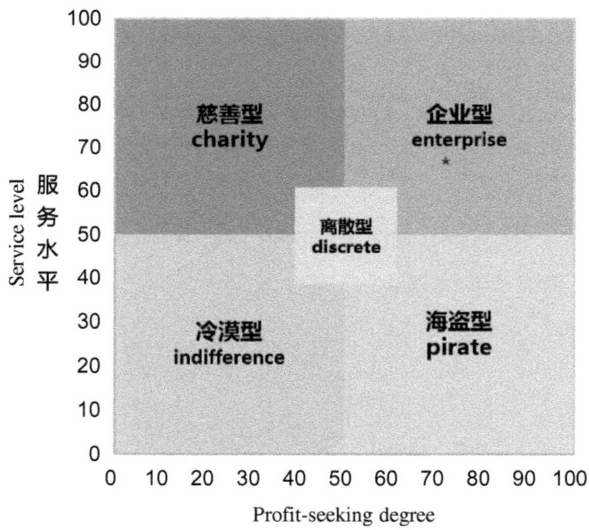

Figure 11.4 Schematic diagram of the cultural type of Tanzhong People's Hospital of Liuzhou City

culture type and also provides the basic tool for planning the direction of hospital cultural improvement and objectives achieved.

Figure 11.4 shows the result of the final diagnosis of the hospital culture type when the second hospital culture construction project was conducted at Tanzhong People's Hospital of Liuzhou City, Guangxi, China, in 2018. Tanzhong People's Hospital of Liuzhou City got scores of 67.1 and 71.9, respectively, in service and profit-seeking degree, suggesting an enterprise-type hospital culture.

Chapter 12

Formulating Measures of Improvement for Hospital Culture Construction

Measures — The Carrier of Responsibilities

Formulating a feasible system improvement program plays a decisive role in the smooth and effective implementation of future hospital culture improvement work. On the basis of the convenience, service, management, environment and etiquette problems presented in the hospital's cultural diagnosis, specific improvement measures must be put forward to address each issue.

It needs to be emphasized that all employees, especially leaders at all levels, should understand that hospital culture construction is a very systematic project. The primary premise behind this project and the actual effect is a set of systematic measures to solve problems and improve the level of functioning of the hospital. With the right measures taken, responsibility can be allocated to different carriers and then be implemented through assessment. Thus, the measures will be implemented piece by piece, and the level of hospital culture construction will be effective day by day, which is the basic logic of doing one thing well.

To develop improvement measures, persistence in the principle of meeting patient needs, satisfying industry standards, implementing the requirements of the local administrative department and ensuring feasibility are requisites.

To solve the problem of "difficulty and high cost in receiving medical treatment", it is of great significance to provide convenient measures and improve the service processes. The emphasis on formulating measures to improve the service level is meant to standardize the service; the reason behind formulating measures to improve management is to execute and implement the systems; the emphasis on formulating measures to change the environment is done to better provide and improve environmental reconstruction; and the necessity to improve the entire service etiquette is to strengthen training and enable strict assessment.

It is important to classify such measures based on experience and sensory categories to establish leading teams for each cultural improvement measure. Relevant senior managers and functional departments of the hospital are responsible for mobilizing all employees to participate in putting forward improvement measures, and for summarizing, organizing, analyzing, supplementing and improving these measures to form a systematic plan to achieve improvement objectives of hospital culture in a phased manner. This method is not only an educational process to comprehensively improve the level of hospital culture construction but also a process of comprehensive self-examination and comprehensive proposal of improvement measures.

It can be seen from Table 12.1 that this hospital has a total of 1196 improvement measures. When classified into feeling and experience measures, it can be observed from Figure 12.1 that the proportions of indicators and measures in patient's vision and service improvement are the largest, which provides a basis for the upcoming hospital culture improvement with data support.

Improvement Measures for Convenience

The continuous provision of convenient medical and health services for patients is a permanent issue that needs work. With the development of science and technology, especially the development of the Internet and intelligence, the provision of convenient medical services has undergone fundamental changes in both content and form.

Table 12.1 Summary of cultural improvement measures of Cengong County People's Hospital of Guizhou, China

S.N.	Indicator classification	Touch	Vision	Hearing	Taste	Smell	Perception	Total
1	Convenience	2	163	16			93	274
2	Service	24	193	41	3		158	419
3	Management	1	201	17			45	264
4	Environment	2	122	3		4	4	135
5	Etiquette		87	14			3	104
6	Total	29	766	91	3	4	303	1196

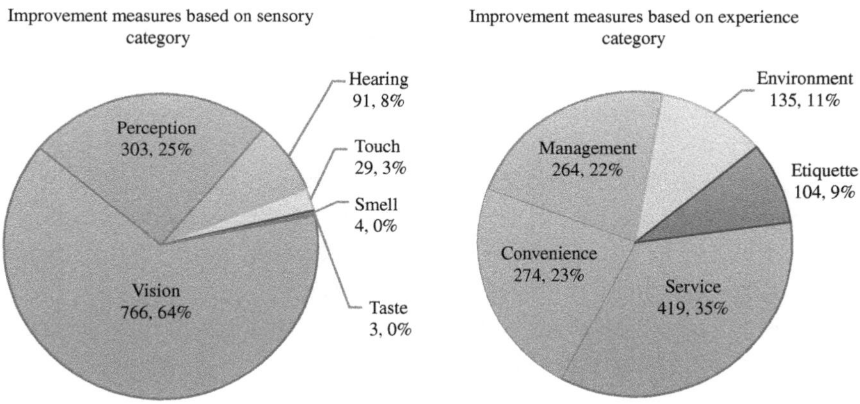

Figure 12.1 Data analysis of hospital culture improvement measures

In terms of patients, medical treatment is the primary link, and in this case appointment registration is the first problem they face. Under ideal conditions, if a medical service system implements hierarchical diagnosis and treatment, appointment registration can be completed in the community. With the development of artificial intelligence medical technology systems, the number of patients who book an appointment for registration will be greatly reduced, and the number of outpatients in large hospitals will rise. However, appointment registration with Internet technology is still the main means of solving the problem at present.

Second, there are convenience-related problems in all links of the doctor-seeing process, such as payment, inquiry, drug intake, settlement, transfer, and scheduling return visits. How to continue to provide convenient and efficient services in every link is a question that all hospitals must think long and hard to arrive at a solution.

In the consultation service for a hospital, it was found that very few people knew that the hospital existed, which is the largest inconvenience in terms of patients seeking medical treatment. How can the residents seek help if they don't know that there is a hospital? In order to improve the awareness rate of regional residents as quickly as possible, 12 specific measures have been proposed, which are as follows:

1. Timely update of publicity materials in the hospital based on integrity;
2. Distribution of relevant publicity materials outside the hospital (hospital profile, expert introduction, department profile, department features, new project introduction, health knowledge publicity, emergency telephone number, etc.);
3. Regularly conducting gratuitous diagnosis activities and distribution of publicity materials in the service area;
4. Strengthening of exchange and communication with township health centers, pharmacies, clinics, community service centers, village doctors and other channel personnel in the region, and placement of hospital billboards;
5. Paying return visits to inpatients, outpatients, and Emergency Department patients;
6. Letting the residents know about the hospital through media, such as radio, TV, newspapers and the Internet;
7. Advertisement on the WeChat Official Account, and holding WeChat promotional activities, service star selection, micro-movies, etc.;
8. Publicizing of hospital staff in QQ zone, QQ group, Weibo and Moments;

(Continued)

9. Enabling word-of-mouth publicity by patients;
10. Establishment of a patient exchange group by each department, and also regular holding of patient exchange meetings and inviting relevant functional departments to participate in the same (Medical Department, Nursing Department, General Affairs Department, Service Department, Cultural Management Department and other functional departments or hospital leaders);
11. Giving special lectures on health knowledge;
12. Setting direction signs at the main intersection of the region, with the hospital telephone number, website address and WeChat QR code.

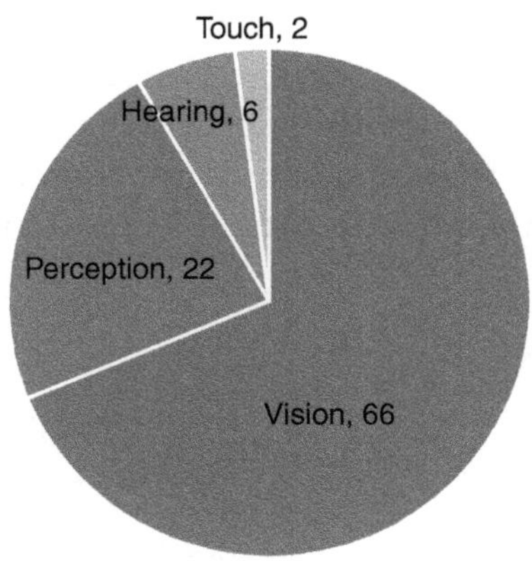

Figure 12.2 Analysis of the impact of a hospital's convenience measure improvement on patients' feeling

Implementation and execution of these improvement measures related to convenience are of great significance for improving the overall hospital culture construction level. Figure 12.2 shows that 66 measures are for improving the visual feeling of patients, accounting for 69% of the total number of all measures. Obviously, the implementation of these measures can make patients feel much more satisfied visually. Twenty-two measures are aimed at improving patient's perception, and 6 measures for improving hearing; 2 measures are aimed at for at improving touch. If these measures are carried out successfully, the satisfaction of patients and their family members will be significantly improved.

Improvement Measures for Service

Service is the most important part of patient experience, it runs throughout all aspects of the medical service process. When a hospital is formulating service improvement measures, the 419 measures that were proposed, and distributed in 30 processes of the hospital's medical services, should be taken into consideration (see Table 12.2). Thus, the formulation of improvement measures for each link and each indicator will have an impact on improving patient satisfaction, especially on the problems that patients are very sensitive about, such as "the frequency of annual theft complaints in hospitals". Although this complaint is not reflective of the treatment process, it will greatly reduce a patient's trust in the hospital if there

Improvement measures to reduce the annual occurrence of theft complaint in hospitals include the following:

1. Strengthen security management and formulate a patrol system for security personnel;
2. Security personnel should strengthen the inspection tour of the hospital during the day and night, check into and inquire about suspicious characters in a timely manner;
3. Improve the theft records, and cooperate with relevant departments to actively deal with any theft incidents;
4. When performing admission publicity and education for patients, they should be reminded to take care of their valuables;
5. Improve the monitoring system and monitor the hospital from all dimensions without compromising patient privacy.

Table 12.2 Distribution of hospital service improvement measures in each process

S.N.	Link	Touch	Vision	Hearing	Taste	Perception	Total
1	Arriving at the hospital		20	5		20	45
2	During treatment	7	19	10		2	38
3	Inpatient ward	3	19		3	8	33
4	Doctor	3	6			24	33
5	Discharge		14			13	27
6	Nursing	7	2			16	25
7	Physical examination			2		17	19
8	Consultation		9	3		6	18
9	Outpatient treatment		11	2		5	18
10	Operation	2	3			12	17
11	Recovery		11	2		3	16
12	Reservation		14				14
13	Medical technician		10			4	14
14	120 emergency call			3		11	14
15	Hospital guidance	2	7			4	13
16	Payment of fees		4	6			10

(*Continued*)

Table 12.2 (*Continued*)

S.N.	Link	Touch	Vision	Hearing	Taste	Perception	Total
17	Emergency		5			2	7
18	Admission Office		3	4			7
19	Before admission		7				7
20	ICU		5			1	6
21	Transfer		3			2	5
22	Self-driving		3			2	5
23	Emergency transfer		3	2			5
24	Registration		4				4
25	Waiting for diagnosis		4				4
26	Taking medicine		2	2			4
27	Patient death					3	3
28	Handling of admission procedures					3	3
29	Home		3				3
30	Return visit		2				2
31	**Total**	**24**	**193**	**41**	**3**	**158**	**419**

is a feeling that the place where medical treatment is sought is unsafe, further reducing the degree of dependence.

Improvement Measures for Management

With poor services, the decline in patient satisfaction is actually caused by poor management, which is mostly caused when regulations are completely absent or not abode by. There is a saying that the main reason for the low management level is that leaders attach little importance to it. In fact, it is the leaders who should be blamed for any poor management.

Measures for improving the management level, according to the number of improvement factors affecting the objective improvement, can be divided into single and systemic measures. The so-called single measure, formulated for a certain phenomenon with numerous single influencing factors, is a simple improvement measure that is easy to implement with quick returns. The systematic measure, formulated for a certain phenomenon with many complex factors, is a systematic improvement measure that can show effects only through long-term persistence.

It is commonly seen that the social media websites of some hospitals are poorly maintained, with the content not having been updated for several months or even a year or more. In the information era, this is a serious indication of poor service quality to close the Internet service window. It is rooted in unclear responsibility, an imperfect system and unrealistic assessment. In the event that immediate effect can be seen by strengthening the management, then this measure belongs to the single type category.

Significant management is involved in the medical service process, for example, if the rate of complaint against 120-related first-aid personnel is reduced, systematic measures to improve 120 emergency services need to be formulated. However, if technical level, communication skill and rigorous assessment are involved, continuous long-term efforts are required to improve the service level and satisfy patients and their family members. Such a measure is of the systematic measure category.

Measures to reduce the rate of complaint against 120-related first-aid personnel include the following:

1. Maintain, strengthen and develop a management system for 120 first-aid personnel;
2. Organize 120-related first-aid personnel sessions to conduct regular business studies, such as skill training, service training, doctor–patient communication skill training, etc.;
3. First-aid personnel should communicate with patients and their family members as much as possible during the first-aid process to explain the situation and earn their recognition;
4. The director and head nurse of the department should regularly assess relevant personnel;
5. Any complaints should be registered and timely research and feedback is imperative.

Improvement Measures in Environment Link

Funds are required to formulate measures for improving the medical environment. The period of time for implementation of these measures, the amount of investment needed and the requirement for volunteer or government support matter a lot.

Is there a speed bump near the hospital? Are there 'zebra stripes' at the hospital entrance? If not, suggestions for improvement need to be proposed to the relevant government departments. Importantly, guidance signs should be set on roads near the main hospitals in the region to help residents quickly find the hospitals. The government should undertake such responsibilities; however, the administrative departments in some regions of China fail to perform well, and may confuse the responsibility for people's livelihood with hospital advertisements, which reflects the poor awareness of the local government and low-level management towards people's livelihood. As a solution to this problem, it is necessary for the hospital to repeatedly explain the facts and reasons to relevant administrative departments until a satisfactory response is achieved. Sometimes it can be very simple to solve similar problems; however, it can sometimes get extremely complex. The solution to such problems rely on the concern about people's livelihood and the work efficiency of relevant administrative departments.

It is the obligation of such departments to solve environmental problems faced by the hospitals, for example, in case the noise decibel in the inpatient ward exceeds the standard. It sometimes seems difficult to control noise; however, the problem can be solved by taking requisite measures, enhancing management or adopting necessary reconstruction measures.

Here is a true story. There is a hospital in Guangxi, China, whose Obstetrics Department inpatient ward is situated in close proximity to the Outpatient Hall due to space limitations. The inpatient ward is extremely noisy, which seriously influenced the recovery of the pregnant women. The hospital leaders felt that there was almost nothing they could do to make a difference. However, when the consultant proposed to replace the glass window with a double-layered window, these leaders realized that they could do something.

Improvement measures taken by Cengong County People's Hospital to reduce the noise level include the following:

1. All hospital staff must develop the habit of talking softly in the workplace, find out which personnel speak loudly or at high tones, and put forward special tips and requirements;
2. Medical staff of the department should remind family members of the patients to not shout loudly in the ward and so as to help maintain silence in the ward;
3. The nursing staff should inform patients and their family members that they cannot squat and fight in the ward during admission publicity and education, so as to avoid disturbing other patients;
4. The Cultural Management Department should randomly test the sound decibels in the department at different time intervals (e.g. 10:00 a.m., 04:00 p.m. and 10:00 p.m.).

It may have seemed like there was nothing they could do, but actually the "patient-oriented" value was not firmly established. Of course, noise in hospitals is usually caused by the medical staff and patients or their family members, which can be easily solved by formulating relevant improvement measures.

Improvement Measures for Etiquette

It is well known that hospital etiquette mostly refers to medical care etiquette. The overall etiquette level of a hospital reflects not only the management level but the harmonious relationship between the hospital and the society, and even the relationship among the internal staff. With a harmonious relationship, many external and internal contradictions can be solved, through which good community relations and a pleasant work atmosphere can be established, thus leading to naturally cumulative positive energy. Therefore, hospital etiquette is of great significance, and it is something that must be done and done well over a long period of time.

Institutionalized long-term training should be first established to improve the overall etiquette of the hospital, followed by the establishment and assessment of standards.

It cannot be expected that one or two training sessions will improve the level of etiquette. The training content covers communication, image, language, behavior, smile rate, pushing of stretchers, holding a chart file, and carrying of treatment plates, with all staff being trained.

It is a better way to cultivate internal trainers, and for any change in hospital staff from time to time, it is necessary for hospitals to develop their own trainers, and it is essential to conduct pre-job training on etiquette for freshers.

Measures to improve the smiling rate of hospital guides in a hospital include the following:

1. Strengthen training on service etiquette and code of conduct;
2. During the vocational learning time in the department, take 10 minutes to practice "professional smiles";
3. Put a dressing mirror in the department, stick a "smiley face" on it, and mark it with the words "Did I smile today?";
4. Remind each other of serving patients with a smile. The team leader is responsible for inspection of every day, which is included in the performance assessment;
5. Practice "professional smiles" in front of a mirror at home.

Chapter 13
Implementing Hospital Culture Construction

Any great organization will definitely show a strong driving force in scheme implementation, no matter how difficult it is. The implementation of the hospital culture construction scheme first depends on the leader's awareness of the impact of hospital culture construction on the hospital development. If hospital leaders realize that hospital culture construction is strategically a top-level design, they will unswervingly implement various measures and constantly pursue medical and health services at higher levels in the process of implementation. Otherwise, the plan will be constrained, the effects are severely weakened, the assessment is ineffective and the implementation is dispensable in the process of hospital culture construction. Eventually, the hospital culture construction begins with a vigorous start and putters out at the end. Of course, what we need is continuous improvement of the hospital culture construction, not a flash in the pan.

Empowering Management Functions to Hospital Culture

Clear management functions must be given to major strategic tasks, which should not be assigned as part-time work to relevant departments. The so-called part-time work refers to the work done after the main work or in leisure time, which are considered less important compared with the main work. The hospital culture construction, with characteristics of long-term continuity, systematic approach and sociality, is an important task that involves continuous improvement of medical service level, and it is not a part-time job; thus, it needs to be given a clear management function. A cultural management office needs to be set up for hospital culture management, and this is the primary task of implementing hospital culture construction.

Here is a true story. In 2014, the management consulting program on hospital culture construction was carried out in one hospital. At our request, the hospital established the Cultural Management Department and assigned a very responsible director of the Nursing Department to be a full-time director. For a long time, the management was being carried out very well, and the overall service level of the hospital obviously improved. To our surprise, local administrative departments then intervened unreasonably in the setting of the hospital management department, and therefore the hospital had no choice but to dismantle the Hospital Cultural Management Department; after this, a departmental leader took the 'part-time' job. Accordingly, problems arose, and the function of

Job responsibilities of the Hospital Cultural Management Department

1. Draw up work plans for hospital culture construction at all stages, and formulate the cultural construction indicator system, implementation standards and evaluation plans for the entire hospital.
2. Strengthen the "patient-oriented" philosophy and related indicators in a variety of ways, including indicator explanation in a WeChat group and conference highlight.
3. Inspect and give feedback on the implementation of cultural improvement in all departments of the hospital, propose rectification suggestions and assist various departments in the implementation.
4. Develop and organize necessary trainings on service quality and hospital culture construction.

(Continued)

5. Organize a Quality Control Circle Meeting every month, report evaluation results, and exchange and share experiences of culture implementation teams in various departments.
6. Respond to questions, organize exchanges and guide all departments to constantly improve the cultural improvement work.
7. Conduct necessary spot checks on the satisfaction of discharged patients and outpatients every month or make telephone follow-ups so as to know about the service conditions of the departments and make records of the same.
8. Record and summarize the links that patients found unfavorable or problematic, draft a work plan for improvement and supervise the relevant departments and individuals to implement the improvement.
9. Organize activities related to cultural festival at least once a year.
10. Other work related to cultural construction.

hospital culture construction was greatly weakened. In the end, such a major strategic task quickly faded away, which directly led to lowering of the service level and affected the good development momentum of the hospital. Afterwards, I went to this hospital and put forward a critical opinion. In 2018, the hospital launched the management consulting project of hospital culture construction a second time, and restored the function of the Cultural Management Department. Soon, the service level of the hospital was obviously improved, and the president of the hospital was pleased enough about this to call and invite me to see the new changes in the hospital.

We learn a truth from this story — that important tasks cannot be fulfilled if it is done 'part-time' for a long time. In Chinese hospitals, most leaders of the functional department do part-time jobs, and even do part-time jobs in several departments, which seriously weakens the management role of important functional departments.

Figure 13.1 shows the full-time degree and work capability matrix, in which the relationship between working part-time and work capability is demonstrated.

The first quadrant shows that important tasks must be undertaken as full-time work by personnel with strong work capability so that work quality and efficiency can be further guaranteed, and the work results which we need most will become lion-like.

The second quadrant explains that if there is one full-time management function, due to low work capability of leaders in a specific functional department and slow advancement, the work results will be sloth-like. First, this is because the superior leadership is weak, and there are problems in command coordination and full mobilization of subordinate enthusiasm; second, the problem rests with inappropriate staffing.

The third quadrant denotes that if the full-time work level is low and work capability is poor, work results will become rainworm-like, which means that the working speed is extremely slow. If the important management functions are in such a state, then the outlook is not at all good. Factors causing the situation include dereliction of duty of leaders and inappropriate staffing, which is the last thing we want to see.

The fourth quadrant expresses that when the full-time level of work is very low, that is, when there are more part-time jobs with

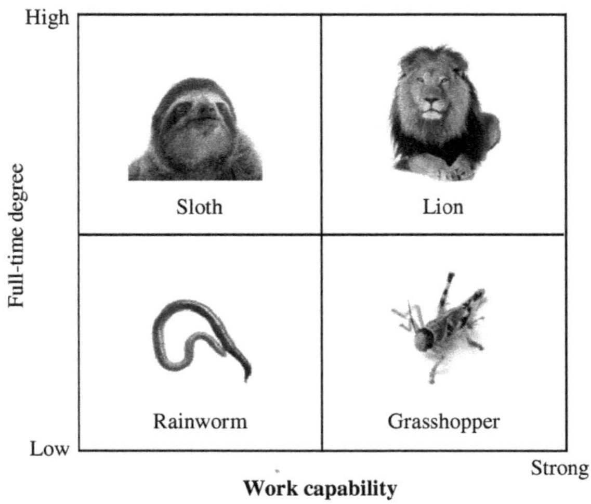

Figure 13.1 Full-time degree and work capability matrix

strong work capability, the job will not be fully done since human energy is limited after all. The work results become grasshopper (locust)-like. It is well known that the grasshopper has two powerful thighs, and it often bites and chews randomly, which symbolizes that if the work is not done in a focused manner, poor results are obtained. There is an old Chinese saying: after the autumn, the grasshopper will die soon. This metaphor is really very vivid. If an important management function is left as part-time work for a long time, its importance will be weakened step by step, leading to serious consequences.

Conclusion: Avoid part-time jobs in the Hospital Management Department!

Organizational Form of Hospital Culture Construction

A corresponding organizational form, as a carrier, must be available to promote the work, especially the hospital culture construction. Only when the corresponding organizational conditions are provided can the hospital culture construction be regularly managed, not just in form due to the lack of carriers to implement various measures.

Over the years, we have been constantly looking into and practicing in order to optimize the organizational form of hospital culture construction, and we have also been summarizing relatively effective and suitable organizational forms of hospital culture construction.

First, a Hospital Culture Construction Committee should be established with the main functions of centralized leadership, command and coordination of hospital culture construction. This is because the management involved in hospital culture construction is different from medical management, nursing management, sensory management, quality management and other functional management tasks of the hospital. The issues involved in culture construction are wider, and it is more focused on management according to the patients' feelings. In particular, the construction of new hospitals has been separated from the more ideological-based preaching management in the past, reflecting that service measures need to be improved in all aspects. These are specific tasks that any functional department working part-time will fail to achieve.

Based on the practices of more than 100 hospitals, we have found out two important lessons. In the hospital where the president is not the first person responsible for the Committee, the advancement of hospital culture construction is obviously slow; in the hospital that does not set up a full-time functional department of hospital culture construction, it is extremely difficult to advance the construction of hospital culture.

The president, as the main person in charge of the Hospital Culture Management Committee, builds the Hospital Cultural Full-time Management Department as the permanent department of the Management Committee, and the first-level management organization is thus formed.

The second-level management organization is mainly based on the division of the departmental responsibility systems for implementing various measures, which is introduced in the next section.

The third-level management organization mainly refers to relevant departments and clinical departments. The Quality Control Circle is established in clinical departments and related departments with a large number of employees, and the hospital culture construction is carried out and advanced according to the implementation measures for the hospital culture construction, thus demonstrating that hospital culture construction requires all employees to take part in the process. For example, in a division of the Internal Medicine Department, all doctors and nurses are divided into five quality control circles, each working on one aspect such as convenience, service, management, environment and etiquette. A job rotation system is adopted along with the development of the management scope of the Quality Control Circle. Improving "convenience" is the focus in the first stage, and in the next stage, it is rotated to "service". This is done to improve the comprehensive understanding of the employee as regards hospital culture construction, so that each employee is active and has innovative ideas and thought processes.

Responsibility List Based on the Implementation of Improvement Measures

A responsibility list based on the implementation of improvement measures is the most important part in the implementation of hospital culture construction. Sub-functions of hospital culture construction are implemented by relevant functional departments of the hospital. These functions, in general, are divided into convenience, service, management, environment and etiquette. As shown in Table 13.1, the hospital divided the 1196 measures for hospital culture improvement based on patient experience into various departments.

All departments of the hospital can form a responsibility system centered on the patient experience according to the above table, and these responsibilities are not set up on the basis of an empty "patient-oriented" concept, but are specific measures with strong improvement objectives.

Table 13.2 provides a classification of the 1196 measures according to patients' feelings, further demonstrating the relevance between the overall improvement measures and patients' feelings. As shown in the table, 29 of the 1196 measures are related to the indicator patient's touch, 766 to vision, 91 to hearing, 3 to taste, 4 to smell and 303 to perception.

Taking the Outpatient Department as an example, there are 80 improvement measures assumed according to the experience category (see Table 13.3). Among them, there are 10 measures to improve convenience, 51 to improve service, 16 to improve management and 3 to improve etiquette. Also, the Outpatient Department is well aware that among these 80 improvement measures, 7 are for touch, 51 for vision, 10 for hearing and 12 for perception. As a result, "the responsibility list based on the implementation of improvement measures" is formed, and the Outpatient Department formulates the requisite implementation plan and measures.

Table 13.1 Implementation of physical examination improvement measures of Cengong county people's hospital

S.N.	Responsible departments	Number of physical examination improvement measures					Total
		Convenience	Service	Management	Environment	Etiquette	
1	All clinical departments	5	164	111	21	30	331
2	General Affairs Department	44	22	16	72		154
3	Service Department	81	17	2	8		108
4	Emergency Department	8	42	34	4	5	93
5	Outpatient Department	10	51	16		3	80
6	Medical Lab	36	12	4	2	12	66
7	Nursing Department	4	16	18	4	20	62
8	Financial Department	12	10	6		10	38
9	Physical Examination Department	8	19	4		4	35
10	Information Department	26	3	5			34
11	All clinical departments and General Affairs Department	10	5		15		30
12	Pharmacy Department	10	4	4		7	25
13	Recovery Department		16	4	1	4	25
14	Whole hospital		5	7		9	21
15	Hospital Office	10		5			15
16	Medical Department	5	5	4			14

17	ICU	2	6	4	1		13
18	Medical Department and Nursing Department		3	5			8
19	Operating Room		1	5	2		8
20	All clinical departments and Service Department		3	3			6
21	Security Department		5				5
22	General Affairs Department and Operating Room				4		4
23	General Affairs Department and Equipment Department			4			4
24	Each department		4				4
25	Cultural Office			3			3
26	Financial Department and Pharmacy Department	3					3
27	Nursing Department, Pharmacy Department and Financial Department		2				2
28	Hospital Guidance Department and Emergency Department		2				2
29	Hospital Guidance and Registration Office		2				2
30	General Affairs Department and Recovery Department				1		1
31	Total	274	419	264	135	104	1196

Table 13.2 Implementation of improvement measures of Cengong county people's hospital according to patients' feelings

		Number of improvement measures according to patients' feelings						
S.N.	**Responsible departments**	**Touch**	**Vision**	**Hearing**	**Taste**	**Smell**	**Perception**	**Total**
1	All clinical departments	13	174	28	1		115	331
2	General Affairs Department	2	142		1	1	8	154
3	Service Department		64	5			39	108
4	Emergency Department		53	15			25	93
5	Outpatient Department	7	51	10			12	80
6	Medical Lab		27	3			36	66
7	Nursing Department	2	50	3			7	62
8	Financial Department		28	6			4	38
9	Physical Examination Department		15	2			18	35
10	Information Department		25	2			7	34
11	All clinical departments and General Affairs Department	3	17		1	3	6	30
12	Pharmacy Department		11	6			8	25
13	Recovery Department		19	2			4	25
14	Whole hospital		16	5				21
15	Hospital Office		12	3				15
16	Medical Department		14					14
17	ICU		12				1	13

18	Medical Department and Nursing Department	1	3				4	8
19	Operating Room		3	1			4	8
20	All clinical departments and Service Department		6					6
21	Security Department						5	5
22	General Affairs Department and Operating Room		4					4
23	General Affairs Department and Equipment Department		4					4
24	Each department		4					4
25	Cultural Management Department		3					3
26	Financial Department and Pharmacy Department		3					3
27	Nursing Department, Pharmacy Department and Financial Department		2					2
28	Hospital Guidance Department and Emergency Department		2					2
29	Hospital Guidance Department and Registration Office		2					2
30	General Affairs Department and Recovery Department	1						1
31	Total	29	766	91	3	4	303	1196

Table 13.3 Responsibility list based on the implementation of improvement measures of the outpatient department

S.N.	Feeling experience	Touch	Vision	Hearing	Perception	Total
1	Convenience		10			10
2	Service	7	32	10	2	51
3	Management		6		10	16
4	Etiquette		3			3
5	Total	7	51	10	12	80

Chapter 14
Various Hospital Culture Construction Activities

Hospital culture construction is by no means a process of making a show, or a complete preaching, but a solid long-term task, which needs to be long-lasting and innovative. Hospital culture construction is not something that can be displayed on a wall but is seen in the healthy and colorful activities year after year; it is not shown in the various improvements within the hospital but in the varied feelings of improvements of community residents and patients; it is not shown in the lip service of the employees but in their sincere services for community residents and patients.

Hospital Culture Construction — Implementation Is Better than Mere Paper Talk

In the long term, the hospital culture that patients and their family members feel should not just be banners and slogans displayed on the wall, nor the hospital motto, hospital song, hospital emblem, ceremony, etc., but the activities carried out by the hospital.

The connotation of hospital culture construction activities is very broad, and it can be divided into online and offline activities. Both categories can further be divided into internal and external ones.

So far, the Internet has already become the virtual space for any organization and individual. Some hospitals that do not attach great importance to online medical practice activities have lagged far behind the development of the times and society. Real (offline) and virtual (online) hospitals are both objective and indispensable for an organization. If the construction of online hospitals is not taken into consideration, offline construction will not be done well either. The same is true for both hospitals and their staff. The best way to check whether a doctor is famous is to see how many fans he or she has. The more fans there are, the more recognized a doctor is, and the more people waiting there for medical treatment. Therefore, such a doctor can be called a "famous doctor." In the future, there will be more and more online activities carried out by organizations, and virtual and real ones will be highly integrated, which thus lay a foundation for dividing hospital culture construction activities into online and offline categories.

Figure 14.1 lists the classification and specific content of hospital culture construction activities. Hospitals should determine their hospital culture construction activities as the case may be.

Yongping County, Yunnan, China, is a multi-ethnic mountainous county with 22 ethnic minority groups; some residents here are Hui People, and Muslims have the habit of praying every day. Therefore, Yongping County People's Hospital set up praying places for Hui residents, which got them much praise. This tells us that the hospital culture construction should be carried out in combination with the actual situation of each place. As long as the hospital cares about the residents and continues to provide residents with all-round services, it will be recognized by the residents.

Conducting Concerts in the Hospital

On the afternoon of August 23, 2017, a public music concert was held in the Outpatient Hall of Xingbin People's Hospital of Guangxi, China (Figure 14.2). This was a music concert especially for children with cerebral palsy, called "Listening to the Voice of the Heart, Playing the Song of the Future".

The WeChat Official Account of this hospital introduced the music concert, which shows high professionalism in both the subject matter and the participants. From the picture, we saw that a piano was

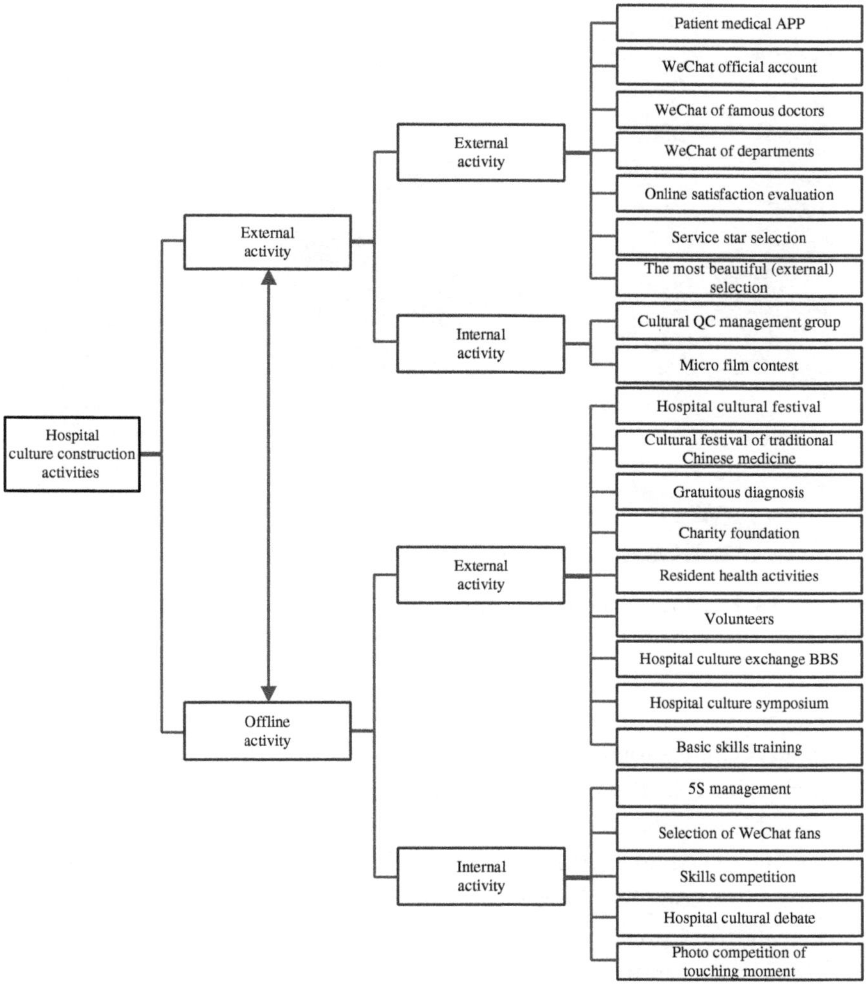

Figure 14.1 Classification of hospital culture construction activities

placed in the Outpatient Hall of this hospital (Figure 14.2). It was not a temporary instrument for the concert but had been there for a long time; professionals played it or it was automatically played every day. When the beautiful music reverberates in the Outpatient Hall, everyone feels calm and appreciates the joy.

Figure 14.2 Music concert of Laibin city Xingbin people's hospital, Guangxi, China

"Every child should be favored, they are our future..." A soulful performance of *Best Future* by medical staff and two children officially started the public music concert "Listening to the Voice of the Heart, Playing the Song of the Future" of Xingbin People's Hospital. The lyrics "Everyone has the right to expect the love. Put love in the palm of your hand and come with me" touched all the members of the audience and aroused waves of applause.

On the afternoon of August 23, 2017, a wonderful public music concert was staged in the Outpatient Hall of Xingbin People's Hospital, held by Xingbin People's Hospital to appeal to the society to pay attention to the growth of children with cerebral palsy. This created a relaxed and comfortable environment for patients and their family members in the hospital, helped them to overcome mental barriers during the doctor-seeing process and to communicate with

(Continued)

doctors and nurses and cooperate with the treatment strategy; it also showed the hope of recovery to patients and helped them build a positive mental outlook.

The famous pianist and national second-grade actor Li Jianmin, Head of the Laibin City Zhiya Public Welfare Orchestra Liu Zhenming, and two teachers of Zhiya Music Orchestra played *Weaving Girl*.

The president of Laibin City Musicians Association, Mr. Hou Hui, played *Horse Racing* together with his students. The rhythmic notes and the high-spirited melody intoxicated the audience who heard it.

"My good mother came home from work, worked for a day, how hard she is, let me kiss you, my good mother..." Two children in the Recovery Department volunteered to sing the song *My Good Mother*. The tender voice, familiar melody and affectionate rendition touched everyone, leaving people in tears.

The concert ended with the performance of two children with cerebral palsy.

The love and dedication of one person can warm others; so, the love and dedication of thousands of people can warm a society. Care for children with cerebral palsy, let us join hands and work together to hold up a sky of love for children with cerebral palsy, so that they can grow healthily and happily in an environment full of love.

The Outpatient Hall was filled with children with cerebral palsy, their family members and other patients. Some children with cerebral palsy were in wheelchairs, listening to the beauty of music quietly under the guidance of their mothers, while some children could only watch in the arms of their mothers because of weak legs; however, they were still cheerful and wanted to participate in the performance. An old man holding his grandson with cerebral palsy couldn't control his tears on listening to the music. But every guardian had received a small towel with which to carefully wipe the saliva and sweat of the children. "Baby, look. She is playing a Chinese zither..."

Figure 14.3 Vestibular indoor setting between the Valley Medical Center in Utah and the parking lot

The same kind of thing happens in such hospitals as Mayo Clinic in America and Valley Medical Center in Utah (Figure 14.3), and this really made residents and patients feel warm.

Region/Community-Rooted Public Relations

In the early stage of establishment, all hospitals aim to provide medical services to the region or the community. Although some hospitals have gradually established a good reputation later, the medical radiation radius is getting longer and longer, and it is still necessary to maintain long-term social public relations. Hospital culture construction activities also involve the formation of good regional or community public relations.

On October 28, 2017, the Hospital of Traditional Chinese Medicine of Jinsha County, Guizhou Province, China staged an excellent textbook-style public relations case.

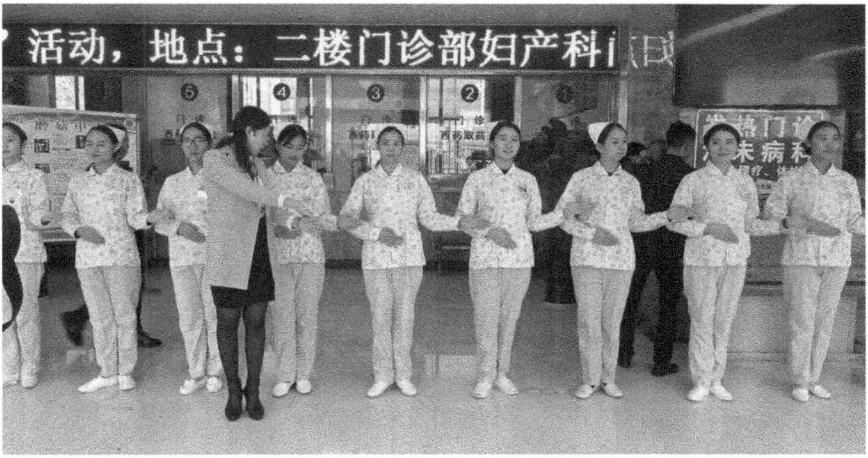

Figure 14.4 Executive director Gu Lili (first row) conducting nursing etiquette training

On this day, the Executive Director of Business Department of JYWJ Gu Lili conducted etiquette training for hospital nurses according to the project plan (Figure 14.4). To improve the performance of nurses on public occasions and improve the effect of the training, the training site was changed to the Outpatient Hall. This was originally an internal training session; however, it was made public.

Patients and their family members saw this and expressed praise for the efforts made by the hospital to improve the service level. Soon after the training started, president Zhao Yong came to the site, so there was the social publicity effect of the etiquette training that the leader valued, as can be seen from Figure 14.5. In general, it is still considered internal training.

At this point, two children, a pair of lovely twins, appeared. They walked forward and curiously watched the beautiful aunts who were seriously undertaking the training. Gu Lili could not help but ask: "Which aunt do you like best?" The innocent children actually became "judges" seriously, which caused a burst of laughter from the onlooker residents (Figure 14.6). This was not deliberately arranged, but was serendipitous. As the media said, it is a speculation.

Figure 14.5 President Zhao Yong came to the site to watch the nursing etiquette training (the 2nd on the left)

Figure 14.6 A pair of cute twins became judges

Figure 14.7 County leaders came to the scene and highly praised the etiquette training

From the perspective of public relations, necessary speculation is needed, and it is indeed understandable.

It was a coincidence that when everyone was enjoying this interesting scene, the main leaders of the county came to the hospital. They gave a high evaluation (Figure 14.7) on observing this training. By this point in time, the original internal training had evolved into a positive public relations event. In fact, most public relations management and planning occur in accidental events. The key is whether the person involved is aware of public relations and has the ability to adapt. Of course, if it is crisis public relations, careful planning is required, which requires immense skill.

Chapter 15
Executive Force in Hospital Culture Construction

The success of any service organization depends on a strong executive force. In particular, successful companies write their own development history with a strong executive force day after day and year after year. During this process, they will definitely encounter rapid imitation of this methodology by competitors, and the competitors can even exceed the original in some aspects; therefore they need to constantly change and innovate to maintain their own advantages, so as not to be eliminated by history. Executive force is needed for change and innovation, and inertia is required for sticking to traditional things. In this sense, the most critical factor determining the effect of the new ideas and practices related to future development is executive force.

Launch of New Hospital Culture Construction Requiring Confidence

Hospital culture construction is essential and necessary for any hospital. However, why are some hospitals are so hesitant to carry out hospital culture construction? First, they don't understand the concept and content of the new hospital culture construction, and indulge in the traditional hospital culture construction based on ideological education. Second, the new hospital culture construction is systematic, and requires corresponding organizational forms and a series of implementation measures with long-term continuity.

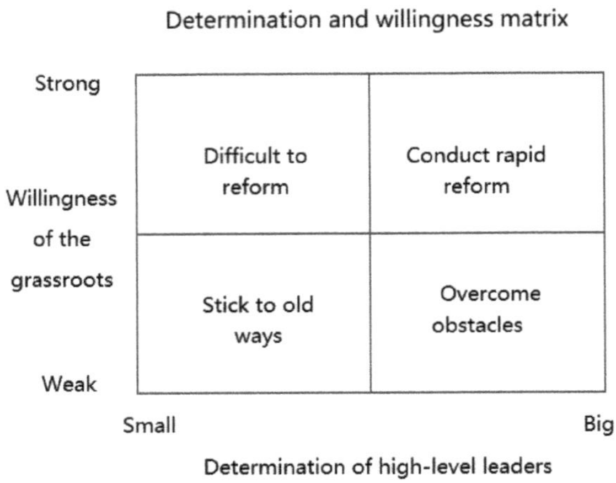

Figure 15.1 Determination and willingness matrix

Hospitals usually lack confidence in the implementation of new hospital culture construction. Third, the construction of new hospital cultures requires passion, but the main leaders are old-fashioned and lack the basic qualities needed to accept innovation. Figure 15.1 shows a determination and willingness matrix that demonstrates the impact of different attitudes of high- and middle-level leaders on reform during the decision of initiating the new hospital culture construction.

When the high-level leader is determined and grassroots leaders and employees have a strong will, major reform can be carried out quickly; however, this is just the ideal picture, as described in the first quadrant of the above figure.

The second quadrant tells us that when grassroots leaders have a strong will to reform hospital culture while the high-level leader lacks determination, it is difficult to reform hospital culture construction. This manifests that the masses are fundamental and leadership is critical.

When high-level leaders have taken no decision to start the new hospital culture construction and grassroots leaders and employees have no intention of doing the same, the hospital is dead, old-fashioned, and has no impetus to provide medical and health services at higher levels for residents. Hospitals in this third quadrant are not desirable.

For most cases, high-level leaders promote reform since grassroots leaders or employees are generally less sensitive to new things than high-level leaders. Even if grassroots leaders and employees have a weak will to reform, as long as the high-level leaders are determined, the obstacles can be overcome and the reform of the new hospital culture construction will be smoothly launched. That is what is described in the fourth quadrant.

Emphasis of President and Executive Force of Leaders of the Cultural Management Department

After starting the construction of the new hospital culture, whether it can demonstrate the required effect quickly depends on the attention paid by high-level leaders and the executive force of leaders of Cultural Management Department. However, it is not enough for high-level leaders to have determination for the new hospital culture construction to succeed. High level of attention is required during the specific implementation process. It needs to be emphasized as the responsibility of the chief leadership because it is a long-term strategic task. The executive force of the person in charge of Cultural Management Department also plays a pivotal role.

When the high-level leaders pay attention and the person in charge of the Cultural Management Department has strong executive force, as shown in the first quadrant of Figure 15.2, the new hospital culture construction will soon be effective and persistent.

The second quadrant shows that although the Cultural Management Department has a strong executive force, high-level decision-making response is slow and the coordination among departments is not smooth as the high-level leaders take no consideration of this. The hospital culture construction will then be effective but not persistent.

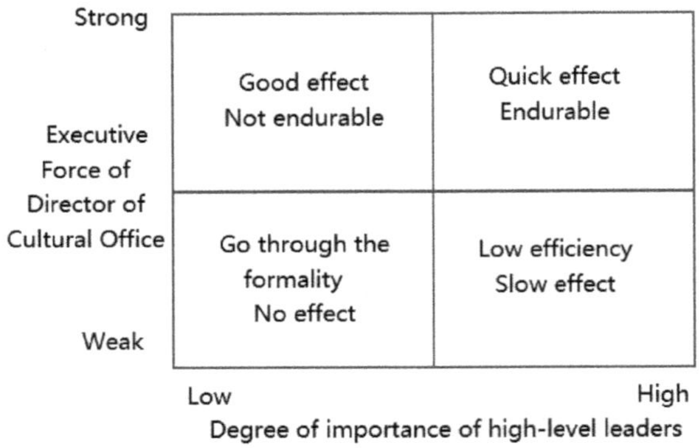

Figure 15.2 Matrix of degree of importance of high-level leaders and executive force of leaders of cultural management department

The third quadrant shows the situation we least want to see. When the high-level leaders don't pay attention to the process and the executive force of Cultural Management Department is very weak, the hospital culture construction work will become a mere formality.

The situation in the fourth quadrant that needs to be avoided is that whereby the high-level leaders attach great importance to cultural construction, but the executive force of the Cultural Management Department is too weak, due to the difficulty in choosing the leader of Cultural Management Department. There are two bases upon which the leader of Hospital Cultural Management Department can be selected. First, a loving heart for the patient, and keen awareness of needs and feelings of the patient; second, a strong sense of responsibility and undertaking responsibility for continuous implementation of various measures to improve service levels.

Prerequisites for Being a Good Leader — Capabilities to Raise and Solve Problems

Based on diagnosis and evaluation results of the current status of hospital culture, comprehensive rectification measures on hospital culture construction need to be formulated. The measures for different hospitals are quite different, which is subject to the difference of the original hospital culture construction level of hospitals, overall quality of employees, customs and habits in different places, etc. However, the "patient-oriented" value never changes. It is extremely important to put forward a set of practical and feasible hospital culture improvement measures, and this shall depend on the problem-raising and solving abilities of all members of the hospital, especially the leaders of the organizations at all levels (Figure 15.3).

Establishing a Quality Control Circle is a good measure to propose comprehensive measures for hospital culture improvement and give full play to complete participation. However, whether a Quality Control Circle can be guided to propose high-quality improvement measures depends largely on the quality and level of the leaders of each unit. It is impossible for a leader with low ability to lead a group of outstanding employees. Specifically, leaders at all levels are required to be quite able to identify and solve problems.

The leader we need most is one who can raise numerous questions and solve many problems, and an excellent leader is as shown in the first quadrant of Figure 15.3.

A leader with strong ability to solve problems but who identifies few problems is not a dedicated one, as shown in the second quadrant of the figure below.

A leader who raises few problems and rarely has solutions to problems must be an incompetent leader, which is the result of

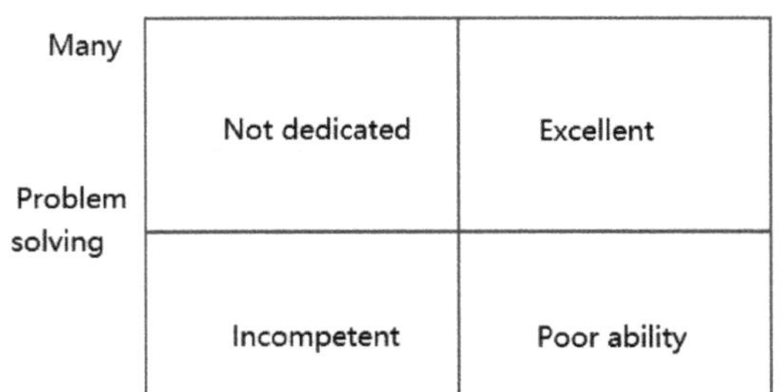

Figure 15.3 Matrix of raising and solving problems

inappropriate staffing by the organization, as shown in the third quadrant of the above figure.

When a leader raises many problems but has a weak ability to solve them, this is a concrete manifestation of poor leadership; therefore, more training is needed to improve the ability to solve problems as soon as possible, as shown in the fourth quadrant of the above figure.

Resolution — The Start of All Practices

Determination is the key factor for implementing various measures well. There are many measures to implement hospital culture construction; some are relatively simple and easy, while some are quite difficult. Simple or difficult, any measure can be smoothly carried out with a strong determination, as is shown in Figure 15.4, titled Determination and Work Difficulty Matrix.

As shown in the first quadrant, for a difficult job, determined people will actively overcome the difficulties and will not give up until the goal is achieved. This is the so-called "overcoming and actively advancing difficulties".

When there are determined people for an easy job, what we see is that the job is immediately advanced and a quick and desirable effect is observed. This is the scenario described in the second quadrant.

When a person is not confident in doing a practically easy job, he or she will find some excuses to describe the difficulty. For a

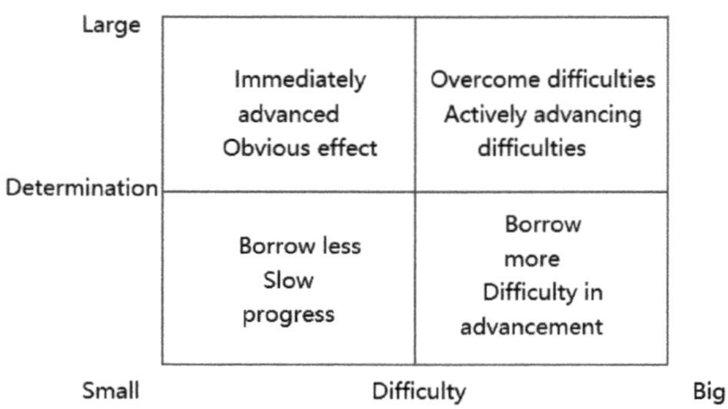

Figure 15.4 Determination and work difficulty matrix

seemingly-difficult job, the difficulty will be reduced when you mobilize the potential of innovative thinking. Or if you are forced to complete the work, there will be fewer excuses and faster progress, as shown in the third quadrant.

In another case, we will see that a job is very difficult, and so people are inherently fearful of the difficulty. So, they will find a lot of excuses to express that this is an impossible task. The situation of many excuses and difficulty in advancement is described in the fourth quadrant.

There are some basic hospitals in China with a "Gynecology and Obstetrics Department", a mixture of gynecology and obstetrics. This is very unfavourable. One of the fundamental reasons for this is that the Obstetrics Department often has great uncertainty as regards the time of deliveries. When dealing with these uncertain births, the main technical staff of the department will be mobilized, including doctors mainly engaged in the Gynecology Department, which will affect the development of gynecological technology in the long run. Thus, we will emphasize that hospitals should divide the original "Gynecology and Obstetrics Department" into a separate "Obstetrics Department" and a separate "Gynecology Department".

The following is a true story. When we were conducting a division of the "Gynecology and Obstetrics Department" for a hospital in Liuzhou, China, many years ago, the main doctors and nursing staff of the Gynecology and Obstetrics Department gathered together for a discussion. Everyone concluded that it couldn't be divided since there were not enough doctors, patients and beds. We asked the president who was present at the time, "What is this meeting about?" The president replied, "The division." We asked again, "Why is division impossible?", and the president immediately realized that this meeting deviated from the theme of "division", so the meeting officially entered the theme of "division", and soon a program of dividing "Gynecology and Obstetrics Department" into "Gynecology Department" and "Obstetrics Department" was formed and reached. The decision to quickly implement this was thus concluded. Though the newly divided "Gynecology Department" has only one doctor and one assistant physician, the construction of the Gynecology

Department has made rapid progress due to the implementation of a series of measures to swiftly improve its construction. In just six months, the number of patients in Gynecology Department exceeded the number in Obstetrics Department. It should be noted that in the original Gynecology and Obstetrics Department, the number of gynecological patients was less than 10%.

In fact, in China, the division of Medical Department in hospitals basically depends on people's determination. No matter how great the difficulty you are facing, as long as you are determined, you will come up with many good ideas to solve it.

Higher Emotional Quotient Required by Leaders at All Levels

"Emotional Intelligence Quotient" (abbreviated as "EQ") was created by several American psychologists in the late 1980s and early 1990s with no authoritative definition. Generally speaking, it refers to the ability to control various emotions. Self-confidence, optimism, positivity, no urgency and strong will are the manifestation of high EQ. On the contrary, someone who does not display the above characteristics has relatively low EQ.

A smile, a look and a word can convey care for the patient, creating an atmosphere of the basic "patient-oriented" value. It is the basic skill of the leaders from various departments of the hospital, especially the leaders of Clinical Department. The EQ level of a department leader determines the overall EQ of this unit, and it is hard to imagine how the mood of the employees in one unit can be and how high the EQ of the department can be if there is a leader who is moody all day. The overall EQ of a department will be conveyed to the patients and their family members.

Figure 15.5 shows such a comparison. To be excellent or outstanding department leaders, they are expected to have higher IQ and EQ.

When IQ is slightly lower and EQ is higher, such a leader is often competent. Studies have shown that people whose job performance is the best are not the ones with the highest IQ but with higher EQ.

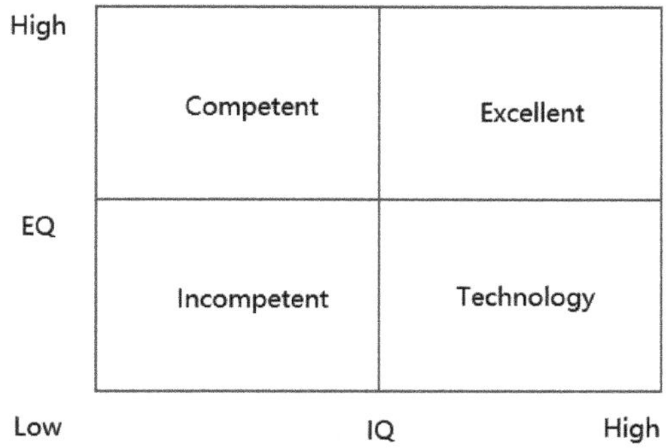

Figure 15.5 Leadership EQ and IQ matrix

When EQ and IQ of a person are at a low level, this person is not suitable for being a leader and is unlikely to lead a good team.

If a person has a high IQ and a low EQ, this person can be competent in terms of providing technical guidance. In a team, it is best not to give leadership to someone with low EQ.

System Destroyer — Leaders Instead of Employees

Hospital culture construction will certainly bring about improvement and perfection of many patient service systems. What impacts the continuity of these systems is not violations, but the violations of a leader. The result of this is not only suitable for the systems of hospital culture construction but also in the places where the system is established.

As regards system implementation, the separation of violation and destruction is a cognitive breakthrough in institutional management (Figure 15.6).

Why is it a breakthrough? "Violation" means "non-compliance", and its antonym is "compliance". A system is created to be obeyed. The meaning of "destruction" is to "destroy" and "damage". There is a big difference between them. A person violating the system does not destroy it. The system is still there. The system can only be destroyed by a leader due to poor implementation.

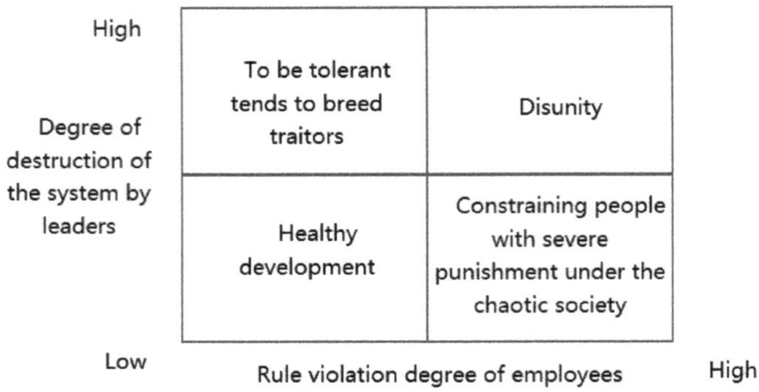

Figure 15.6 Matrix of violation and destruction of systems

As shown in the fourth quadrant of the above figure, when the degree of violation by employees in an organization is relatively high, the degree of destruction by leaders is relatively low. The leaders strictly put the system into effect, which presents the state of "constraining people with severe punishment under the chaotic society". After a period of strict enforcement of the system, employee violation can be greatly reduced. If everyone abides by the system, the organization transitions to the third quadrant of the figure and begins to show a state of "healthy development". When there are fewer violations by employees in the organization, the leaders will become less strict, and the degree of destruction to the system increases. At this time, the organization is in the state of "to be tolerant tends to breed traitors", described in the second quadrant. If leaders in the organization continue to ignore employees who violate the system, more employees are likely to break the rules. Therefore, the degree of violation of the system by the employees is also high, and the organization will enter the state of "disunity" described in the first quadrant. When an organization gets to this stage, it is already hopeless.

From this matrix, we can draw the conclusion that employees can only violate the system, while those who destroy the system are the leaders. When implementing the various systems for hospital culture construction, we do not want to see employees violating the system, and we are even less willing to see the leaders destroying the system.

Chapter 16

Cases of Management and Assessment of Hospital Culture Construction

A cultural improvement management assessment plan from Cengong County People's Hospital, Guizhou, China.

Organization, Division of Labor and Duties of Hospital Culture Improvement

Establish the "Hospital Culture Construction" Leading Team

To guarantee the smooth and effective implementation of this program, the "Hospital Culture Improvement" Leading Team was established to take charge of the comprehensive promotion of cultural improvement. The members are as follows:

Team leader: Yang Zhong

Deputy team leader: Li Hong, Yang Guangyi, Yang Shaohua, Deng Jinqing and Yang Xingyou

Team members: Middle-level cadres and department staff of the whole hospital

The team leader is responsible for the overall improvement of the hospital culture; the deputy team leader for the cultural improvement of the department, and Deng Jinqing, Director of the Party Office directly leads the work of Hospital Cultural Office.

The leading team has Hospital Cultural Office, responsible for leading the daily work of the leading team, and specific implementation, coordination, supervision and follow-up of the hospital culture improvement plan. The members are as follows:

Director of Hospital Cultural Office: Gong Furong
Manager of Hospital Cultural Office: Yang Jingwen

Specific job responsibilities of Cultural Office are as follows:

1. Formulate work plans for hospital culture construction at all stages, and formulate the cultural construction indicator system, implementation standards and evaluation methods for the entire hospital.
2. Formulate improvement plans and assessment plans for each department.
3. Check, assess and give feedback on the implementation of cultural improvement in all departments of the hospital on a regular basis, and put forward rectification opinions and urge implementation.
4. Develop and organize the implementation of necessary service quality training.
5. Respond to questions, organize exchanges and guide all departments to constantly improve the cultural improvement work.
6. Conduct necessary spot checks or telephone follow-ups on the discharged patients every month and on outpatient satisfaction to understand the department's service situation, and keep records for spot check or a telephone follow-up.
7. Summarize the procedures that patients found unsatisfactory or problematic, draft the work plan for improvement and supervise the relevant departments and individuals to implement improvement.
8. Other work related to cultural improvement.

Establishment of "Hospital Culture Construction" Quality Control Circle

For details, please see *Quality Control Circle Management Scheme of Cengong County People's Hospital.*

Workflow of Hospital Culture Construction

1. Cultural improvement path of the hospital (see Figure 16.1)
2. Improvement plans of specific time arrangement about hospital culture in three stages (see Table 16.1)
3. Workflow

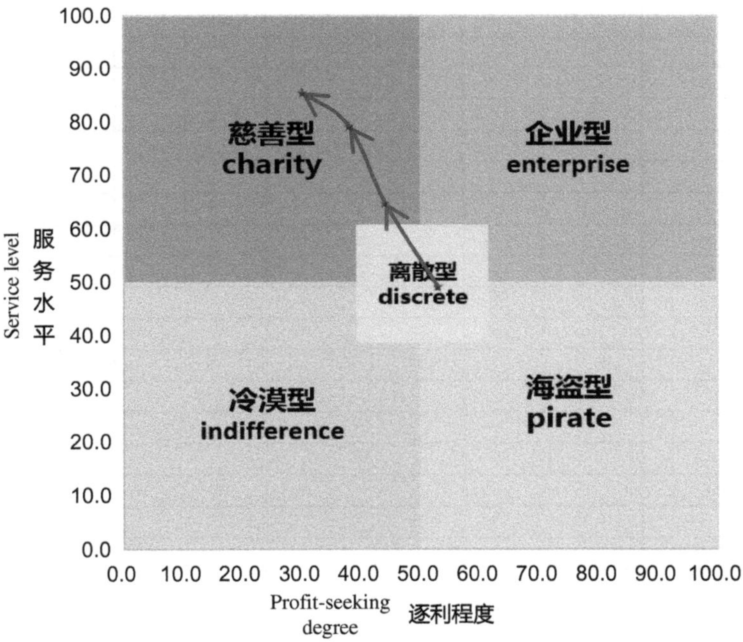

Figure 16.1 Schematic diagram of the cultural improvement path of Cengong county people's hospital, Guizhou

Table 16.1 Three-stage hospital culture improvement plan of Cengong county people's hospital, Guizhou

Stage III			Stage II	
Generate improvement result of Part I in Stage I	Implement cultural improvement of Part I in Stage I	Formulate the improvement content, plan and implementation department	Generate improvement result of Part I in Stage I	Implement cultural improvement of Part I in Stage I

Table 16.1 (*Continued*)

Stage I					Working phase
Formulate the improvement content, plan and implementation department	Generate improvement result of Part I in Stage I	Implement cultural improvement of Part I in Stage I	Formulate the improvement content, plan and implementation department		Working content
				September	2017
				October	
				November	
				December	
				January	2018
				February	
				March	
				April	
				May	
				June	
				July	
				August	
				September	
				October	
				November	
				December	
				January	2019
				February	
				March	
				April	
				May	
				June	
				July	
				August	
				September	
				October	
				November	
				December	
				January	2020
				February	
				March	
				April	
				May	
				June	
				July	
				August	

According to improvement plans of specific time arrangement about hospital culture in three stages of Cengong County People's Hospital, and in combination with the organizational structure and division of labor of the hospital culture construction, the specific workflow of each stage is as follows:

(1) Determine cultural indicators: The sources of cultural indicators are those indicators that have not been completed or have been completed in the previous stage but need to be maintained, as well as indicators that need to be built in the next phase.

This job in Stage I has been completed by the project team.

(2) Investigate cultural indicators and diagnostic results: These two tasks are the basis of all jobs to be done at each stage, and the Cultural Office is required to be completed on time with best quality and in the quantity required.

Document: *Diagnostic Result of Cultural Construction of Cengong County People's Hospital.*

This job in Stage I has been completed by the project team.

(3) Develop and agree upon the improvement plan: The deputy team leader of the department reads the plan and organizes the improvement plan promotion meeting, and the team leader reviews the plan. The main purpose of these three tasks is to determine the task breakdown and assignment of the cultural construction work at the current stage based on diagnostic results.

Developing/agreeing upon the improvement plan means that the Cultural Office will formulate an improvement plan based on the diagnostic results, and then organize an indicator assessment and acceptance department to discuss about the improvement measures and stage targets of the indicators at this stage. The target of each stage is used as the assessment basis for the hospital culture construction.

The review of the plan and organization of promotion meeting by the deputy team leader of the department is to make the hospital leaders understand and control the status quo and promotion plan of the hospital culture construction. And as a backing of the cultural construction advancement work when necessary, this will help solve problems in the process of advancement; the task of promoting cultural construction will thus be released. In this task, the cultural construction advancement plan shall be broken down and released based on necessity to the first responsible department, and the Assessment and Acceptance Department shall be responsible for the supervision and assessment of various indicators.

The main purpose of the team leader's reading is to give the president the overall progress of the culture control and give instructions.

Document: *Improvement Plan of Cultural Construction of Cengong County People's Hospital.*

This job in Stage I is completed by the Hospital Cultural Office with the help of the project team.

(4) Implement the improvement plan: It is implemented by the first responsible department for each indicator, and the Assessment and Acceptance Department plays the role of supervisor and aids in assessment.

(5) Daily supervision/inspection runs through the implementation of the improvement plan: The tasks that the Hospital Cultural Office needs to complete are daily inspection and record, monthly assessment and feedback, and evaluation and feedback at each stage. The daily inspection of the Cultural Office is focused on indicators for which an implementation plan has been made in that month. The indicators with full scores but that need to be maintained also have to be continuously checked. When any problem is discovered, the cultural improvement specialist needs to directly point it out and the individual/department involved needs to correct it and make a record of the same.

Document: *Daily Inspection Record of Cultural Construction of Cengong County People's Hospital.*

(6) Monthly assessment and feedback means that the Cultural Office will summarize and give feedback on the problems examined this month to the first responsible department and inform them on

the assessment results. It is then required to form analysis and rectification measures and focus on improvement.

Rewards or punishments of Financial Department means corresponding deductions based on the assessment result of various departments.

The main purpose of organizing a feedback meeting with the deputy team leader is to inform them of summary results and to praise the departments with good performance and promote good practices and experiences.

Document: *Brief Report on the Cultural Construction Assessment of Cengong County People's Hospital.*

After the documents are created, they will be submitted to the assessment and acceptance departments, deputy team leaders and team leaders.

(7) The staged evaluation feedback refers to forming a complete diagnostic result through the inspection of Hospital Cultural Office, and then department evaluation is carried out according to the completion of the indicators of each department.

Rewards and punishments of Financial Department mean that the Financial Department will make corresponding rewards based on the evaluation results.

The organization of feedback meeting by the deputy team leader is to inform on summary results and diagnostic results, and to praise the departments with good performance and promote good practices and experiences.

Document: *Diagnostic Results of Cultural Construction of Cengong County People's Hospital.*

(8) For indicators in the actual implementation process that cannot be completed according to the plan due to non-person or departmental factors, negotiate and plan the completion time again and include it in the work arrangement.

(9) Staged summary: It mainly refers to reflection and arrangement of the implementation of cultural work at this stage carried out by the Cultural Office. In this way, sort out the precautions and methods for the following work, reorganize the cultural indicators at this stage and prepare for work at the next stage.

Implementation Steps of Hospital Culture Construction:

1. Screening and rectification (September 2017 to August 2018)
   The planned target score for this stage is to reach 654.5.
   Stage I (September 2017 to March 2018)

   Conduct training on etiquette and behaviors and improve them according to the improvement plan under the hospital culture improvement program. First, develop the cultural construction indicator system, implementation standards and evaluation methods of the whole hospital, and guide and supervise the implementation of cultural improvement in all departments; second, the various departments set up five quality control management teams for "hospital culture construction" — environment, convenience, management, service and etiquette. Each Quality Control Circle appoints one responsible person to be liable for the cultural improvement of the department (the responsible person of different teams may be the same person); third, each department is required to organize a lecture on hospital culture-related knowledge internally every month.
2. Stage II (March 2018 to August 2018)
   Continue to select some remaining indicators to improve and consolidate the cultural improvement results achieved in Stage I.
   Consolidation and rectification (August 2018 to July 2019)
   The planned target score for this stage is to reach 807.6. The main task of this stage is to continue to rectify the cultural indicators that have not been improved in the screening and rectification stage, and to consolidate the cultural improvement results that have been achieved.
3. Consolidation and improvement (August 2019 to September 2020)
   The planned target score for this stage is to reach 855.0. The main task of this stage is to continue to rectify the cultural indicators that have not been improved in Stage I and II, and to consolidate and enhance the cultural improvement results that have been achieved.

Annex: Quality Control Circle Management Scheme of Cengong County People's Hospital

The Quality Control Circle, a quality control team, refers to a team of organizing employees who are engaged in various jobs in the workplace for improving quality and people's quality, and carrying out activities under the "patient-oriented" hospital culture construction system by centering on business strategy, policy goal of the hospital and existing on-site problems.

I. Meaning of Quality Control Circle

In order to establish the "patient-oriented" hospital culture, Cengong County People's Hospital hereby sets up a Quality Control Circle to implement the hospital culture improvement work.

For the hospital, this is conducive to establishing the hospital culture based on the efforts of all employees, improving patient satisfaction and enhancing the quality and ability of serving the people. For employees, it is helpful to stimulate the enthusiasm and creativity of the employees and it also provides them with a harmonious cultural environment and a broader platform. For the people, it provides them with a good medical and service environment.

II. Instruction for Hospital Cultural Indicators

(I) *Classification*

1. There are 31 etiquette indicators, of which 27 require multiple observations and multiple inquiries.
2. There are 71 environmental indicators, of which 29 require multiple observations.
3. There are 181 service indicators, of which 114 require multiple observations, multiple inquiries and telephone follow-ups.
4. There are 97 convenience indicators, of which 27 require multiple observations, multiple inquiries and telephone follow-ups.
5. There are 120 management indicators, of which 53 require multiple observations, multiple inquiries and telephone follow-ups.

III. Member Arrangement

(I) *Requirements*

For members of Quality Control Circle, they need to actively participate in cultural improvement work, and pay attention to the implementation of the department culture improvement.

The indicator survey is conducted for etiquette, environment, service, convenience, and management. The survey was done in three phases: 2017, 2018 and 2019.

1. The Cultural Office regularly explains the indicators, and relevant members of Quality Control Circle in the department survey the corresponding indicators and supervise the tasks every day.
2. Keep in contact with Cultural Office every day (such as through WeChat message).
3. Report on the improvement of the department culture and seek help from Cultural Office for difficulties and problems encountered (for example, the photo of the etiquette training in the department is sent to the cultural management group, and the improvement

measures of each department are informed to the Director of Cultural Office in time) in a timely manner.

4. Except special circumstances (off-duty, sick leave and others).

(II) *Staffing arrangement*

1. Each department (except the Administrative Department) is divided into five Quality Control Circles (etiquette, environment, service, convenience management), with one leader for each team.
2. The team leader position is on a monthly rotational basis, and everyone must participate.
3. The Cultural Office records the progress of members of the Quality Control Circle on a monthly basis and maintains these files (getting prepared for the continuous development of the hospital culture construction).

IV. Job Responsibilities of Quality Control Circle

(I) *Work report*

1. Report time: before 5:00 p.m. every Friday, the completion rate of the cultural improvement of the department should be reported to the Cultural Office (including photos before and after the improvement).
2. Report content: improvement plan, plan completion, unfinished reason and improvement photo issued by the Cultural Office this month (requirements: comparison before and after the improvement).
3. Report form: edit We Chat messages and send them to the improvement team, which will be summarized by Cultural Office.

(II) *Daily work*

1. According to the monthly plan of the Cultural Office, the monthly improvement plan for the department will be developed.

2. According to requirements of the Cultural Office, the maintenance indicator arrangement will be released and monitored in real time.
3. In the internal meeting of the department, explain the cultural improvement arrangements for this month and encourage cooperation.
4. The team leader reflects in a timely manner the culture improvement of the department as well as the difficulties and problems encountered, seeks help from the Cultural Office, makes a summary every Friday and sends it to Quality Control Circle.

V. Arrangement of Quality Control Circle Meeting

(I) *Form*

Face-to-face.

(II) *Time*

The last Friday of each month (except in special cases)

(III) *Content*

1. Summarize the monthly results of cultural improvement.
2. All departments need a cultural commissioner representative to report the contents not completed by the department and reasons, problems arisen and difficulties encountered.
3. Present the plan for the next month.
4. In the last week of the month, replace the regular members with new ones. Invite new members to join the WeChat group before the meeting starts. They will participate in the monthly Quality Control Circle Meeting. After the meeting, the regular members will leave the group.

VI. Evaluation Method

1. Organize a Quality Control Circle Meeting to vote on cultural improvement results every three months, to select the best department, grant it the cultural flow red flag and a 30-score as rewards.
2. Annual evaluation: monthly assessment results are used as a reference.

Hospital Culture Building
Group of Cengong Hospital

VII. Establishment Time

Please report to Cultural Office prior to 5:00 p.m. on September 7, otherwise 30 points will be deducted from the monthly management assessment results.

1. Team leaders scan this QR code to join the WeChat group.
2. Please change the nickname in such a format as: Pediatric Department — etiquette group — name.

Annexes to Hospital Cultural Indicators

I. Visual experience indicators

(I) Convenience indicators

1. Rate of hospital publicity material possession in regional households.
2. Whether there are special phone lines for consulting.
3. Awareness rate of hospital consultation phone lines.
4. Whether people can consult the medical service via the WeChat Official Platform of the hospital.
5. Utilization rate of partner hospitals.
6. Whether there is a reservation registration system.
7. Whether there is reservation registration flow chart.
8. Whether the doctor schedule has been updated on time.
9. Whether there is online consultation service available on the hospital website.
10. Proportion of direction signs configured at the main roads providing access to the hospital.
11. Proportion of beds to parking spots.
12. Whether the parking lot is clearly marked.
13. Integrity of road signs inside the hospital.
14. Whether there are reserved parking spaces for bicycles and motorbikes at the parking lot.
15. Whether there is reserved parking space for patients and their family members at the parking lot.

16. Whether there are bus stations near the hospital.
17. Whether there is detailed hospital location map at the bus station.
18. Whether there are bulletin boards for demonstrating the medicine price.
19. Whether there are toilet signboards set in the hall.
20. Whether there are Patient Complaints & Reception Handling Procedures billboards in the hall.
21. Whether notices and announcements are posted on the special notice board.
22. Whether there is medical treatment flow chart.
23. Whether there is a convenience outpatient clinic.
24. Whether there is an outpatient doctor schedule bulletin board.
25. Whether there is self-service registration area.
26. Whether there are independent registration offices in the hospital.
27. Written prompt rate of corresponding Treatment Department.
28. Owning rate of chairs per 100 outpatients in the waiting area.
29. Whether there is free WiFi available in the hospital.
30. Whether there are health education brochures available in the waiting area.
31. Whether there are billboards introducing the possible destination of outpatient doctors.
32. Whether there is expense inquiry system available.
33. Whether there are POS machines.
34. Whether internet payment is acceptable.
35. Whether there is price publicity.
36. Proportion of payment system equipment at the inpatient wards.
37. Whether there are ATMs.
38. Whether there are special windows (for family members of revolutionary martyrs and servicemen and the elderly, the weak, the sick, the disabled and pregnant women).
39. Whether there is examination result query and printing system.
40. Proportion of marking the time of issuing the examination results of medical lab.
41. Whether there are disposable paper cups available at the water tap.

42. Whether there are presbyopic glasses available at charging windows and medicine-dispensing windows.
43. Whether there are regional maps and bus routes posted in the hospital.
44. Whether 24-hour service is available at the Emergency Department.
45. Whether there are signs directing the way to the Emergency Department at night.
46. Whether there are striking signs directing the way to the Emergency Department.
47. Whether there are medical staff on-duty 24-hours at Paramedical Units of Emergency Department.
48. Proportion of convenient bags/boxes (needles & nail clippers, etc.) configured in the ward.
49. Proportion of sockets configured at the bedside.
50. Proportion of wardrobe configurations in the ward.
51. Whether there are microwave ovens in canteens.
52. Whether there is drinking water available in each ward.
53. Proportion of beds (chairs) for caretakers.
54. Proportion of pedestal pans configured in the toilet of ward.
55. Proportion of armrests besides the squatting pans in the toilet.
56. Proportion of the number of hooks for transfusion bottles in toilets to the number of toilets.
57. Whether the hospital canteen provides meal delivery service.
58. Control rate of chair configuration in the waiting area for family members of patients undergoing operations.
59. Whether there is drinking water available in the waiting area for family members of patients undergoing operation.
60. Whether there are display screens showing the operation status in the waiting area.
61. Whether there are tips for patients' family members, visiting schedule, ICU introduction chart and staff profile in the waiting area.
62. Whether transport of patients unable to move freely home via ambulance is possible.

63. Whether the physical examination services can be reserved online.
64. Whether there is physical examination flow chart.
65. Whether there is physical examination information inquiry system.

(II) Environment indicators

66. Whether there are special channels for the blind at the main roads providing access to the hospital.
67. Whether there are speed bumps on the roads providing access to the hospital.
68. Whether there are zebra stripes set on the roads providing access to hospitals.
69. Whether there are green channels for patients seeking emergency treatment.
70. Whether ambulances are clean, free from sundries.
71. Whether there is a hospital plan sketch.
72. Whether there are barrier-free passages.
73. Prompt rate of silence-keeping reminder every 20 meters.
74. Proportion of "no smoking" warning signs.
75. Whether there are cigarette butts on the ground of the Outpatient Hall.
76. Number of wall ads.
77. Whether the logo of hospitals has been lit up at night.
78. Serviceability rate of lighting equipment in the public area.
79. Rate of glasses cleaned in the service area.
80. Degree of cleanliness of public toilets in the hospital.
81. Proportion of garbage cans every 10 meters.
82. Proportion of cleaned areas surrounding the garbage cans.
83. Whether there are plants within the hospitals.
84. Whether there are resting chairs set in the corridors.
85. Whether there are anti-collision armrests in the corridors of Outpatient Department.
86. Whether there are breastfeeding rooms for mothers and their babies.

87. Proportion of cushioned chairs in winter.
88. Proportion of having perfect handwashing facilities in toilets.
89. Whether there are hospital guides/triage nurses.
90. Proportion of cleaned hospital guide desks.
91. Whether there are TVs equipped in the waiting area of the Outpatient Hall.
92. Whether there are drinking water devices installed in the waiting area.
93. Whether the waiting area is clean and tidy.
94. Whether drinking water is available in the B-ultrasound Room.
95. Whether there are independent transfusion rooms for children.
96. Number of chairs for outpatients waiting area for getting medicine.
97. Whether TVs are available in the transfusion room.
98. Whether there are chairs set outside of the rescue room.
99. Whether the environment of the Admission Office is clean.
100. Whether there are chairs set in the Admission Office.
101. Serviceability rate of bedding.
102. Proportion of taking the initiative to pick up sundries in the ward.
103. Whether there are any cigarette butts in the inpatient ward.
104. Proportion of cleaned TVs in the ward.
105. Proportion of cleaned desks in the office of the Clinical Department.
106. Proportion of cleaned walls in the wards.
107. Proportion of cleaned chairs and desks beside the bed.
108. Proportion of ward curtains.
109. Interval of cleaning the ward curtains.
110. Whether there is sewage on the toilet ground within the ward.
111. Owning rate of toilets in the ward.
112. Proportion of installing TVs in the ward.
113. Average number of beds in the ward.
114. Rate of security protection facilities in the ward.
115. Whether there are recreation facilities in children's wards.
116. Whether there are cartoon walls in the Pediatric Department.
117. Proportion of the setting of armrests in ward corridors.

118. Proportion of the setting of safe escape signs.
119. Whether the environment of the Catering Department in the hospital is clean and tidy.
120. Proportion of cleaned desks in the nursing station of the Clinical Department.
121. Ratio of neatly placed brochure shelves of all departments.
122. Frequency of replacing mattress.
123. Proportion of the setting of bed partition curtains.
124. Frequency of replacing bedsheets and quilt covers.
125. Whether the construction of operating rooms meets the requirements.
126. Whether there is a waiting area for patients' family members in front of operating rooms.
127. Whether there is a waiting area for patients' family members in front of ICU.
128. Whether there are recreational facilities in the Recovery Department.

(III) Service indicators

129. Ratio of followers on hospital's WeChat among local residents.
130. Follow-up ratio.
131. Whether there are expert-to-door services.
132. Whether there are all-around appointment registration methods.
133. Whether there is alert for appointment registration.
134. On-time working ratio of experts.
135. Proportion of the setting of hospital billboards in administrative villages/communities.
136. Whether there are uncivilized slogans in the hospital.
137. Ratio of pasting promotion contents at striking positions for serving patients.
138. Whether there are backup wheelchairs in the Outpatient Hall.
139. Whether there are suggestion-collecting boxes set in the hall.
140. Owning rate of signboards introducing chief physicians and nurses in charge on the door of wards.
141. Ratio of prompting the position of water cups for direct drinking water.

142. Proportion of designating full-time elevator operators.
143. Visiting rate of guiding patients to the Treatment Department by hospital guide.
144. Whether there are convenience service boxes at the hospital guide desk.
145. Whether there is an all-purpose card system available in the hospital.
146. Whether there are specially assigned persons in the self-service area.
147. Priority prompt for special groups at the registration office.
148. Whether there are outpatient doctor profiles.
149. Whether there are orderly doctor-seeing prompts set.
150. Whether there are TVs equipped in the waiting area of the Outpatient Hall.
151. Ratio of outpatient doctors wearing stethoscope.
152. Attendance ratio of chief and higher physicians.
153. Attendance ratio of department directors.
154. Accessibility ratio of outpatient service at weekends.
155. Recognizability ratio of diagnosis reports and prescriptions.
156. Ratio of doctors playing with their phones during work.
157. Whether there are one-stop services for patients to cancel registration, return medicines or get refund.
158. On-time ratio of outpatient doctors.
159. Accessibility ratio of outpatient clinics.
160. Off-duty ratio of outpatient doctors.
161. Owning rate of independent outpatient consulting room for each outpatient doctor.
162. Whether patients and their family members are apprised of the payment method.
163. On-the-job rate of toll collectors.
164. Whether examination results are delivered to inpatients.
165. Whether there are backup wheelchairs available in the Medical Lab.
166. Ratio of prompting the possible destination of staff in the Medical Lab.

167. Whether there is an examination flow chart and precautions posted in striking positions.
168. Whether there are chairs available outside of the Medical Lab.
169. Bed–chair ratio in the transfusion room.
170. Whether there are recreation facilities and newspaper in the outpatient transfusion room.
171. Whether there is hot drinking water available.
172. Whether there is an "emergency priority" notice posted on the medicine-taking window.
173. Whether there are gifts.
174. Ratio of the same doctor for return patients.
175. Ratio of transferred patients coming back.
176. Whether there is an Emergency Department.
177. Whether there are emergency knowledge booklets in the Emergency Department.
178. Rate of patients being accompanied by medical staff when being transferred to another hospital.
179. Whether there are publicity and educational materials for inpatients.
180. Proportion of setting patient monitors.
181. Serviceability rate of patient monitors.
182. On-the-wall rate of warm words in inpatient ward.
183. Proportion of floor safety signs.
184. Proportion of inpatients dining in hospital canteens.
185. Proportion of wheelchairs in inpatient wards.
186. Whether the phone number of the Catering Department in the hospital has been known by patients or not.
187. Power outage rate in the ward.
188. Whether there is a remote consultation facility.
189. Awareness rate of consultants.
190. Satisfaction rate of consultation results.
191. Feedback rate of consultation results.
192. Ratio of rounds doctors wearing stethoscopes.
193. Control rate of ward rounds by chief physicians.
194. Chief surgeon's visiting rate before the surgery.

195. Whether there are patients expressing their gratitude to medical staff.
196. Examination-accompanying rate for patients who need critical or Grade I care.
197. Post-surgery visiting rate of anesthesiologists.
198. Diet guidance rate of postoperative patients.
199. Whether mental health education materials for patients' family members are provided in ICU.
200. Whether there is video communication between patients and their family members in the ICU.
201. Whether there are brochures about recovery knowledge in the departments.
202. Rate of (treatment) monitoring on special recovery patients.
203. Control rate of inspection frequency during physiotherapy.
204. Usage rate of partition curtains and big towels in the recovery treatment room.
205. Guidance rate of therapists during the treatment.
206. Proportion of recovery materials on the walls.
207. Issuance rate of the department contact card to discharged patients.
208. Rate of escorting discharged patients.
209. Rate of follow-up service via WeChat/SMS.
210. Rate of greeting discharged patients on holidays and festivals.

(IV) Management indicators

211. Frequency of gratuitous diagnosis.
212. Update frequency of hospital website.
213. Perfectness of the hospital's WeChat Official Platform.
214. Article releasing frequency on the hospital's WeChat.
215. Unblocked rate of access for ambulances.
216. Rate of standard ambulance parking in the hospital.
217. Configuration of emergency stretchers.
218. Proportion of GPS equipped on 120 ambulances.
219. Driving record rate of 120 ambulance drivers.
220. Control rate of home visit staff number.

221. Whether ambulance drivers received special trainings on emergency knowledge.
222. On-schedule work rate in the morning.
223. On-schedule off-duty rate in the afternoon.
224. Perfection rate of opinion book in each ward.
225. Proportion of hospital guides receiving professional etiquette training.
226. Control rate of hospital guide number per 100 outpatients.
227. On-the-job rate of hospital guides.
228. Average age of the hospital guides.
229. Rate of visiting doctors with secondary senior title per 100 outpatients.
230. Control rate of the specialist clinic construction.
231. Whether there are information signs or isolation strips for queuing in the registration area.
232. Whether the self-service system remains intact.
233. Whether there is any payment information billboard at the registration office.
234. Whether there is any security monitoring equipment in the outpatient clinic.
235. Rate of standard writing of medical records by outpatient doctors.
236. Proportion of doctors with secondary senior title and above among the outpatient doctors.
237. Whether the outpatient is surrounded when receiving diagnosis or treatment.
238. Whether there are any privacy protection facilities in the outpatient clinic.
239. Error rate of toll collectors.
240. Rate of equipping service evaluation device in the charging window.
241. Number of charging windows at peak hours.
242. Whether there are any privacy protection facilities in Medical Lab.
243. Whether there are charging standard bulletin boards in the Functional Department, Clinical Lab and Radiology Department.

244. Whether the transfusion chairs are cleaned and disinfected every day.
245. Control rate of routine inspection interval of nurses in the outpatient transfusion room.
246. Whether there is any service evaluation device in the pharmacy window.
247. Whether there is any return visit SMS notification system for patients.
248. Whether security monitoring equipment is provided in the Emergency Department.
249. Whether facilities in the rescue room of the Emergency Department meet standards.
250. Proportion of physicians and nurses having intermediate titles in the Emergency Department.
251. Whether the checklists of the Emergency Department and ordinary departments are separated.
252. Whether there are systems and standards for emergency transfer.
253. On-the-job rate of staff working in the Admission Office.
254. Rate of wristband-wearing of inpatients.
255. Serviceability rate of security monitoring equipment in the ward.
256. Timely facility maintenance in the ward.
257. On-the-wall rate of department introduction.
258. Completion and clearness rate of the department introduction content.
259. Configuration proportion of department brochure shelves.
260. Serviceability rate of the hospital publicity logos.
261. Whether the hospital issues a uniform hospital gown.
262. Frequency of changing and washing of the hospital gown.
263. Qualified rate of fire extinguishers in the hospital.
264. Error rate of medical record management.
265. Timely filing rate of discharge medical records.
266. Satisfaction rate of medical record copying.
267. Whether the bed is equipped with curtains.
268. Patrol rate of security personnel.
269. Whether there are people prohibiting smoking in all departments.
270. The rate of arriving on-time for urgent medical consultations.

271. Whether the remote consultation facilities are in good condition.
272. Configuration rate of bedside boards introducing the medical staff in charge, disease diagnosis and nursing level.
273. On-the-job rate of department directors.
274. Rate of making ward rounds of the department directors.
275. Whether there is the system of making ward rounds at night in the hospital.
276. Execution of ward rounds at night for critically ill and perioperative patients.
277. On-the-job rate of night shift doctors.
278. Class A medical record rate.
279. Actual bed-to-doctor rate in the ward.
280. Shift handover rate of critically ill patients in front of the bed.
281. Proportion of certified doctors.
282. Whether departments regularly organize the Concern Group.
283. Actual bed-to-nurse rate in the ward (1:0.4).
284. Actual doctor-to-nurse rate in the ward (1:1.2).
285. On-the-job rate of head nurses.
286. Rate of making ward rounds by head nurses.
287. On-the-job rate of night shift nurses.
288. The head nurses carry out weekly training on nurses in the department.
289. Proportion of qualified nurses.
290. Proportion of care workers in the department (1:0.1).
291. Ratio of beds to nurses in the ICU (1:2.6).
292. Proportion of providing tahe doctor–patient communication manual.
293. Whether ward channels are reasonably divided to avoid interference.
294. Whether the recovery equipment is in good condition.
295. Rate of holding contrast scale for pre- and post-recovery conditions.
296. Whether recovery is subject to quality control inspection.
297. Whether there are medical records or therapeutic regimens for recovery.

298. The rate of presenting the discharge process and materials required.
299. Error rate of physical examination results.

(V) Etiquette indicators

300. Control rate of the appearance of 120 related personnel.
301. Rate of eye salute to patients coming across.
302. Rate of eye salute to colleagues (medical staff) coming across.
303. Neatly dressed rate.
304. Rate of wearing name badges.
305. Proportion of hospital guides receiving professional smile training.
306. Smiling rate of hospital guides.
307. Rate of hospital guides working with proper make-up.
308. Whether hospital guides are provided with special working clothes.
309. Smiling rate of staff working at the registration window.
310. Rate of registration personnel receiving professional training on service with a smile.
311. Smiling rate of outpatient doctors.
312. Smiling rate of toll collectors.
313. Rate of charging window personnel receiving professional training on service with a smile.
314. Rate of toll collectors seeing people off politely.
315. Smiling rate of staff in Radiology Department.
316. Smiling rate of inspection personnel.
317. Smiling rate of function inspectors.
318. Smiling rate of medicine dispensing staff in the Pharmacy.
319. Smiling rate of staff in the Admission Office.
320. Rate of neatly dressed staff in the Admission Office.
321. Smiling rate of residents.
322. Rate of nurses wearing proper make-up during work.
323. Appearance control rate of nurses.
324. Rate of nurses wearing special shoes.
325. Smiling rate of nursing staff.

326. Smiling rate of therapists during the treatment.
327. Smiling rate of staff in the Physical Examination Department.

II. Auditory experience indicators

(I) Convenience indicators

328. Consultation call answering rate.
329. Rate of noticing the location of the Treatment Department.
330. Whether there is an electronic queue management system.
331. Whether the Medical Lab is equipped with an electronic queue management system.
332. Serviceability rate of bedside call system.
333. Awareness rate of the reservation phone number for physical examination.

(II) Environment indicators

334. Noise decibel level in the ward.

(III) Service indicators

335. Follow-up rate of emergency call patients.
336. Rate of medical staff answering all questions asked.
337. Telephone politeness rate of staff.
338. Rate of outpatient doctors actively inquiring after patients.
339. Rate of patients and their family members being notified before prescribing any precious and self-paid medicine.
340. Prompt rate of "follow-up at any time when you are not well."
341. Rate of the patient's complaint process being interrupted by something irrelevant to the current diagnosis and treatment.
342. Usage rate of the automatic voice player at cashier.
343. Active greeting rate of toll collectors.
344. Whether there is an intercom loudspeaker at the charging window.
345. Rate of presenting post-treatment precautions.
346. Rate of describing the use and dosage of drugs.

347. Whether to inform family members of critically ill patients regarding precautions during a transfer.
348. Rate of publicity and education on common knowledge about hospitalization.
349. Rate of staff actively inquiring about inpatients.
350. Rate of noticing family members of patients before consultation.
351. Whether background music is played during recovery.
352. Telephone follow-up rate of discharged patients.
353. Telephone follow-up rate after a physical examination.

(IV) Management indicators

354. Rate of following up transferred patients.
355. Whether to deny diagnosis and treatment of other medical staff in front of patients or not.
356. Call completing rate of clinical department directors at night.
357. Call completing rate of chief physicians.
358. Rate of communication with patients during a bedside shift turnover.
359. Whether to actively inform about the operation status during the operation.

(V) Etiquette indicators

360. Control rate of polite expressions used by 120 operators.
361. Control rate of polite expressions used in the Medical Lab.
362. Rate of pharmacy staff seeing people off politely.
363. Rate of using civilized expressions by staff in the Admission Office.
364. Rate of using polite expressions to see people off.

II. Olfactory experience indicators

365. Whether there is an unpleasant odor in toilets.
366. Whether there is an unpleasant odor in ward toilets.
367. No irritating smell in the ward.

III. Gustatory experience indicators

368. Whether there is an unpleasant taste in the drinking water.
369. Rate of nurses helping children take medicine.
370. Satisfaction with food provided by the Catering Department.

IV. Haptic experience indicators

(I) Convenience indicators

371. Owning rate of bath equipment in ward toilets.
372. Rate of 24-hour hot water for daily use in each ward.

(II) Environment indicators

373. Rate of air-conditioner equipped in the transfusion and observing rooms.
374. Whether there are skid-resistant carpets on the floor of the Recovery Department.

(III) Service indicators

375. Rate of supporting patients unable to move freely.
376. Rate of stethoscopes used by outpatient physicians.
377. Rate of looking, touching, knocking and listening by outpatient Western-style doctors.
378. Rate of warming stethoscopes in winter.
379. Proportion of mosquito and fly repelling equipment in the ward.
380. Whether disposable toiletries are available in the VIP ward.
381. Rate of doctors touching patients during ward rounds.
382. Provide hand warmers during transfusion in winter.
383. Rate of supporting patients unable to move freely to use the toilet.
384. Rate of one-puncture for transfusions.
385. Infection rate of operative incisions.

(IV) Management indicators

386. Rate of secondary anesthesia on operative patients.

V. Multisensory experience indicators

(I) Convenience indicators

387. Hospital awareness rate of residents in the region.
388. Emergency call awareness rate of residents in the region.
389. Hospital expert awareness rate of residents in the region.
390. Whether the hospital has an exclusive website.
391. Awareness rate of hospital website.
392. Whether the hospital has a WeChat Official Platform.
393. Department awareness rate of residents in the region.
394. Rate of knowing registration appointment.
395. Control rate of per capita waiting time for outpatient payment.
396. Average waiting time for assay.
397. Average waiting time for radiologic examination.
398. Average waiting time for function examination.
399. Control rate of result-issuing time of ultrasonic examination.
400. Control rate of result-issuing time of large equipment examination items.
401. Control rate of result-issuing time of routine tests, such as blood, urine, stool, electrocardiography and radiological image.
402. Control rate of result-issuing time of biochemical, coagulation and immunological tests.
403. Control rate of result-issuing time of the bacteriological test.
404. Control rate of result-issuing time of intraoperative frozen pathology tests.
405. Whether the hospital decocts traditional Chinese medicine.
406. Control rate of waiting time for taking Chinese medicine.
407. Control rate of waiting time for taking Western medicine.
408. Satisfaction rate of patients with drying clothes.

(II) Environment indicators

409. Filter-cleaning rate in using air-conditioners.

410. Rate of installing air-conditioners in the ward.
411. Whether the hospital has a hall or area for recovery patients to do exercises.

(III) Service indicators

412. Active greeting rate of gatekeepers.
413. Rate of 120 related first-aid personnel comforting patients and their family members.
414. On-time working ratio of 120 home visit staff.
415. Driver-assisting rate of 120 ambulance.
416. Control rate of observing time in emergency.
417. Control rate of patients' waiting time for elevators.
418. Responding rate to complaints.
419. The number of annual medical disputes.
420. The annual occurrences of theft complaints.
421. Whether patients have been reminded to take care of their valuables.
422. Active inquiry rate of hospital guides.
423. Rate of "looking, listening, questioning and feeling the pulse" used in clinic of traditional Chinese medicine.
424. Warm prompt rate before examination.
425. Notice prompt rate after blood drawing.
426. Proactive-helping rate of nurses in transfusion room.
427. Whether there are heating equipment in Outpatient Treatment Room.
428. Whether there is equipment for warming hands in the outpatient transfusion room.
429. Rate of introducing the basic information of the to-be-transferred hospital.
430. Rate of comforting the family members of patients being rescued.
431. Rate of guiding regarding the hospital admission formalities.
432. Proportion of VIP wards configured in hospital.
433. Frequency of broadcasting videos about health knowledge.
434. Rate of comforting inpatients on important holidays and festivals.

435. Proportion of adjustable hospital beds configured in hospital.
436. Rate of informing consultation results in a timely manner.
437. Rate of knowing therapeutic regimens after consultation.
438. Rate of knowing implementation of therapeutic regimens after consultation.
439. Rate of knowing chief physicians.
440. Whether accompanied delivery is available.
441. Rate of patients' family members knowing the therapeutic regimen.
442. Rate of calling to remind pregnant women of physical examination 42 days after delivery.
443. Rate of Obstetrics Department calling for pregnancy examination.
444. Rate of cesarean section.
445. Rate of information about therapeutic regimens, expected results and expected expenses provided by doctors.
446. Rate of transferring medical information of transferred patients (department or hospital transfer).
447. Rate of compliance between therapeutic regimen made by doctors and actual treatment demand of patients.
448. Rate of preparing complete discharge summary for all inpatients.
449. Rate of informing patients and their family members on laboratory test and treatment.
450. Whether each department provides related trainings for patients and their family members to participate in the treatment decision-making and treatment process.
451. Rate of admission publicity and education.
452. Rate of knowing nurses in charge.
453. Rate of answering the hospital bed bell punctuality.
454. Rate of guiding and helping patients to take medicines.
455. Whether there are quarrels with the patient when dealing with doctor–patient conflicts.
456. Rate of propagandizing emergency knowledge to patients.
457. Rate of psychological guidance before and after the operation.
458. Rate of medical disputes upon operation.
459. Rate of providing post-operative complication guidance.

460. Frequency of ICU medical staff informing family members of critically ill patients.
461. Whether to provide on-site recovery services.
462. Satisfaction rate of recovery patients.
463. Rate of publicity and education upon discharge.
464. Control rate of time required to complete the discharge procedure.
465. Article loss rate of discharged patients.
466. Complaint rate of discharged patients about hospitalization expense.
467. Rate of medical staff comforting family members when the patient died.
468. Rate of noticing physical examination precautions.
469. Whether there is a meal service after the physical examination for patients who are examined with an empty stomach.
470. Whether to provide optional physical examination packages.
471. Whether there are health-consulting specialists to help those showing any positive findings in physical examination.
472. Whether there is a community for a single disease (WeChat, Twitter, etc.).
473. Whether there is knowledge publicity about a single disease.
474. Whether there are physical examination reservation & express services.
475. Rate of timely notification of physical examination results.
476. Whether to provide follow-up services after physical examination.
477. Rate of telephone follow-up after physical examination.

(IV) Management indicators

478. Frequency of patient consultations held by the hospital.
479. Rate of complaint against 120 related first-aid personnel.
480. Feedback rate of patient opinions.
481. Control rate of mastering the basic knowledge for hospital guides.
482. Proportion of hospital guides receiving professional triage training.

483. Control rate of patient waiting time for registration during peak hours.
484. Average waiting time of the patient during peak hours.
485. Average inquiry time of patients.
486. Rate of receiving professional training on doctor–patient communication skills.
487. Rate of doctors answering phones during work.
488. Patient complaint rate about outpatient doctors.
489. Rate of training on emergency patient transfer system.
490. Owning rate of bed tables.
491. Improvement rate after consultation.
492. Proportion of clinical department directors with secondary senior title and above.
493. Usage rate of antibiotics.
494. Usage intensity of antibacterial agents.
495. Number of doctors who smoke in the ward during work.
496. Rate of respecting the privacy and confidentiality rights of patients over medical treatment and information.
497. Rate of informing patients earlier regarding any operation, anesthesia, blood transfusion, use of blood products, and other high-risk treatments and operations.
498. On-time rate of the first operation every day.
499. Rate of patients participating in the marking of operative or invasive site.
500. Awareness rate of discharged patients about bed doctors.
501. Control rate of quantity of physical examination equipment.

Sincere Gratitude

The evaluation model of hospital cultures was established in June 2013, and after that, a hospital culture construction system based on the new evaluation model was quickly set up. In the following five years, the personnel of JYWJ seriously practiced and made a lot of supplements and improvements to the hospital culture construction system. They greatly enriched the methodology during the study of hospital culture implementation; so, let us extend our sincere thanks to them again. The personnel are:

Jian Bingbing, Lan Xiaofeng, Ma Wufu, Gu Lili, Zhang Shujun, Xie Zhichang, Cui Baohui, Yang Shuanping, Wang Zhiqiang, Wang Tianqi, Liang Chenguang, Wang Zhifen, Zhang Hongtao, Yang Dongdong, Cui Guotao, Sun Longqing, Zhang Liguo, Zhao Ning, Ma Xinxin, Guo Ran, Xu Juan, Liu Lu, Qiu Lixue, Wang Shuang, Wang Shanshan, Lin Chang, Chang Xu, He Xulong, Li Jiuhe, Zhou Chengda, Feng Yun, Wang Minglei, Jia Ning, Liu Taiyong, Qiu Yanpeng, Wu Aixian, Zhang Yunpeng, Zhang Guo, Cheng Songlin, Liu Hongmin, Wang Youcui, Li Qiming, Xu Xin, Zhang Xiaolong, Wang Ce, Song Qi, Cai Shizhen, Gao Caicai, Zhou Xinyu, Jia Wei, Zhang Meilin, Feng Guizhi, Wang Mingjun, Zhu Zhaojun, Gao Tian, Pan Dexin, Wen Shuyun, Feng Min, Wei Xiaohan, Zhang Ying, Yuan Yingfei, Li Tingting, Yuan Chongyu, Zhang Yongjin, Lan Ziyuan, Gao Yanwei, Lin Changyun, Huang Yi, and Zhang Jucai.

What impressed us the most was that the presidents and all the employees of the hospitals were daring enough to practice this innovative theory. Without their recognition, support and courage to follow this practice, even the best theory will be ignored. They have tested the practicality of this new theory. We are very pleased that these hospitals have achieved remarkable results in the hospital culture construction and conveyed these results to patients and their family members, who feel the love and warmth brought by the hospital changes. It is hard to name all the participants, but we list some of these hospitals.

We would also like to sincerely thank the Management Consulting Committee of China Enterprise Confederation. Leaders and experts of the Committee have heard of the innovative research results we have made, and recommended our practice cases in 2016 and 2017 as part of China's excellent management consulting cases.

S.N.	Hospital name	S.N.	Hospital name
1	Guangxi Pingguo Aluminum Industry Hospital	20	Hunan Baojing Hospital of Traditional Chinese Medicine
2	The People's Hospital of Fengqing, Yunnan	21	Guizhou Jianhe Hospital of Traditional Chinese Medicine
3	Tianzhu County People's Hospital, Guizhou	22	Cengong County People's Hospital, Guizhou
4	Suiyang County People's Hospital, Guizhou	23	Guangxi Debao Hospital of Traditional Chinese Medicine
5	Henan Gushi Hospital of Traditional Chinese Medicine	24	Guangxi Xincheng People's Hospital
6	Xishui County People's Hospital, Guizhou	25	Guangxi Yangshuo Maternal and Child Health Hospital
7	Chongqing Jiangjin Maternal and Child Health Hospital	26	Chongqing Xiushan Maternal and Child Health Hospital
8	Guangxi Binyang Maternal and Child Health Hospital	27	Hunan Xinhuang Hospital of Traditional Chinese Medicine
9	Guangxi Tiandong Hospital of Traditional Chinese Medicine	28	Guangxi Xiangzhou Hospital of Traditional Chinese Medicine
10	Maternal and Child Health Hospital of Aksu Prefecture, Xinjiang	29	Guangxi Tianyang Maternal and Child Health Hospital
11	Guangxi Liuzhou Xijiang Hospital	30	Guangxi Liuzhou Tanzhong People's Hospital
12	Guizhou Qianxi Center Hospital	31	Songtao County People's Hospital, Guizhou
13	Guangxi Liuzhou Erkong Hospital	32	The People's Hospital of Shuangjiang, Yunnan
14	Guangxi Liuzhou Second Maternal and Child Health Hospital	33	Chongqing Rongchang Hospital of Traditional Chinese Medicine
15	The People's Hospital of Shiping, Yunnan	34	Guizhou Sansui Hospital of Traditional Chinese Medicine
16	Hunan Linwu Hospital of Traditional Chinese Medicine	35	Yunnan Fengqing Hospital of Traditional Chinese Medicine
17	Guangxi Long'an Hospital of Traditional Chinese Medicine	36	Guangxi Debao Hospital of Traditional Chinese Medicine
18	Hunan Liuyang Maternal and Child Health Hospital	37	Guangxi Lingchuan Hospital of Traditional Chinese Medicine
19	The People's Hospital of Jingdong, Yunnan	38	Guangxi Liuzhou Red Cross Hospital

39	The People's Hospital of Wuding, Yunnan	58	Shaanxi Shenmu Second People's Hospital
40	Guangxi Rong'an People's Hospital	59	Yunnan Gejiu Maternal and Child Health Hospital
41	Hunan Anxiang Hospital of Traditional Chinese Medicine	60	The People's Hospital of Xinping, Yunnan
42	Guangxi Wuming Hospital of Traditional Chinese Medicine	61	Guizhou Libo Hospital of Traditional Chinese Medicine
43	The People's Hospital of Binchuan, Yunnan	62	The People's Hospital of Yongping, Yunnan
44	Xinjiang Wusu Hospital of Traditional Chinese Medicine	63	Guangxi Guiping People's Hospital
45	The People's Hospital of Ning'er, Yunnan	64	Guangxi Xingbin People's Hospital
46	Yanhe County People's Hospital, Guizhou	65	Guangxi Rong'an Maternal and Child Health Hospital
47	Zhoushi People's Hospital, Kunshan, Jiangsu	66	Zhenning County People's Hospital, Guizhou
48	Guizhou Weng'an Hospital of Traditional Chinese Medicine	67	Fujian Changting Maternal and Child Health Hospital
49	Hunan Nanxian Maternal and Child Health Care Hospital	68	The People's Hospital of Chenggong, Yunnan
50	Guangxi Wuming Maternal and Child Health Hospital	69	Baoshan Anli Hospital
51	Hunan Nanxian Hospital of Traditional Chinese Medicine	70	Guizhou Zheng'an Maternal and Child Health Hospital
52	Guangxi Yizhou Maternal and Child Health Hospital	71	Yunnan Yanshan Maternal and Child Health Hospital
53	Guizhou Zunyi Xiazi Health Center	72	Guizhou Dejiang Hospital of Traditional Chinese Medicine
54	Guizhou Jiangkou Hospital of Traditional Chinese Medicine	73	Guizhou Liping Hospital of Traditional Chinese Medicine
55	Zhijin County People's Hospital, Guizhou	74	The People's Hospital of Yanshan, Yunnan
56	Hunan Qiyang Hospital of Traditional Chinese Medicine	75	Guangxi Hezhou Hospital of Traditional Chinese Medicine
57	Guizhou Chishui People's Hospital	76	People's Hospital of Dejiang, Guizhou

(*Continued*)

(Continued)

S.N.	Hospital name	S.N.	Hospital name
77	Henan Maternal and Child Health Hospital	91	Sansui County People's Hospital, Guizhou
78	The People's Hospital of Weixin, Yunnan	92	Guizhou Jinsha Hospital of Traditional Chinese Medicine
79	Pingba County People's Hospital, Guizhou	93	Yinjiang County People's Hospital, Guizhou
80	The People's Hospital of Menghai, Yunnan	94	Sixth People's Hospital of Nanning, Guangxi
81	Guangxi Guiping Maternal and Child Health Hospital	95	The People's Hospital of Mojiang, Yunnan
82	Guizhou Dushan Hospital of Traditional Chinese Medicine	96	Guangxi Liuzhou Tanzhong People's Hospital 2
83	Chongqing Pengshui Maternal and Child Health Hospital	97	Yunnan Xishuangbanna Maternal and Child Health Hospital
84	The People's Hospital of Tonghai, Yunnan	98	The People's Hospital of Lianghe, Yunnan
85	Meitan County People's Hospital, Guizhou	99	Guangxi Pingle Maternal and Child Health Hospital
86	Zheng'an County People's Hospital, Guizhou	100	Jinsha County People's Hospital, Guizhou
87	Yunnan Weixin Maternal and Child Health Hospital	101	Guangxi Tianyang Maternal and Child Health Hospital
88	Xixiu District People's Hospital, Guizhou	102	The People's Hospital of Ximeng, Yunnan
89	Pingtang County People's Hospital, Guizhou	103	Yunnan Qiubei Renji Hospital
90	Cengong County People's Hospital, Guizhou	104	The People's Hospital of Nanjian, Yunnan

The author, Jian Di, outside Mayo Clinic.

The author and his team inside the Mayo Museum.

The author presenting his book, *Destruction and Reconstruction of the Hospital Culture*, to the Mayo Museum.

Index

A

120 ambulance, 129, 242, 251
active greeting rate, 129–130, 247, 251
active inquiry rate, 133–134, 251
affordable excellence, 15
American Joint Commission International (*see also* JCI), 35
asset–liability ratio, 37
average waiting time, 148, 150, 250, 254
awareness rate, 123–124, 176, 234, 241, 247, 250, 254

C

calculation method, 48, 61–62, 64–65, 68, 70, 74, 79, 95, 106, 110–111, 118, 127, 133, 139, 147, 150
control of annual medical disputes, 131–132, 251
core values, 3–4, 7–10, 30
cultural management department, 93–94, 177, 188, 197, 211–212
culture control rate, 165, 167

D

data analysis, 69, 175
determination and willingness matrix, 210
doctor–patient conflicts, 61
doctor–patient office, 92
doctor–patient relationship, 77

E

emotional intelligence quotient (*see also* EQ), 216
employee-centered, 6
empty words, 6
evaluation method, 18, 48–53, 57, 68, 71, 77, 79, 81, 92, 96, 99, 106, 110, 115, 125, 128, 132, 135, 139, 141, 148, 150, 220, 227, 233

F

food satisfaction rate, 106
frequency of broadcasting health education videos, 142
frequency of patient consultation, 148
full participation, 15
full-time degree, 190

G

Gu Lili, 92, 205, 255

H
healthy development, 13, 218
Hospital Cultural Management Department, 93–94, 188, 212
hospital culture, 1, 4, 6–13, 16, 19, 23, 26–28, 34, 40, 75, 98, 107, 136, 157, 159, 171, 174, 187, 191–192, 199, 209, 213, 217, 221, 227, 255
hunger breeds discontentment, 106

I
ideological preparations, 114
ideology, 13, 16–17, 19, 27
improvement direction diagram, 41
improvement objective, 48–51, 53, 55–58, 60, 64, 68, 75, 78, 80–81, 87, 89, 92, 99, 102, 106, 110–112, 119, 124, 128, 137, 140, 147
indicator, 25–26, 29, 31, 34–36, 39, 47, 50, 53, 63, 67, 77, 92, 95, 113, 117, 126, 129, 137, 147, 153, 174, 224, 230, 246, 249
investigation method, 48–51, 53, 55, 62, 72, 77, 79, 95, 106, 113, 118, 125, 133, 137, 143, 150

J
Jiang Zongshun, 121–122, 156

L
leadership EQ and IQ matrix, 217

M
matrix of raising and solving problems, 213
matrix of violation and destruction of systems, 218
Mayo Clinic leaflet, 10
medical experience, 67, 111, 148
medical service, 14–15, 21–25, 30, 35, 47, 62, 178, 181, 188, 234

N
normativity, 27, 147

O
Outpatient Hall, 11, 55, 114, 148, 183, 200–201, 205, 237–240

P
patient-oriented, 3–9, 12, 14–20, 24, 47, 98, 107, 116, 133, 184, 188, 229
pirate-type hospitals, 34
proactive helping rate, 135–136, 251
process, 5, 17, 21, 26, 30, 43, 54, 64, 88, 91, 112, 135, 178, 199, 202, 247, 252
professional smiles, 185
profit-driven, 4, 12
profit-seeking, 11–12, 14–15, 29, 33, 35, 37, 39, 42, 159, 170, 221
proportion of VIP wards, 140, 251
public-benefit hospitals, 33

Q
Quality Control Circle, 189, 192, 213, 221, 230–232
quantified, 26

R
rate of interaction, 143
rate of introducing basic information, 139

rate of secondary anesthesia, 118–119, 250
rate of TCM methodology, 135
responsibility list, 198

S

satisfaction, 6, 13, 21, 24, 63, 71–72, 79, 84, 86, 91, 99, 106, 136, 147, 157, 189, 229, 241, 249
secret prescription, 121
self-consciousness, 27
service marketing, 26
service oriented, 4
source of money, 38
S–P hospital culture evaluation model, 29–30

T

transfusion room, 56–58, 135–138, 238, 241, 251

W

warmth retention rate, 117
WeChat, 32, 35, 176, 188, 200, 232, 239, 242, 253
work capability matrix, 189–190
work difficulty matrix, 214

Z

zebra stripes, 53–54, 182, 237
Zhao Yong, 205–206
Zhou Xianjing, 157

Lightning Source UK Ltd.
Milton Keynes UK
UKHW020749120320
360226UK00001B/29

9 789811 211638